Praise for
All the Ways We Kill and Die

"A must-read for military buffs and a should-read for anyone who has given even a cursory thought to the U.S. efforts in Afghanistan and Iraq. . . . The search for the story behind an IED death leads to the history of the post-9/11 wars and the lives of the men and women who fight them. . . . Completely absorbing from beginning to end."

—*Kirkus*, starred review

"Castner takes us through a kind of moral detective work, uncovering not only private griefs but also the broader military and social context of our country's response to such deaths. A brilliant, moving, and troubling portrait of modern American warfare."

—Phil Klay, author of the
National Book Award-winning *Redeployment*

"Like the best of storytellers, Castner transports us into the world of the men and women who fight and die and grieve: a struggling widow, two amputees, the exhausted pilot, the contractor for hire, a talented female biometrics engineer, even the jihadist bomb-makers. An extraordinary work of nonfiction that reads like a suspense novel."

—Gayle Tzemach Lemmon,
author of the *New York Times* bestseller *Ashley's War*

"Brian Castner has written an intimate, heartfelt, and rending portrait of the American family at war and at home; and he's done so in a totally surprising and captivating way. . . . Deftly reported and elegiac in its language, this is a story every neighbor, every parent, every soldier, and every school civics class ought to consider required reading. *All the Ways We Kill and Die* has much to tell us about how to live."

—Doug Stanton, *New York Times*
bestselling author of *Horse Soldiers*

"A powerful and gripping take on modern war. *All the Ways We Kill and Die* is a stirring inside look at the deadly dance between EOD and bomb makers on the battlefields of Iraq and Afghanistan. Written in crisp, unflinching prose, the book is one of the definitive accounts of our decades of war."

—Kevin Maurer, author of *Hunter Killer* and *No Easy Day*

"Provocative, riveting, and uncommonly insightful in addressing both sides of the story, Castner writes in the tradition of Orwell and Kapuscinski . It is impossible to read his book and not be moved by the predicament of the shadow wars we're mired in. Infused with the knowledge of an insider, this is a bravura performance."

—Joydeep Roy-Bhattacharya, author of *The Watch*

"*All The Ways We Kill and Die* reads like a good work of fiction with a rich cast of characters and well developed whodunit plot line, all set in a postmodern military genre of special operations forces, robots, and drones. . . . It provides a unique perspective of warfare in the 21st century and for that reason alone, *All The Ways We Kill and Die* should be cataloged in the annals of modern American military history."

—Commander Jeremy Wheat, USN,
Center for International Maritime Security

"Castner solemnizes a small but recently critical section of America's armed forces, and powerfully acquaints readers with the risks run and the sacrifices made by EOD personnel in Iraq and Afghanistan."

—*Booklist*

"A tautly written, first-person look . . . in the style of a thriller. This is a fast-paced, personal tale that examines some little-known aspects of the wars in Iraq and Afghanistan and how they have influenced the current fight against al-Qaeda and ISIS."

—*Publishers Weekly*

"[A] deeply-reported tale of the costs of war. . . . Castner works like a translator."

—*Consequence Magazine*

"*All The Ways We Kill and Die* occupies a space somewhere between rage and redemption, a purgatory of loss reported as unflinching testimony. . . . To call it intense is to cheapen its power. Castner's writing is as horrifying as it is illuminating. Castner's writing shines because of his willingness to hold his readers' faces toward the abyss when they would rather turn away. We would all do well—as veterans, as citizens—to be so brave."

—*Task & Purpose*

"*All the Ways We Kill and Die* display[s] Castner's considerable talent for both in-depth reportage and more imaginative forms. . . . There's as much for the armchair military history buff in Castner's exploration of IED technology and tactics as there is for fans of literary nonfiction."

—Matthew Komatsu, *The Millions*

ALL THE WAYS
WE KILL AND DIE

ALL THE WAYS
WE KILL AND DIE

A PORTRAIT OF MODERN WAR

BRIAN CASTNER

With a New Foreword by C. J. Chivers

Arcade Publishing • New York

First Paperback Edition

Arcade Publishing books may be purchased in bulk at special discounts for
sales promotion, corporate gifts, fund-raising, or educational purposes. Special
editions can also be created to specifications. For details, contact
the Special Sales Department, Arcade Publishing, 307 West 36th Street, 11th
Floor, New York, NY 10018 or arcade@skyhorsepublishing.com.

Arcade Publishing® is a registered trademark of Skyhorse Publishing, Inc.®,
a Delaware corporation.

Visit our website at www.arcadepub.com.
Visit the author's website at www.briancastner.com.

10 9 8 7 6 5 4 3 2 1

Library of Congress Cataloging-in-Publication Data

Names: Castner, Brian.
Title: All the ways we kill and die : an elegy for a fallen comrade and the
    hunt for his killer / Brian Castner.
Other titles: Elegy for a fallen comrade and the hunt for his killer Description:
New York: Arcade Pub., [2016] | Includes bibliographical references.
Identifiers: LCCN 2015040029 | ISBN 9781628726541 (hardcover: alk. paper);
ISBN 9781628729078 (paperback) | ISBN 9781628726572 (ebook)
Subjects: LCSH: Afghan War, 2001—Personal narratives, American. | Schwartz,
    Matthew, 1977–2012. | United States. Air Force—Officers—Biography. |
    Improvised explosive devices—Detection—Afghanistan. | Ordnance disposal
    Units—Afghanistan. | Castner, Brian. | Afghan War, 2001—Campaigns.
Classification: LCC DS371.43.S39 C37 2016 | DDC 958.104/748—dc23 LC
record available at http://lccn.loc.gov/2015040029

Cover design by Erin Seaward-Hiatt
Cover illustration: iStockphoto

Printed in the United States of America

To my brothers in arms, still at war,
for all the reasons contained herein

Remember, remember!
The fifth of November,
The Gunpowder treason and plot;
I know of no reason
Why the Gunpowder treason
Should ever be forgot!
Guy Fawkes and his companions
Did the scheme contrive,
To blow the King and Parliament
All up alive.
Threescore barrels, laid below,
To prove old England's overthrow.
But, by God's providence, him they catch,
With a dark lantern, lighting a match!
A stick and a stake
For King James's sake!
If you won't give me one,
I'll take two,
The better for me,
And the worse for you.
A rope, a rope, to hang the Pope,
A penn'orth of cheese to choke him,
A pint of beer to wash it down,
And a jolly good fire to burn him.
Holloa, boys! holloa, boys! Make the bells ring!
Holloa, boys! holloa boys! God save the King!

—English Folk Verse, c. 1870

Contents

PART IV: HUNT AND KILL

PART V: THE DEAD REVISITED

FOREWORD
BY C. J. CHIVERS

THE FIRST EXPLOSIVE ORDNANCE DISPOSAL team I recall seeing, nearly thirty years ago on a Marine Corps base, was typical of its time. Our infantry platoon was out patrolling in southern California's hilly scrub. One of us came upon what looked like a rusting mortar round in the dirt. We'd been told that the hills of our base were littered with unexploded ordnance, remnants from firing practice for earlier wars, and that these old bombs and shells were not to be disturbed in any way, lest they explode and kill us where we stood. So we followed the drill. The grunts backed away, a base supervisor was notified, and we were told to wait in place until EOD arrived. Training briefly stopped.

A short while later a pair of explosive ordnance disposal technicians showed up in a truck and asked to see what we had found. We were infantry Marines, which means that in many ways we could be a bunch of stiffs, a regimented band of young men who followed strictly enforced social codes that covered just about everything — how we dressed, how we talked, how we deferred (at least on the surface) to rank, how we presented ourselves to each other and to everyone else.

The two enlisted Marines who arrived from EOD shared our service but carried themselves differently. They wore their uniforms casually, spoke informally, and observed their own rules. They were not just unimpressed with rank, they seemed to have no interest in it. Their attitude was both cocky and beyond discussion. *Where we are needed, we are in charge.*

They approached the mortar round and conferred over it. Then one of them bent down and picked up this supposedly fearful item and carried it to the truck as if it were a misplaced toy. No doubt what he did was carefully considered and safe. These men had their reasons, which later I would come to understand. Maybe they recognized the mortar round as a practice munition with no explosive fill. Maybe they saw that it contained no fuze. Maybe it was a familiar item on this base, something they encountered many times and knew was not a threat. I don't recall them telling us much. EOD came, EOD worked, and EOD was gone, barreling away in the EOD truck, two enlisted guys who seemed to have more authority and insider knowledge than the rest of us combined.

I remember them as a phenomenon unto themselves. They were the first two Marines I'd met who kept their own clock. They managed to seem both dialed in and loose. *Fucking snake handlers*, I thought. They had their piece of military life and their own way of living it. A sideshow, a subculture. We went back to being grunts.

Roll the clock forward fifteen years, to the start of an era when the United States military would in short order occupy both Afghanistan and Iraq, beginning a period of open-ended wars against irregular foes. One feature of these wars is that improvised explosive devices—makeshift bombs, in the language of laypeople— would cement themselves as the primary source of American battlefield casualties and also kill civilians in extraordinary and indiscriminate fashion. Here was a weapon capable of both agonizingly local and strategic effect.

The bombs would take many forms. Some were built from conventional military ordnance—unfired artillery shells, abandoned aviation bombs, and the like. Others were made from scratch. Some would be detonated by a victim who unwittingly would activate a switch. Others would be detonated by a triggerman in hiding, often by means of remote control. Still others would be rigged to timers or strapped to suicide bombers or rushed at their targets by the drivers of explosive-packed trucks and cars.

All would have a shadowy origin, the products of bomb makers who stayed, as best they could, out of their enemies' view and grasp. Afghanistan and Iraq became their killing grounds. Both countries were warped into the new shapes that the bomb makers' dark crimes demanded. Checkpoints and blast walls rose like weeds. Fear and grief settled into the collective psyche. The very experience of being in public changed.

Improvised explosive devices had another effect. They pulled EOD technicians out of their underappreciated roles in the American military and thrust them into a central position of modern warfighting. In my own travels in Afghanistan and Iraq, I would encounter EOD teams repeatedly. Their jobs had grown and assumed an importance of outsized scale— defeating the weapons that were claiming lives at an unrelenting pace. These teams could still seem like a tribe apart, a clique that did not follow everyone else's rules. But they were no longer grudgingly tolerated. They were revered and sought after for their courage and skills. Most everyone wanted them around. On many days, the battlefield could seem as if it belonged to them.

This book, by former EOD officer Brian Castner, covers the emergence and experiences of this class of warriors, who have shaken off the relative obscurity of the recent past to become one of the most essential participants in the wars in our times. EOD techs, as they call themselves, hail from all four American military services, each with their peculiar missions and traits. But no matter their branch, since 2001 they have combined to form a roaming body of bomb hunters and bomb disablers—the most effective defense yet against a weapon that has given current conflicts much of their sinister form. They are a brain trust, a cadre of emergency responders, and an intelligence and evidence-collection service.

Set in parallel narratives, Mr. Castner follows an elusive bomb-making instructor (the "Engineer") and the American military's frustrating pursuit of him as he seeds the battlefield with his lethal handiwork and protégés and presides over the killing of one of the Air Force's committed and experienced young EOD techs. In doing so, Mr. Castner presents a character—Technical Sergeant Matthew S. Schwartz—who personifies the EOD experience and whose path positioned him between two killing machines, one jihadist, the other Western, which together foretold his death and assured the efforts of his brothers and sisters to avenge it. The result is a journey into the EOD tribe and the many strands of investigators and killers who support it, for a view of a war within the wars in Afghanistan and Iraq.

Mr. Castner's complex portrait of his fellow EOD techs is a service unto itself. But his thorough sketching of the conditions in which they have been working since 2001 is more valuable than the account of Sergeant Schwartz and the hunt for his killer. It shows a shape of war today, and how land wars amid populations that produce a cohort of bomb makers have become grimly unwinnable—campaigns with no clear end, in which the next bomb can always seem minutes away. It shows how EOD techs, like medevac crews, are lifesavers—people whose effects are tangible and real.

That last point is necessary. Bomb making is a fluid and transferrable skill, not confined to countries at war. The age of the improvised explosive device is here and will not end any time soon. Read *All the Ways We Kill and Die* as profile and elegy. But understand it as a glimpse of a future. As makeshift bombs proliferate and spread, men and women like Matthew Schwartz will be quietly trying to keep the rest of us alive, even as we puzzle, as I once did, over who they are.

November 2017
South Kingstown, R.I.

Author's Note

THE FIELDS OF WAR, INTELLIGENCE, and medicine—the primary topics of this book—are notoriously filled with dense jargon and acronyms. Every attempt is made in the course of the text to explain such terms as they arise, but to maintain the authenticity of the voices of the primary characters, unfamiliar terminology will inevitably appear. To assist the reader, a glossary and notes are provided at the back of this volume.

ALL THE WAYS
WE KILL AND DIE

PROLOGUE

IN THE NAME OF ALLAH, the Most Gracious, the Most Merciful, all praise be to Him who commands to fight and slay the pagans wherever ye find them, seize them, beleaguer them, and lie in wait for them in every stratagem; and blessings for His Prophet, peace be upon him, the Messenger of the Holy Book, where we are enjoined to fight them until there is no more oppression and all submission is made to Allah alone; for in the words of our Sheikh, may Allah accept his martyrdom, all who are able must kill them in every country upon the earth until all Muslims are free.

But how shall it be done? God had not yet granted him the power to kill them all today, so whom should he choose? And how? Decades had taught him this: patience is the gift of zeal, persistence the true mark of fervor, and Allah ultimately rewards both.

His soft hand on the *mujahid's* shoulder, and the youth lowered the thin wire leads.

Be still, Khalid, he said. Not yet. Those are not the *kuffar* we will kill today.

The *albuyah nasiffah* lay in the road in the center of the village. Not a road, a pockmarked track. He had seen real roads, highways even, if the youths had not.

The bomb lay in the road, and a *kuffar* armored truck was perched right over it. It just sat there and idled and did not move, like a lamb with a knife at its throat submitting to the *dhabihah*. The trucks were strung in a line down the road, sitting and watching, like him, while a small robot hurried about and undid more of his designs.

The bomb that lay in the road was not the only bomb in the road. The *kuffar* had found the other, but not this one, not the one that could be detonated via the thin automobile wire held in Khalid's hand.

He and Khalid had been squatting behind the *qalat* for half a day, hiding, out of sight of the sensitive cameras mounted on the *kuffar's* trucks. Their third man—no, a boy really—was the spotter, also in hiding but much closer, on the other side of the road, with a direct view of the bomb and clutching a small Yaesu radio. There were three of them total, then, he and the two local Afghan youths. They were interchangeable martyrdom-seekers. He was not.

They had waited for the trucks to arrive. They didn't know the trucks were coming, or at least not this particular group. The trucks always came, though, if you waited long enough; patience and persistence. The *kuffar* preferred the highway to the south, but very recently they had begun to use this road, so he had moved here as well. It was only to wait until the right truck drove over the bomb. They all looked the same to the younger men, but not to him.

They sat and waited, for two hours they waited, while the *kuffar* searched and preened and strutted about. Khalid drank from a bottle of water, but he had politely refused. It was a bad habit, leaving one's fingerprints about. Occasionally, he leaned out from behind the mud wall of the *qalat* and used a pair of black binoculars to observe the small lead portion of the column. He had taken the binoculars from a Soviet soldier's corpse when he was still a young man, as young as the corpse in fact, as young as the two *mujahid* colts he shivered with today.

It was cold, even in the afternoon, cold in a way his homeland never was, and despite his years away and travels to the northern high mountains, his blood had never thickened. These youths were in nothing but their *shalwar kameez*, not even bundled in their shawls or *patu*. One was wearing light slippers, the other black high-tops worn through with holes. He cinched his Western jacket tighter.

It was rare for him to accompany common *mujahid* on their ambush. He was an emir, though an emir with no militia, a marshaler of expertise rather than foot soldiers. He need not be out today, but how else to ensure this *katibat* was correctly employing his wares? He need not be out today, but he was, and he was the emir, and so he would choose. He knew that not all the *kuffar* were the same, that some were worth killing more than others.

They are putting the robot back in the truck, *agha sahib*, his spotter said over the radio.

That is the one we want. Tell me when they are in position, he said.

Through his binoculars he could see several small figures returning to their vehicles. From watching for so many years, he knew that in a moment the convoy would finally move.

Get ready, he said, and Khalid began chanting quietly to himself, praising God in an ever rising voice, until he put his hand out again and the youth went quiet.

I want to hear, he said, and then silence but for cold wind over rock.

He stared through the binoculars. The line of armored ants began to crawl. A particular knobby ant, the one that bore the robot, appeared in his sights, disappeared behind a hut, reappeared in another gap. It was in the center of the column, and it was approaching the marker.

Now, *inshallah*, his radio said.

Now, he repeated.

The *mujahid* youth touched the bare wires to the main terminals of the car battery. A second delay, then a cloud of fire and ash above the horizon of mud walls, the spine of a massive armored truck briefly breaching the roofline like the hump and flukes of Yunus's whale, a moment of anticipation, near silence, and then a blast wave crack that shook his thin bones and echoed across the open country of the river valley.

Khalid looked up at him in wonder, then back at the battery leads.

Allahu Akbar, the youth said quietly to himself.

The Engineer said nothing.

PART I
THE DEAD

"My lands are where my dead lie buried."

—Crazy Horse

1 · BLAST WAVES

A WESTERN MOUNTAIN WARM SPELL had stolen the modest Christmas snows, and the home of Matthew and Jennifer Schwartz sat among bare trees and dying grass, a pale house on a brown lawn.

The house was nearly empty. The girls were off at school. Jesus and his radiant Sacred Heart stared from the living room wall at a blank television and forgotten couch. Duke the chocolate Lab slept at the foot of the stairs. The only sound in the empty house was the mechanical hum of the treadmill and the regular beat of a runner's footfalls.

The house was often empty. A new pickup truck and trailer filled the driveway, camping equipment filled the garage, dirty dishes filled the sink, Duke shuffled and huffed about the backyard, the three girls laughed and sang songs, but Matt was gone, always gone, and the hole remained. A toothbrush here, a T-shirt there, the small reminders of him were strewn about the house like so many pretty gold rings, and she but the amputated stump of a hand with no fingers.

That morning Jenny was finishing another long run on her treadmill. She had discovered running on Matt's second tour. At the start of his deployments, she ran four or six miles. Now that he had been gone three months, she was up to ten and barely out of breath.

Jenny had learned long ago not to pine by the phone; it only made the hours crawl. But she had also learned to save the last recording on the answering machine, not to delete the last email. Matt had been out on a long-distance patrol for over a week, and had managed only a quick and broken sat phone call. So more than anything, it was a last email that kept tumbling through her head. It bothered her that it read like a last email. Heavy zippered sweatshirts in the dryer, tumble, tumble, the email always in the back of her mind as she ran.

Jenny was soaked when she got off the treadmill, dripping the sweaty, unwashed funk that comes from not having showered since, well, who keeps track of these things when your husband is gone and the girls need you? She paced and began her stretching routine, and the doorbell rang. Under no circumstances would she ever answer the door smelling like she did, but she did look out the window.

She saw a sea of uniform blue hats stark against the dry Wyoming prairie.

If I don't answer the door, she thought, *he's not dead. He's not dead yet*.

The doorbell rang again. Perhaps a third time. They weren't leaving.

Jenny disconnected her mind and entered a dream. She felt herself drifting across the floor as her feet, under their own programming and direction, moved her body to the door.

"Ma'am, are you Mrs. Jennifer Schwartz?"

Yes, the empty body answered.

"Ma'am, on behalf of the United States government, we regret to inform you that your husband has been killed in action in Afghanistan."

THAT JANUARY EVENING, soon after the New Year, when darkness comes early to New York State's northern tier and the chill clamps tight, I finished a walk in my woods and shed my snowshoes at the back door to find my wife curled up under a knitted blanket on the couch, nestled in front of the Christmas tree as one would sit before a fire, a still twinkling in an otherwise unlit room.

The kids busied themselves with an embarrassment of new toys, recent Christmas gifts from all members of the family. A pile of papers, my wife's half-edited PhD dissertation, lay abandoned next to her in this, her favorite of post-holiday spots; Jessie's efforts to work were stymied by the softness of the seat and the comfort of the blanket, the pleasant glow from so many small white lights and the snow outside. I kissed her and snuggled in and felt the warmth from her back and neck and no one had tried to kill me in five years.

We sat together on the couch, and I pulled out my phone, an unconscious habit. My thumb moved through various Facebook status updates, past children at Disney World, a four-year-old's birthday party, a new hairstyle and car, political memes like modern prayer cards. I checked on Dan Fye, who had lost a leg half a year earlier and was struggling through rehab with a halo of pins and screws erupting from joints. I checked on Evil, to see if he had time to update while flying out of Bagram. I checked on three dozen other friends, brothers really, closer than any friends, who were in Afghanistan, about to leave for Afghanistan, just back from another tour. Jessie asked me what I was looking at, and I lied and said, "Nothing," as she stared at the tree in peace.

I was thumbing through my phone, my wife's head across my chest, my children distantly playing some electronic game in the basement, when it happened. No telegram arrived. The phone did not ring. There was no knock on the front door. The tiny screen on my phone simply flickered as I scrolled to more recent updates.

First, a more distant acquaintance changed his Facebook profile photo. His smiling suntanned face became the bomb squad's ordnance-and-lightning badge with a thick black band across it, the universal symbol for mourning. Someone had died. Then a second friend changed his photo as well. Someone had died recently, or at least, the news was only now getting out.

So I started over, reviewed when everyone in Afghanistan had last checked in. It was an exercise in frustration. For some it had been weeks; when on patrol in the mountains, a civilian Internet connection was hard to find. I checked the updates of those who normally announce bad news, but there was silence from the Chiefs and commanders. As a last resort, I rechecked the wife network, for offers of vague support and prayers. Nothing from Amanda, but her husband was still recovering from his gunshot wound. Nothing from Monica and Aleesha. Jenny had been silent for hours, which was unlike her, and her husband Matt was deployed. Had he called and told her who it was?

Then a new status update popped up. "Fuck you Afghanistan."

This was from Pinkham, a much closer friend. My chest clenched. A choke collar around my neck tightened.

Then immediately a direct message to me, from one of the few female techs I served with, Angela Olguin: "I assume u r in the know?"

No, I wanted to shout, I was not in the know. The crossover potential between Pinkham and Angela was small. We had all been assigned to the same unit in New Mexico, a small company of sixteen. Who was there? Kermit, already killed in Iraq. Bill Hailer, retired. Dee, retired. Garet, in Japan. Beau, shot and home. Hamski, already killed. Pinkham, Angela. Matthew Schwartz, who was deployed. Wes Leaverton, was he deployed? Laz? I thought he was in Guam. Piontek, no he got out. Burns too. Who else?

I grew agitated and fidgety, broke the Christmas tree spell.

"What is it?" asked Jessica as she sat up, wary, defensive, holding the blanket to her chin.

"We, we lost someone," I fumbled.

"Please don't let it be Matt," my wife pleaded.

Why Matt? Why did she say Matt?

As fast as my fingers and thumbs could work, I messaged back to Angela: "No, fuck, what happened?"

My mind raced. Who was it? Who's the worst it could be? Imagine him or her, imagine the worst outcome, and then whoever it is will be a relief.

In our job, we knew there would be casualties. Well, not at first, not when Afghanistan started. But eventually we grew to understand that while our vocation had provided a new family of brothers and sisters, it did so on the condition that too often they would die young. We had all by now learned how to lose acquaintances, a guy you had trained with, a guy you met once on a range clearance or Secret Service mission, a guy whose face appeared in every group photo.

But in time most of us developed a list, buried in the subconscious until moments like these. Five or ten names. The guys you *can't* lose. The guys that have to make it back. It is a bargain with Satan. If I have to lose brothers, you tell yourself, I can bear it all as long as you spare these few. Matt and Josh and Phillips and don't make me say them all. Please, just don't take this small list that I am hiding in a place I am terrified to look.

Why did Jessie say Matt? Why did she have to say his name out loud?

I sat and shook and repeated my names like a mantra, and Jessie clutched the blanket, and I stared at my phone until it rang not ten seconds later. It was Angela.

"Matt died this morning," she sobbed.

I nodded my head to Jessie. Her face broke into a thousand pieces, and she collapsed on the floor in front of the glowing Christmas tree.

I DIDN'T GET it right away, but it makes sense now when I look back on it. Of course I would do an investigation. The training kicked in, subconsciously. Grief drove me to unusual lengths, but the old instincts informed the process.

I was an Explosive Ordnance Disposal officer, a leader in the military's bomb squad. We call it a brotherhood, and there are so few of us we're all connected by only one or two degrees of separation. The brotherhood is a mindset, an affection, a burden, a bond that endures long after the crucible of EOD school and deployments around the world are over. It's the covenant we keep with those in the ground, our responsibility to those hobbled before their time, the standard by which I secretly measure everyone I meet.

In EOD, our job is to make bombs safe. Sometimes we can disarm the device before it goes off. Too often, though, the bomb works as designed, and we're left picking up the pieces, human and mechanical, to figure out what happened. Collecting the forensic evidence, recreating the scene, imagining the attacker's intentions, noting the effect of each munition on the human body. This is all fundamental to how we are trained to think.

There are so many ways to die, and right away, from the first moment, I wanted to know how Matt died, every last detail. It's a basic human response magnified by my professional calling. It was January of 2012. We thought Iraq was over, but Afghanistan was still bloody, and Matt was just the latest in a terrible string of killed and crippled. Fifteen of my fellow EOD brothers had died in the previous twelve months, a killed-in-action rate of 5 percent, over ten times the average for American soldiers at the time. The year before that had been even worse, and I had lost track of the number of amputees created. For a while there, it seemed like every few days you heard someone lost a leg.

Some of us slip through the war unscathed, and some are lost to it, and some step up to the brink and then are pulled back from the abyss.

War can be random; you can die from bad luck, wrong place at the wrong time. But other times they pick you out of the crowd, and it's intentional and premeditated. If it weren't a war, we'd call that murder.

I needed to know which it was. Was Matt unlucky or targeted?

So I did an investigation. In EOD, you always work as a team, and so I started with my teammates. I talked to the maimed, the too often forgotten survivors of both the random and deliberate bombs, and the medics who treated them. I talked to the detectives, the intelligence analysts and interrogators, who work the forensics and build the profile of the bomber. I talked to the hunters and killers who finish the job. I collected evidence from all of them, the same as I would from a blast site. And in the end, I learned that the story of Matt's death was also the story of the Surges in Iraq and Afghanistan, that both we and the jihadists have fundamentally changed the methods by which we fight, and that Matt was fatally caught up in all of it.

That's the story I'll tell here. All the ways we die, and nearly die, and who and how we kill in response.

But first I had to bury the dead.

2 · ROAD TO PERDITION

JENNY SCHWARTZ WISHED SHE WAS wearing a T-shirt that bore the news. That would make life just a little easier, save her the trouble of constant explanation.

If she had a T-shirt, it would be like wearing dark sunglasses and holding a white cane. Some small part of her brain would calm, as everyone around her would instinctively know that beginning yesterday, and for the rest of her life, the context of every future breath had been irreparably altered.

Instead, she felt the need to tell everyone around her, every stranger she met. It was like a mouthful of too-hot coffee. It had to come out.

And so as she sat on that commercial airplane from Cheyenne to Delaware, flying via a hastily arranged ticket that probably cost more money than she made in a month, she couldn't help herself. She just said it to the man vacuum-sealed into the seat next to her.

He was fat. He spilled over the armrest. He was in his early thirties probably, about her age. He was sweating slightly. He had not stopped talking since they took off. Her eyes may have been red and puffy; was that why he kept going on and on, relieving some perceived social awkwardness? All at once, it was too much. She cut him off.

"I'm sorry, but I just need to tell you this. My husband died yesterday morning in Afghanistan. We're going to meet his body at the morgue."

Silence.

And then a flood from the fatty mouth. I'm so sorry. I had no idea. I can't imagine. I just want to give you a hug. You just look like you need a hug. Do you need anything? Please, can I buy you a drink? Do you need somewhere to stay in Delaware? Here, here is my card. You can call me any time. Just to talk, if you need someone to talk to. You know, for now, just to talk.

Widow, she thought, not for the last time. *It would be easier if I just had a T-shirt that said "widow."*

She would tell everyone by the end of the day. The flight attendants. Taxi drivers and waitresses. The clerk at the Fisher House and the maid on the way to her room and the guys at the EOD unit who already knew and her friends who kept calling and texting her phone and filling her Facebook wall with prayers. She would tell all of them the same thing. "I'm sorry. My husband died yesterday."

But for now, she just sat in her seat on the plane and waited and looked out the window. She had just left a town at war; Cheyenne has two military bases within a mile of city hall. Her destination, Dover, Delaware, was a similar small town with a large base, the debarkation point for thousands of dead. Dover was also at war. But were the lands in between? For years Jenny had felt she was living a separate life, a parallel track from the America that she saw on the news or from her few nonmilitary friends on Facebook. The feeling of isolation was only growing.

Isolation, and anger. She was furious at him, for dying, for leaving her to bury him alone.

Jenny would eventually ask why. After a year or two, she would. It would take time, longer than her friends imagined, but she would. That day, though, and for many long months that followed, asking why didn't make sense. There was only a how, and on that airplane, the day after he died, this was how.

JENNIFER O'BRIEN AND Matthew Schwartz had grown up together in Traverse City, Michigan. Back then it was a poor and shrinking cluster of houses on a frozen lake, not the beach town and artist retreat it is today, and they were two kids largely left to make their own way. Jenny's parents had died in a car accident on Christmas Eve when she was very young, and so her much older sister had raised her. Matt's mother and father had divorced, and were only occasionally part of his life as a child. Not abandoned, not estranged, but also not consistently present. Day-to-day he was raised by his grandparents, a chore they embraced. His grandmother always called Matthew by his full name, because it means "Gift of God."

Jenny and Matt met in a local grocery store where they both worked, she fifteen, he a year older. His hair was long and he partied too much, but he was goofy, "a giant goober" she would call him, and she liked that. Neither was dedicated to school. No family member or guidance counselor intervened. Neither thought about where they were headed. Both college and career remained unconsidered paths. After high school, Matt worked as the night security guard at the local Sara Lee factory. Jenny got a job at the front desk of the Grand Traverse Resort. She sat and answered phones and watched the massage therapists make more money. I could do that, she thought. But she didn't. Matt took a couple of classes to get his private pilot's license, but quickly ran out of money. Aimless and unsatisfied, Matt and Jenny broke up, and as he was now free of his primary Traverse City attachment, Matt enlisted in the military in late 1999 for reasons common to countless numbers of young men before him: the simple need to leave.

When Matt returned for a brief visit later that year, Jenny didn't recognize him. The boy who left for Air Force Basic Training had come home for Christmas a man. He was now stationed in Fort Walton Beach, training to become a bomb technician at the EOD school at Eglin Air Force Base. He was already a generation removed from the Sara Lee factory and the grocery store, doing things no one in Traverse City did. He didn't ask her to follow him to Florida, not really. It was understood; this was her chance to escape rural Michigan.

You better treat her right, her older brother told Matt, and that was that.

There was a massage therapy school in Fort Walton Beach. It was six months long, the same length of time as the remainder of Matt's training. It seemed like a sign that things were possible in other places that were not possible at home. That it would all work out.

She left Traverse City for good. She joined him on the road to a marriage, to three children, to an Air Force career. It was 2000, the new year had come without a computer crash, the world was at peace, the Clinton boom showed little sign of stopping, and they were moving to sunny Florida.

MATTHEW SCHWARTZ WAS shot on his second combat tour and died on his sixth, and that story, like so many others, begins on September 11, 2001.

On that morning, Jenny was in bed with a toddler and Matt was at the Cannon Air Force Base gym, doing physical training before dawn. It is still hot that time of year on the utterly flat prairie of eastern New Mexico, and so his unit woke early to build their sweat in the cool mornings, avoiding the acrid breeze off the feedlots brought on by the afternoon heat. Never a runner, Matt usually got in a lift and then hit the basketball court, where most days they played a quick pickup game in which elbows were freely thrown and fouls rarely called. Matt wasn't much of a shot, but his deceptive height and growing bulk frustrated driving point guards.

The morning of 9/11 was like any other morning until the towers fell, and then Matt asked the same question a million other military souls asked: "Where we will go, and how soon?" No one knew the answer, just as they didn't yet know that the real question was, "How long will we be there?"

Matt had finally graduated from EOD school only eight months prior, and as the youngest and least experienced member of his unit, his answer to "where" was not Afghanistan but the presidential ranch in nearby Crawford, Texas. He spent the weeks before Christmas assigned to the Secret Service, searching visitors' bags and vehicles while F-16s from Cannon patrolled overhead. Two weeks later, he was off to Camp Snoopy, the American outpost at the international airport in Doha, Qatar, one of the rapidly expanding bases strategically sandwiched between Saddam and the Taliban. Matt spent the first half of 2002 watching cargo come in for the war in Iraq and special operations wide-bodies go out for missions in the Hindu Kush in Afghanistan. He never got any closer to the real fight than the humid flight line, and then he went home.

His second tour came a year and a half later, to Kuwait. Ali al Salem Airbase is a rocky speck in the emptiness that forms several natural borders in that part of the world, past the western outskirts of Kuwait City but off the main roads that lead to Saudi Arabia and Iraq. Salem was a radar station and sleepy C-130 hub during the long decade of Operation Southern Watch—the United States' name for the mission to ensure Saddam Hussein didn't kill the Marsh Arabs and other Shiites near the river deltas of the Tigris and Euphrates—but it expanded quickly to support the invasion north. The bermed border was only forty miles away.

By the time he arrived, though, major operations were already winding down. The worst Matt would have anticipated from such a posting were occasional trips into the desert to dispose of old unexploded ordnance, a daily drudgery of flight line standby, and sleepless nights listening to sortie takeoffs. It was early 2004, before the four contractors were hung from a bridge in Fallujah, and throughout the military the sense still pervaded that Iraq would be done as quickly as Afghanistan, and you had better act fast if you wanted to see any action. Stuck at Salem, Matt could only hope that he'd be called north to augment a unit doing real work.

But the call never came, and Matt watched the Iraq War on cable news. Salem was emptying; coalition countries that had partnered with the United States in the invasion, including the British, were packing up to go home. But shipping munitions is a costly and hazardous process, and once delivered it is usually best to leave them wherever they are. When the main UK forces left Salem, several bunkers worth of ordnance stayed behind.

Bill Hailer was the chief of the Air Force EOD unit at Salem, and thus tasked with cleaning up every other country's munitions mess, and when he wandered into the British bunker he discovered a puzzle that did not please him at all. Bill was a craggy ranch hand with a graying fifties flattop and wind-pitted face. He had grown up in southeastern New Mexico, near Cannon, where he was stationed with Matt. He was a master sergeant nearing his twenty-year retirement mark, and in those twenty years Bill had been just about everywhere an EOD technician could deploy, including Kandahar in Afghanistan immediately after the initial October 2001 invasion. Bill preferred straightforward missions and cut-and-dry procedures, and before the improvised device war in Iraq he found it in a professional lifetime of working with military ordnance, using established techniques and explicit safety precautions. But this bunker was different and presented a problem: it was full of rockets he did not recognize.

The Brits had beat feet out of town so quickly they barely had time to leave Bill a metaphorical note: "Gotta go—please blow these up for us. Brilliant! Cheers!" The few ammo troops left behind were clueless. Bill had expected 1,000-kilogram aircraft bombs, No 1 Mk 1 dispenser cans, something of an aerial nature to match the forces that had been stationed at Salem. Instead, he found infantry weapons: a few dozen stacks of wooden shipping crates cradling shoulder-launched rockets. Bill inspected further.

They almost looked like American Light Anti-Tank Weapons (LAWs). They were the right basic cylindrical shape, the right length, a door on each end of the tube. But the trigger assembly was bulky and a little odd, a foreign lever-actuated system. And they were too big around; American LAWs are only 66mm in diameter, and these were much bigger. Probably even bigger than the US Army's 84mm AT-4. And newer looking than both of those systems for sure. Bill took a picture of an open crate using a bulky digital

camera containing a 3.5-inch floppy disk and went back to the shop
to investigate the cipher he had inherited.

He searched for the rockets in a computer program called
AEODPS (pronounced "AID-ops"), the master database of all
munitions known to the US intelligence services. Like a Christmas
catalog of Civil War cannonballs and Russian surface-to-air missiles,
it is an international arms dealer's wet dream. It is also the bible for
bomb techs, and trusted as if God bequeathed a million specific
commandments. AEODPS delineates each piece of ordnance in
excruciating detail: sizes and weights, key markings for identification, the firing mechanism with blown-out diagrams as you would
find in a grease-stained car repair manual, historical use by countries
and organizations, and, of most concern, detailed instructions for
disarming the fuze, disposing of the explosives completely, and staying alive while doing so. Collectively, it is every EOD trade secret in
one place, and thus classified and highly controlled, one of the more
closely overseen sets of documents in the US military.

Hailer punched the British rocket's measurements into the database, and nothing popped up. He tried searching by nomenclature,
the thing's name, stenciled on the launcher. Nothing. He searched
for British rockets and found pictures of old blasting machines.
AEODPS was newly digitized—it had been available only in micro-
fiche or individual paper records not long before—and so a few of
the younger techs, more comfortable with computers and the new
system, tried their hand. Still nothing. Months later, Bill would
learn that the only way to find the thin publication in the database
was to already know the number under which it was filed.

He emailed his bosses at headquarters but got no answer.
He emailed the EOD technical development center outside of
Washington, DC, the publishers of AEODPS, for more detail. They
confirmed they knew the rocket existed, but provided little additional help. So Bill and his team made a disposal plan on their own.

The morning of the job, Bill stayed back at the base to pull
standby, and Matt Schwartz and three other members of the EOD

team arrived at the Salem munitions storage area before dawn. They loaded C-4 and det cord and time fuze and pull-ring detonators and the British anti-tank rockets onto two trailers towed behind their two unarmored Humvees. Then they drove out to the demolitions range, a featureless expanse of fine sand desert even emptier and lonelier than that upon which Salem was built.

The war was causing a global shortage of explosives, and ground combat units in Iraq and Afghanistan were the first priority to receive meager shipments, either newly manufactured C-4 or old satchel charges deposited in obscure stateside depots during the Vietnam War. They had some C-4, but Bill was concerned they didn't have enough, so the night before they all discussed whether they should gently remove each warhead and solid propellant motor from the launcher before detonation. The rockets could then be packed together more tightly, requiring fewer additional blocks of plastic explosive. Bill didn't like the idea; he was afraid removing the rocket could ignite the motor. Other members of the team thought it necessary. By the end of the talk, each side thought they had convinced the other.

As the oppressive early-spring sun climbed off the horizon, Schwartz and his teammates got to work. Half the team still thought they were removing the rockets from the launchers, and before anyone could stop them, slipped one out slick as could be. The process worked so unexpectedly well that they decided to download the rest. They passed each rocket slowly down into the hole, a pit explosively dug by a decade's worth of disposals. Once every rocket was in a dense line, a strip of C-4 was run across the stack. Finally, each tube was discarded into the back of an awaiting empty trailer, tossed aside as harmless scrap.

Matt stood in the back of that last trailer, snatching empty tubes and pitching them in a pile as fast as he could. Lunchtime temperatures were already typically well over one hundred degrees. His eagerness to be done and out of the heat made him and his team blasé and careless, but why be careful with trash that presented no hazard? They would not have tossed those tubes so recklessly if they had known they were being reckless, if they had known that cleverly concealed in a strip of black plastic on the underside of each launch tube was a gun barrel and magazine of high-power 9mm tracer rounds. They were throwing and kicking a pile of rifles with their hammers cocked. But Matt knew none of this until one fired and a clap of thunder struck the trailer.

In 2016, one can read the Wikipedia article on the same rocket launcher to learn of the concealed 9mm tracer rounds.

But in 2004, the first person on the Kuwaiti disposal range to learn of them was Matt Schwartz, when through random happenstance and nothing else, the projectile entered the top of his tan boot, burned through fiber and muscle, and burst in a bloody mess out of the bottom of his foot.

THE MILITARY WIFE fears the surprise knock on the front door as she would a viper in the cradle. Jenny has heard that knock twice. The first time it was me at the door.

Staff Sergeant Brown and I had not put on our dress uniforms before visiting Jenny Schwartz. We didn't want to scare her. Starched coats and a chest of medals says death. Rumpled camouflage says luck and life. Matt would be fine. He would recover and serve out the rest of his tour in Kuwait, be back running on his rebuilt foot in a few short months—but appear in the wrong uniform and there would be no time to explain that. The sight of us in blue would be a stronger message than any verbal reassurances we could give later, too late to prevent the anxiety and dizziness a vomit-inducing uniform brings.

"I haven't met Jenny, have I? It is Jenny, right?" I said to Brown as we parked and got out of the truck, smoothed our front pockets and adjusted our hats, walked the short walk from driveway to front door. I had been put in charge of the unit at Cannon only a couple of months prior, and I was already doing a casualty notification about a man I barely knew.

"Yes, it is Jenny, and you might have been introduced to her last year at the base Labor Day picnic," answered Brown.

"I don't remember."

"I know her very well, it'll be fine."

Brown knocked, I adjusted my uniform, my hands shook, a baby cried inside, a young woman in blue jeans with an infant on her hip opened the door, and I started speaking before I lost my nerve.

"Jenny? My name is Captain Castner. I'm your husband's commander here. I'm sorry to have to tell you this, but . . ."

She cut me off.

"Oh, I already know. Matt called this morning. He's fine. He's an idiot, but he's fine. Told me he's saving that stupid boot as a souvenir. That's the thing he's most worried about. Come on in and have some iced tea."

We did go in, sat on couch, I held the baby, Brown and Jenny chatted like old friends, I looked in that little girl's eyes and knew her daddy was fine and that in no time he would come home and that the war would be over soon and so everything would be all right.

BUT THE WAR didn't end. It was evolving, metastasizing even as I knocked on Jenny's door.

Behind that door, Jenny struggled to create a normal life for herself and her girls, always conscious that financially she was better off than she would have been had she stayed in Traverse City. Financially and every other way too. Leaving Michigan had propelled her to adulthood. She had completed massage therapy school in Florida, and after they moved she got a part-time job at the gym on base. Jenny made friends with my wife and others, all of them with young children and separated from extended family in that remote corner of America's high plains.

Cannon Air Force Base in Clovis, New Mexico, was their first real assignment, and Matt and Jenny would be stuck there for six years. Clovis is ten miles from the Texas border and four hours from anywhere you might want to be, a town so small and landlocked that when a local Walmart finally opened—the next closest was over one hundred miles away—it caused a sensation. The land there is utterly flat; stand on a tuna can, the joke goes, and you can see the back of your own head. Such a flatness yields no natural creeks, and so the water pools on the ground the few times a year it rains. It is a land of slaughterhouses and dairy farms and the smothering flocks of brown-headed cowbirds they attract. It is a place where the only thing in abundance is space, enough space for cowboys and cattle drives and alien abduction tales, enough space and privacy for miles of concrete runway and parking ramp and fighter planes. Out there range was both for grazing and bombing; Matt Schwartz worked the latter.

A camaraderie develops among those who undertake coopera-tive hostile labors, who trust others with the safety of their life and limb as a regular part of their day. Firefighters and police, rousta-bouts and ranch hands, grunts and EOD technicians each have their culture-specific élan that springs from the nature of their work. But the poor wives of these men develop their own sisterhood, an aban-doned cohort worthy of Milton: "They also serve, who only stand and wait."

The brotherhood of EOD is not all men, and the sisterhood of spouses is not all women, but the ratios are stark, thirty and forty to one, and gender roles perpetuate out of sheer practicality. From all over the country, such similar stories: married young, children young, off the traditional college track. They had all joined a peacetime mil-itary and saw their plans derailed by 9/11. Add an assignment to a lonely austere speck on a map, and the in-group effect is only magni-fied. Clovis sat on the prairie of the Llano Estacado, which as far as they could tell was Spanish for Flat Shitty Place, and there were only two ways to make the best of it: drinking and making babies.

"Most people don't join the military because they have a great life growing up," Jenny would observe, looking around her living room of early twenty-something couples bingeing on canned beer and plastic jugs of vodka. The assignment in New Mexico was full of such fests, families in base housing taking turns hosting so they could put their young children to bed and not drive home drunk. Such excessive partying bonded not just the EOD brothers before war, but—in a modern egalitarian spirit that has dispelled any potential stigma—their wives as sisters as well. None of their husbands told the whole story about Iraq or Afghanistan, so the wives would compare notes and find truth in the mosaic. The pile of empty bottles at the end of the night proved they knew what was coming. As her girls got older, Jenny gradually left that scene behind, but it had done its job.

It was in those years that my wife and Jenny grew close. Jessie connected with her like no one else we had met in my military service. They were the same age, same fit build and sandy-blonde hair, both from little towns in Michigan. Their names were so close they often answered for each other. The three Schwartz girls were nearly the same age as three of our boys, regular playmates when we were all stationed together in New Mexico and at reunions afterward. Jessie and my boys went to the Schwartz's house nearly every night for dinner while I was deployed in Iraq in 2005. We tried to return the favor when Matt was gone, but once we moved to separate parts of the country, occasional trips to visit had to suffice. Jenny and Jessie did drift apart, would go months without talking, but then would be attached on the phone for hours when one needed the other.

We got more of those phone calls when Matt was deployed, and his tour to Kuwait would be his last rearguard assignment. He had four more trips in him, two to Iraq and two to Afghanistan, and they would grow progressively more dangerous. In Iraq, he was in some of the worst neighborhoods the country had to offer, ugly towns north of Baghdad during the height of the Surge. His last tour was with the Marine Corps at Camp Leatherneck in Helmand, the bloodiest province in Afghanistan by a two-to-one margin.

He could see the trend, noted the danger increasing on each of his deployments, but still he went back. Why?

The earnest patriot, looking for a story of love and brotherhood and the triumph of the human spirit, will be disappointed by the answer. Matt and his family needed the money. He needed the reenlistment bonus; if he timed it right, and signed the contract while overseas, the six-figure check would be tax-free. Three girls to raise, a Great Recession on, no college degree between him and Jenny. He looked for jobs: the Secret Service, the ATF, working construction for his brother in Michigan. Nothing panned out, and so he signed up for another hitch. His modest upbringing had taught him the value of the steady paycheck and the full retirement to follow.

After his reenlistment, Matt tried to mitigate his combat exposure and failed. After the New Mexico fighter base known for its high-tempo deployment rate, Matt requested an assignment at a career-freezing backwater. He got F. E. Warren Air Force Base, a forgotten outpost on the Wyoming prairie, the home of Intercontinental Ballistic Missiles with nuclear warheads. Training to disassemble nukes is tedious and unpopular work, but Matt took it anyway, since it meant no more trips to Iraq or Afghanistan. Soon after he arrived, the Air Force changed its policy. There were too few EOD technicians military-wide, too many deployment slots in theater to be filled; missile bases like F. E. Warren could no longer shelter its support personnel.

Matt was headed back to combat, where there are no bills and paychecks don't matter.

Matt was caught in a certain generational band, a group of EOD technicians who enlisted in the few years before 9/11 and saw the worst of each stage in the war. He was still young during the invasions of Iraq and Afghanistan, when the danger was statistically more modest. He rose in rank and took on increasing responsibilities just as the IED threat spiked and the EOD technician's job evolved; not only were there more and deadlier hidden devices, but the EOD team leader's job required more personal exposure to them. If Matt had been younger, he would have had fewer years in the trenches. If he was older, he would have been promoted into leadership and administrative positions that required fewer route clearance missions and no more long walks in the bomb suit. Instead, he was stuck in the middle, counting the years to retirement. Only seven more, the day he died.

The simple mathematical odds were stacked up against him. One trip to Qatar, one trip to Kuwait, two to Iraq, now two to Afghanistan. Matt was sober enough to recognize the winning streak and know he should cut it off while he was ahead, but it's hard to step back from the table when you are betting for rent money.

Matt acted like a dead man walking as his deployment approached. Seven EOD techs died in the three months just prior to his tour, and Matt surely saw the post-blast investigation reports on each. He knew what was coming, and his family felt the vibe and internalized it. There was no way to jinx a sixth post-9/11 deployment, so they did things they never did before, said things they never said before. Matt had gotten shot and lived; his luck had run out a long time ago.

Jenny had consciously avoided getting family photos on any particular schedule—before deployments or after, on holidays or summer vacations—and it had developed into a superstition. But they broke that rule before this last tour, all sitting for one formal portrait. Emily, their middle daughter, seven years old, declared that that it was nice to get "one last family picture."

Messages came in from around the country. Bill Hailer felt compelled to contact Matt when he found an old photo of their EOD unit at Cannon and got a chill. In the picture, three men kneel in front of the main group, Matt with two others who had already died in combat. The photo seemed like a warning. Bill was long retired from the military but still felt responsible for getting Matt hurt on the range at Salem. His last words to his old teammate were: "Stay safe."

The grandmother who raised Matt called often in those months, but surprisingly, his grandfather did as well. Jenny wasn't sure the man even knew how to use a telephone; she had never seen him dial one. He called Matt to say good-bye and that he loved him.

Matt's biological father, unreliable for large portions of Matt's life, insisted on visiting the family in Wyoming, insisted on traveling to Florida to see his son in predeployment training.

"They aren't on vacation down there," Jenny told him on the phone in exasperation. "This isn't a party. He doesn't have time to see you."

"I promised my son we would have a drink before he shipped off to war, and goddamn it, we will!" he said.

"Do not contact him. Do not go down there. He is in training to go to Afghanistan. He cannot see you," she said, and he listened, but as she was saying it, she realized that she was the one to make sure Matt's father would never have the chance to say good-bye.

Matt and Jenny and the girls packed into the trailer and went camping on one last family vacation, and they called it that. They all felt what was coming, but even as the family violated every super-stition, did the last of everything, Matt's coldness and emotional distance was implacable. He didn't laugh. He was never goofy any-more. He came home from work every day, drank a bottle of wine in front of the television, and went to bed. He and Jenny fought constantly. She cried and begged, "When is the old you coming back?" Her goober was gone.

The gears of the military machine ground on, without consid-eration for intuitions or unease. The draft military of World War II and Korea and Vietnam was young and often unattached. The mod-ern all-volunteer military is professional, full of career officers and sergeants, and so we deploy more and more mothers and fathers, fewer and fewer single men. The average age of a US soldier killed in Vietnam was twenty-three. The average in Iraq and Afghanistan was twenty-six.

The final jinx was Jenny's last visit with Matt. "These weird premonitions are too much," she said. It all felt like Fate or God's will or both. So though she had never done it before, she left the three girls with family and flew to San Antonio where Matt, having finished his final training cycle in Florida, was awaiting his flight to Afghanistan. They spent his last few days in the United States together, in a suburban motel room.

Jenny was miserable, but Matt said she just had to deal with it, she just had to suck it up and she did, Jenny dealt with it, she dealt with it all, until the end of December of 2011, after Christmas, when Matt mounted up for a route clearance mission out of Camp Leatherneck and east and north across Helmand Province. Their job was to drive the highways, attract attention, get shot at, clear IEDs, and close with and defeat any resistance they encountered.

Before Matt left on the mission, he sent that last email to Jenny, the email she had been replaying in her head for the long week of near-silence that followed. This is what it said:

"If I don't come home, know I've lived a happy life."

THE DAY AFTER she was informed of Matt's death, Jenny flew from Cheyenne to Delaware and spent three days at the Fisher House at Dover Air Force Base, waiting for him to come home. Three days of blur, three days of sitting at a kitchen table but not eating, three days of filling out insurance forms, three days of hiding in the non-denominational chapel in silence.

If you've died in an American war over the last several decades, Dover has almost certainly been your first stop upon return to the United States. It hosts the Department of Defense's only port mortuary in the Lower Forty-Eight, the only place red, white, and blue caskets are carried off of military transport planes.

No, not "caskets." They weren't called that at Dover. Jenny was learning so many new terms, and she tried speaking them out loud to see how they fit in her mouth. Port Mortuary. Ramp Ceremony. Dignified Transfer. And not a casket with Matt but a Transfer Case with Remains. These new words burned and made her gag, like some cruel Tabasco-flavored medicine that somehow must be choked down twice: first for Matt's death, then for the inability to name it.

Since that knock on the door, Jenny had been so anxious to see him, to see his body and what state he was in, to make sure it was all true. But Matt was late leaving theater, and so she had an extra day to wait at Dover for the dignified transfer. But even then—and she had only just discovered this upon arrival in Delaware—she wouldn't actually be able to see him. It was against policy. She was allowed only to see the transfer case come off the plane from a distant viewing area. The morgue did allow her control over other decisions, a thousand logistical concerns including this: was it okay to destroy parts of Matt they might find later, or did she want the odd toe or kneecap that might crop up? Jenny asked her priest about that one.

Jenny and the girls kept vigil at the Fisher House, a large private boarding house for military families. A bum leg kept Zachary Fisher from enlisting in World War II. Instead, he became a leading New York City real estate developer, and after spending the first half of his life making his money, he spent the second half giving it away, to create a museum out of the USS *Intrepid*, to the families of the victims of the Beirut Barracks bombing in 1983, to a foundation to open free long-term residences for families of service members undergoing treatment at military hospitals. He would open twenty-four Fisher Houses in his lifetime, from Bethesda, Maryland, in 1990 to Fort Hood, Texas, in 1999. He died before 9/11, before the homes were flooded by families of casualties from the wars that followed. There are now sixty-five such houses, including the one at Dover, where there is no major hospital but there is a morgue.

With nothing to do but sit and think, Jenny found it hard not to regret getting married so young, getting pregnant so young. The military encourages you to marry, she could see that now. You have to live in the barracks if you're single, but if you get married you get to live anywhere you want and get a big extra check for rent besides. No way to live together first. No testing it out. There was too much money to lose. Together and married, and their first daughter was on the way in no time. Amazing it didn't happen before the move to Florida, honestly. And now three daughters to raise, suddenly, on her own.

Well, maybe not so suddenly. Everyone thought he was a family man, but he worked late, made the military number one, never took off to watch the girls, always made her find the babysitter if she had something to do for herself, take a class, accept an evening massage appointment. She was the one that made the family. What did he do? He just came home, took a big shit, ate dinner, went to bed. He never cooked. He never cleaned the kitchen. They had been on their own a while.

She was so angry at him, but at least now he was coming home.

The sun was out the day of Matt's arrival, pleasant despite a January chill. They stood on the Dover flight line in a small group, Jenny and the girls and Matt's parents and brother and sister. The girls got excited as the gray C-17 approached, jumped up and down and yelled, "Daddy's home! Daddy's home!" In some ways it felt like any other deployment; always a day late, she and girls dressed up in their fancy clothes to welcome him.

The back ramp opened. A small blue honor guard removed three transfer cases. Then it was done. They returned to the Fisher House.

She had one final decision to make before she left Delaware: where would Matt be buried? Certainly not New Mexico, nor Cheyenne where they lived now. For years he was adamant that he wanted to be buried at Arlington, that it was the fitting end of his military life. But ambivalence had crept in during that last summer, that time of last family photos and the last vacation, and he had suddenly announced that he didn't care anymore. Bury him anywhere. Rather than provide her freedom, though, this new lack of guidance was a straightjacket.

In the end, only Matt's grandparents had an opinion. They had raised him, had said good-bye, were not bound by martial concerns nor hearts hardened by six deployments. Their request was simple.

"Bury him here with us," they said. "Bury him in Traverse City."

She would, she decided. The Air Force was his job, but he wanted to be a good father and husband at heart, she thought. So she would bury him in Michigan. That first road to Florida, a highway to

beaches and youthful opportunity, had somehow looped around in
the distance and brought them back to where they started. After a
dozen years of military life, and almost as many years of war, they
could claim nowhere for themselves, nothing felt settled and right,
not even their childhood home. That wasn't a time of innocence
anyway. But Traverse City was home to people who loved him, so it
would have to do.

She bought a plot at the traditional family cemetery. She bought
the plot next to her parents' graves. And then, at the age of thirty-
three, she bought another, the one right next to him, for herself.

3 · A FROZEN FUNERAL

MATTHEW SCHWARTZ DID NOT DIE alone. Bryan Bell and Matt Seidler, the two younger members of his team, died with him, making January 5, 2012 the EOD community's worst ever day in Afghanistan. The last comparable loss in a single incident was five years earlier in Iraq. On April 6, 2007, a 107-millimeter rocket struck an armored Humvee and killed the entire Navy EOD team inside: Chief Greg Billiter and two petty officers, Curt Hall and Joseph McSween. They were near Hawija in the northern part of the country, traveling in the protected center of a convoy, when the projectile was shot from the side of the road. The warhead struck the weakest seam, the joint where the front door, side plating, and roof come together. The odds against such a precise strike are incalculable; it was luck that killed them. We know this because another EOD team did an investigation afterward, collected evidence, processed the data, and wrote a report. But that takes time, and on the day of Matt's death and the several days after, most of us had almost no idea what killed him and his team.

There was no question that Jessie and I would go to Matt's funeral, only how soon we would leave and how many of our children—the Schwartz girls' former playmates—should we bring. Jessie wanted to leave that night, as soon as we found out. She wanted to go, somewhere, anywhere, to immediately close the miles between her and the Schwartz family. But we didn't know if Jenny was going to the morgue in Delaware. We didn't know where the funeral was. We didn't know anything. So we did the things you do, we called and Facebooked and told everyone who might not have already known, and then we kissed our children in their beds where they slept. Jessie packed until I stayed her nervous energy, and it was far into the night that we finally lay side by side in bed, staring at the ceiling in the dark.

It was then that I asked the question that had been gnawing at me from the moment of my phone's first fell buzz.

"Why did you ask if it was Matt before?" I said.

"What do you mean?" she replied.

"When I got the message and we didn't know who died, you asked if it was Matt. How did you know?"

"I was always a good nurse because I knew," she said.

"But how? Did you just pick the worst possible name you could think of?"

"No, I was thinking about Matt this morning."

"Did he come visit you today?" I asked. She understood what I meant.

"No. Don't you just have days where someone weighs on your mind, on your heart, and then you call them and find out there was horrible news or they had a bad day?"

"That doesn't happen to me," I said and rolled over to go to sleep.

ON THE MORNING of Thursday, January 11, my wife and I and my two oldest boys climbed into the family van and drove the many hours from Buffalo to the top of the mitt of Michigan. The wake was scheduled for Friday evening, the funeral Saturday morning. A recent storm had left behind a heavy blanket of snow that made rounded barrows out of parked cars. The drifts and piles only deepened as we crossed the low Canadian farmland and gradually climbed into the glaciated hills and thick pine forests of northern Michigan. The highway ended, the roads narrowed and slickened, the mounds of snow grew ever higher, the woods ever wilder, and

I was reminded again that a winter's journey into the north is also a journey back in time to a harder past. In a northern winter, the natural world still holds sway, and human exertions are kept to the limited concerns of warmth, sure footing of boot and tire, and the next belly-filling meal. The thermometer was thirty degrees lower and the snow two feet higher by the time we reached the huddle of silently smoking chimneys on the frozen East Arm of Grand Traverse Bay.

All out-of-town family and friends were staying at the Grand Traverse Resort, where Jenny had worked answering phones as a teenager half a lifetime before. For the first time, she returned now as a guest, for free, a comp provided by the hotel's owner.

We parked the car in the hotel's unplowed parking lot, and with careful stutter-steps began to unload bags and carry them through the knee-deep snowdrifts and across the icy sidewalk to the entrance and check-in. The lobby was an empty vault, oversized in the off-season, and as we stood in line at the check-in counter, wet below the knee and holding wet bags, Jenny and the girls appeared on the far side of the space.

I learned something in that moment. The lonely years together at remote bases, late-night phone calls, playdates while husbands were deployed, months of meals prepared to ensure the spouse left behind would eat, the encouragements and support to go back to school, the commiserations about unsanitary base housing, the secretly crafted mutual plans to leave unworthy husbands, the rituals and schedules, the endured deprivations and disappointments, the practiced grief, all those trials that form the bonds of military wife sisterhood, all was in preparation for this:

The two women caught sight of each other, and with no hesitation or shame, ran into each other's arms.

"I'm so sorry, Jenny," Jessie said.

"When they told me, I didn't want to believe them. I kept asking, 'Are you sure? Are you sure?' I would have punched someone if they were wrong. I wanted to punch someone so bad. I think I threatened to punch the chaplain if they were wrong. But they said they were sure, and they were right."

"I love you, Jenny," Jessie said.

"But I didn't believe them, because I said, 'If he's really dead, then where is the shop? Where are his EOD brothers? Where is everyone? They would all be here if he was really dead.' But they weren't. It was just the commander and the first sergeant and the chaplain, and I barely know them. Why didn't any EOD guys come to tell me?"

"I'm sorry, Jenny."

"They said, 'Is there anyone we should call,' and I said they should call you. But the Air Force couldn't find your number. They couldn't call you. And I, I didn't know what I could do. But I thought, if he was really dead, you would have already been there somehow. But you weren't."

"I'm sorry, Jenny. We're here now."

UNFORTUNATELY, THE COMMANDER and the first sergeant and the chaplain were right, and Jenny knew this because earlier that day she and the girls had finally been allowed to see Matt. The Air Force conducted a second dignified transfer, transported him from Dover to a funeral home in Traverse City, and it was there that they and the rest of Matt's family finally got their first look.

Jenny and her three girls passed through the decorated public front of the parlor and into the EMPLOYEES ONLY preparation rooms in back. Matt was in a casket, and as one, all four peered in over the lip.

They looked at one another. Then they laughed. This wasn't their daddy. This wasn't her husband.

Matt's beard had been shaved and his hair had been trimmed, but into a style he had never worn, faded along the sides with trendy sideburns. They were thin and narrow, unlike anything he had in life; Matt preferred a standard-issue, seven-dollar high-and-tight from the Base Exchange. His jaw was set oddly forward and shifted to the right, giving his head a boxy look. There was a massive bruise around one eye. The undertaker had filled him full of embalming fluid but hadn't yet applied makeup, so he was puffy and pallid. But none of those inconsistencies compared to the most obvious flaw.

"Why doesn't Daddy have his glasses on?" one of the girls asked.

Yes, that was it. No glasses. Matt was blind without them. The thought of him buried without his glasses was too much. Jenny sought out the funeral director.

"Sir, what happened to his glasses?" she asked.

"I'm sorry, ma'am, he didn't have any when he arrived," the older man said.

"Please, do you have any more? He needs his glasses."

The funeral director did keep a store on hand, for cases such as this, but all were bifocals in elderly styles. He had no glasses for a man in his thirties. He certainly didn't have the type Matt always wore, a round, steel-rimmed pair issued free by the military hospital; Matt was too cheap to go buy his own.

In the end Jenny selected a style Matt's grandfather would have been more comfortable in. They were as close as she could get. At least he had something.

THE WAKE WAS the next day, on Friday, and the first to arrive at the church that afternoon were not clergy or family or military officials but rather strangers, large, bearded men, clad in black leather, riding coughing motorcycles the color of an Iraqi burn pit. They were not modern riders of pale horses but rather protection, and comfort.

Since 2005, a relatively small group of citizens have exercised their right to free speech by protesting at military funerals, using the semi-public occasion as a platform to spread a political message linking dead soldiers and the civil marriage of homosexuals. In response, a much larger group of citizens, over two hundred thousand total at last count, have exercised their Constitutional right to counterprotest, forming a much larger human wall to block the sightlines between the fundamentalists and the friends and family of the deceased. Since that first protested funeral, the Patriot Guard

Riders have literally ridden around the country, from tragedy to tragedy, flags unfurled from the backs of their bikes, standing shifts at memorial services and interments from Maine to California. They even brave Michigan in January.

The Riders set up for the wake hours before the event officially began. They fitted flags on poles. They straightened their jackets and vests, dressed in padded overcoats of Cold War Army camouflage to keep out the worst of the chill. They parked their bikes in the most remote corner of the lot, and when they approached the church, few smiled and few spoke. Many were old enough to be Jenny's father. They were already in formation, two lines forming an impenetrable corridor from parking lot to church's front door, before the first guest arrived.

By design, Jenny and the girls also arrived at the church early, to claim a few solitary minutes before the two days of public performance would start. Family and close friends kept a respectful distance at the back of the nave, where a table had been set up with news clippings and memorial testimonies and the traditional large, framed photo of the deceased. Eschewing modern military norms, in his death mask portrait Matt has no beard from a month on patrol, no rifle and body armor, not even an American flag in the background. Instead, Jenny chose a close-up, her goofy Matt with a toothy smile that lights up his entire face.

I recognized the photo. This one had been cropped, but the larger version was put on Facebook months before. In the full view, he is grabbing a fellow EOD brother in a side bear hug, their faces close, Matt reaching his left hand across to secure his bro's right nipple for a playful twist. In the background are rows of aircraft seats and overheads bins; the photo was taken on the rotator from Baltimore, Matt's last flight to his last deployment. There is a sense of anticipation, a tender deviousness, a joy, a love. But no such context for this solemn memorial, and no titty grabs in church.

While her friends waited, Jenny and her three daughters walked up the aisle to the open casket alone, to spend a last family moment together. The girls carried the prayer shawls given to them at the Fisher House. In a cluster of oddly linked arms and hand-holding, they approached the box and stood and held one another and looked.

His makeup was on and the bruise was covered and the glasses were there, but she still didn't recognize him, not really, lying there in the coffin. But she didn't know the man who had left, either. Not the one that had left the last time.

One night, in the summer before his final deployment, after the girls had gone to bed and the house had grown quiet, Jenny and Matt stayed up alone, watching television. It was a typical show common on America's commercial networks, involving police and terrorism and homeland security. In that particular episode, a woman was forced to drive a car with an IED in the back. She was forced to be a suicide bomber. Matt got agitated, restless, and then loud, far too loud for a quiet house with three sleeping girls.

"This is bullshit!" he yelled. "That never would happen."

"Honey, be quiet, please," she urged, trying to soothe. "What would never happen?"

"The police. They've stopped the car. They're talking to her. You never do that. They should have shot her."

"What are you talking about?"

"If they think a bomb is in the car, everyone needs to get back, and you need to shoot her!"

"Matt, this is America. You can't just do that!"

"Jenny, I think I know something about this. I think I know what you should do. And I'm telling you, I don't care where you are, you shoot her in the fucking head!"

Which man lay in this box? The perpetually smiling goober from the memorial photo? Or the other one?

Jenny led her girls back to Aleesha and Amanda and Jessie, the small group of EOD wives waiting for her at the end of the aisle. They hugged her, and like a child she put her head down on Aleesha's chest.

"Are you okay?" they asked.

"I want to crawl in the casket with him and fall asleep," she said.

THE MIND IN grief seeks safe harbor in the sure detailed facts of the death. But no longer connected to any official channel or source more reliable than vague DoD press releases and Internet reports, I was adrift and still knew nothing. It was not until the wake, a week after Matt's death, that I could finally corner a fellow EOD guy and ask some detailed questions, to relieve some of the anxiety of ignorance.

"I don't have access anymore," I said. "All I've heard is that he was in a convoy. I haven't seen the report. Have you?"

"Yes, I've seen it," said Pinkham, an old friend from Cannon. "The initial report anyway. He died midsentence."

"What do you mean?"

"They were mounted, in the JERRV," said Pinkham. "Blast hit between the driver and team chief up front. Vented through the hull, into the cab. Massive blast over-pressure. Threw the JERRV twenty feet in the air, I heard. So it was big, it was quick. It wasn't . . . *that*. You know, what you worry about. What you think when you hear they were in the truck."

Yes, I knew what he meant. All of the worst ways to die had been in the front of my thoughts as well. Like the doctor treating their own sick child, too much knowledge and insight can consume. That headache could be meningitis. Lethargy could be leukemia. If it was another child, it would be easy to dismiss. But your own . . .

Fire is the night terror of every armored vehicle occupant. The JERRV, the massive six-wheeled and V-hulled armored truck used by EOD forces whenever the road allows, used to carry a spare tire up front, bolted in place right behind the team chief's passenger side door. New trucks from the factory still bear it, but it's the first thing to come off when the JERRV arrives fresh and clean at your compound's parking yard. No one ever drives them in combat like that anymore, not since one took a rocket-propelled grenade square on the four-foot-tall tire. The armor absorbed the blast, but the tire burst into flame. It melted through the door seals and rapidly moved inside the truck, spreading through the flammable interior, a wind-whipped desiccated grassland of seat covers and uniform fabrics. The crew fled in time, that time.

But we've all done a post-blast where they didn't. The meat slides off the bone like greasy pork short ribs cooked all day in an Alabama smoker.

In my worst fears, Matt's truck was hit by a smaller bomb, or one placed less perfectly. It could have caught the fuel tank or ignited the bang stored on the outside of the truck or pushed the hot engine block into the cab. Thrown toward the ceiling or side wall by the blast, striking his head against the armored can, Matt could have been knocked unconscious as the JERRV nosed into a dirt berm. Slumped, crumpled, neck unnaturally overextended as his heavy helmet pulled his head to the side, radio crackling, *Are you okay are you okay*, as smolders swell to open flame, and red and orange forms flash to life around him.

A minute passes, and nothing.

It would be the coughing that finally rouses him, his lungs filling with the acrid black and green smoke of burning plastic and electronics. Half-blind, his glasses slipping from his nose, not knowing whether to fumble for his harness first or the door. He would have woken up waist deep in the Phlegethon, the river of fire and boiling blood that comes for the violent of this earth. His feet are hot inside his boots. He violently slaps his thighs, momentarily staving off the flames that crept up his pants.

He yells at his driver. He yells at his robot operator. They still slumber.

Matt could have fumbled with the nylon restraining straps on his seat as a face appears in his window. It's his security. They shout and wave to get him to open the door, shut tight with two heavy metal combat locks, drive bar activated at the top and bottom of the frame by a massive swinging handle. He reaches for it, but misses in a wave. His right arm is pinched against the seat and the truck hull, and his left isn't responding like it should. He yells at this security. They yell back at him. All is muffled, as the flames intensify and noxious smoke shuts out the light.

Like a hurricane, the rescue MRAP could have arrived. The last truck in the convoy, massive drag chain attached to the front chassis and wrapped up and about the hood and front grille. In a flash that chain is unwound, solid tow hooks attached to the D-ring latches on the outside of the JERRV door. *Get out of the way*, the platoon sergeant barks, as the driver of that MRAP grinds the transmission into reverse, buries the pedal, and speeds backward to tear that armored cage limb from limb.

And snaps the chain. The combat locks hold. The MRAP bumper bolts hold. The rescue D-rings on the JERRV, proudly spark-welded in place by a veteran craftsman at the factory in South Carolina, doing his part to fight the war and bring our boys home safe, they hold as well. The chain snaps, and the MRAP nearly backs into a ditch, and the fire rages and the platoon sergeant yells to grab the spare out of the back of the command Humvee.

Driven mad from panic and pain and heat and blindness and choking poisonous breaths, Matt could have cursed his God and his ravaged arm that doesn't have the strength to twist the release on the secure combat lock. Locked in to keep the hostile crowds out. To keep an Afghan mob from pulling open the doors and dragging your body through the streets and hanging you from a bridge. Those heavy locks could have done their job. No one can get in.

His security on the outside can't hear him screaming, but they can feel the pounding against the door, see his fist beat against the armored glass of the porthole-like window, the hull of the JERRV hot to the touch now as they desperately take a crowbar to the door. The soldiers will work to free him long after the pounding stops and the smoke completely blocks their view inside, long after he stops moving at all, his nose and lips blackened craters, only the metal plates of his body armor recognizable among his gear. When they finally get the door off, the smoke will pour out anew, the soldiers vomiting from the smell as they desperately claw inside and take a hold of the first exposed limb available, in their haste forgetting the manner in which that arm is going to fall in their lap. Short ribs.

This was my nightmare. Matt could have died in a fire. But he didn't. He died midsentence. I knew that for sure when I finally glimpsed his perfect, pale face propped on a clean, soft pillow, and the tears ran undammed off my cheeks and down the side of the casket and onto the floor. Thank the Lord.

WHEN THE CROWD lined up at the sanctuary door, Jenny put on her face and braced a mask of brave smiles. All night, the stream of mourners never slowed, greeting her, then filing past into the main aisle and reception area and cafeteria space in the basement. There was family, of course, and military friends from previous assignments, local police and firefighters and National Guard, concerned citizens and local politicians. Traverse City is not so large that the native sons it has sacrificed in the post-9/11 wars are anonymous or uncountable; Matt is the fourth of five.

They pity me, Jenny thought. She could see it in their red eyes and stooped shoulders, the tears meant for her and her daughters. They wonder how we'll make it. They wonder what will happen to our family. Jenny didn't want to be pitied, but there was no help for it. All she could do was be stronger than them. She decided she wouldn't cry, not until the show was done, and she and the girls were alone.

Jenny stayed at the wake until the very end. The girls had long since gone back to the hotel, taken by Matt's brother and her sister-in-law, who had assumed the lion's share of the babysitting, feeding, bathing, clothing, and entertaining duties as Jenny's empty body proceeded as required through all expected duties and rituals.

Jenny walked out of the back of the church as the lights were being shut off, her breath momentarily taken away as she stepped into the frigid, snowy darkness of the northern Michigan winter.

The door was opened for her by a middle-aged man with a long mustache and riding leathers. His fellow Patriot Guard Riders were each in exactly the spot she had left them hours before. Most held an American flag, a few the black and silhouetted image of the Prisoner of War/Missing in Action memorial. Each stood in a little hole; they had stayed off the shoveled sidewalk to make space for mourners, and so through occasional shuffling and stamping of cold feet, they had packed down a small space in the adjacent knee-high snow. Four hours in the single-digit dark.

"Thank you for coming," she said to each in turn.

"It is our honor, ma'am," they replied one by one.

That night her sisterhood of fellow EOD wives stayed with her in her hotel room. Jenny took off her mask and drank as fast as she could until sleep finally took her.

ON THE MORNING of Matt's funeral, the sky was empty and pale. The snow-producing cloud cover of the last several days was finally gone, and like an insulating blanket suddenly ripped off the bed while you sleep, a shocking cold set in, that particular sharp-eyed cold that assaults the interior of your nose, squeezes your sinuses shut, and makes your head throb as the roof your mouth begins to freeze with each breath.

We all returned to the same church we had left only hours ago. Every pew was full, and the back wall of the church filled with the overflow. Two priests said the funeral Mass, an abundance of clergy in this time of national shortage, an elderly semiretired man and the comparatively younger current pastor of the parish. The older priest had overseen Matt's conversion to Catholicism, had answered all of his probing and barbed questions as Matt determined if a life in this church was right for him, had married Matt and Jenny in that same church more than a decade before, had baptized their oldest daughter.

Perhaps in times past it was commonplace for priests to bury those they have married. Perhaps priests used to specialize in taking out those they had brought in, when an unkind harvest would shorten the lives of those in the fields. But priests are out of such practice now. They are unused to seeing the full span.

The younger pastor led the service, gently cued those unfamiliar with the rituals and responses, the standing up and sitting down. There is comfort in being told what to say; one's own words never sound more hollow or insufficient than in requiem. The priest presided with pride and regret and perspective and exhaustion.

"More than any pope or theologian," he said in the homily, "more than any biblical scholar, more than anyone in this church, Matt knows the Truth of it now."

Matt knows the truth. Everything for him has been answered, but I still had so many questions, starting with this practical matter: is the bottom half of him in that casket?

I didn't think about it until I had left the wake the night before. Only the top half of the casket was open. Why was that? Was his bottom half not in there? Pinkham said the JERRV took the blast between the driver and team leader up front. Did it shear Matt in half? If I had thought about it the night before when I last saw him, I would have checked. I would have put my hand in and checked. Is the bottom half of him in the casket? Who could I ask now? Not Jenny, not now, but who else would know? Is the bottom half of him in the casket?

I could think of little else during the service until nearly the end. As he intoned the final prayer, the priest's stoicism finally cracked, and I heard a catch in his voice. Surrounded by Jenny and the girls, he laid a hand on the draped casket and begged that Matt have angels to lead him and martyrs to welcome him, to Paradise, where Lazarus is poor no more.

Matt and Jenny led the procession out of church, past more Patriot Guard Riders already mounted for the processional convoy from the church to the cemetery. It was a seven-mile drive, and the January sun was too feeble to break the cold, yet still the streets of Traverse City were full of mourners and well-wishers and sign holders, flag wavers, and small children and saluting old men in one unbroken chain the full length of our journey.

This welcome-home parade offered no Manhattan ticker tape, only rest for a servant good and faithful.

The snow was thick and unspoiled at the cemetery, white clumps clinging to the boughs of the encircling pine trees. We parked in a line, tromped a path through the white to a small fabric tent and deep trench it sheltered.

I looked about. All of the gravestones were covered in a blanket of snow. I couldn't read any of the names.

There were a few chairs in the tent, and Jenny and the girls and Matt's parents took them. An honor guard carried the casket ahead of us and set it upon the belt and winch suspension system that straddled the hole. The priest continued his prayers, and the honor guard prepared their rifles, and I wondered how much of Matt we were burying, and then the general stepped forward.

Lieutenant General James Kowalski, three stars on his shoulder, shaved gray hair and lips a line. General Kowalski was the commander of all intercontinental ballistic missile and nuke-capable bomber units in the United States Air Force. He started flying B-52s in the Carter administration. He led the sole bomber wing that pounded Baghdad in 2003 and had not done a combat tour in the Middle East since. That wasn't his fault; it was to him to prepare for another war while burying the casualties of this one.

The honor guard approached with a flag folded into the triangle shape of the hat worn by the soldiers of our country's first war. The general got on one knee and looked Jenny right in the eye. He spoke under his breath, muffled and intimate despite the mourners crowded all about.

Jenny told me later that she felt bad for him. He was distraught and holding back tears.

"On behalf of the President of the United States," he said, on the edge of hearing, "the Department of the Air Force, and a grateful nation, we offer this flag for the faithful and dedicated service of Technical Sergeant Matthew Schwartz."

Jenny took the flag, and she nodded, and the general stood up, and when he stood up we all let out a sigh, all of us shoulder-to-shoulder against the cold, grateful that the worst was finally over. But we were wrong. The general turned sharply to his left, moved one seat down, and prepared to present another flag. Three more, one to each daughter. He abandoned the script, spoke to each of them in turn, said things only they could hear. It was another ten minutes before he finally got off his knees.

A bomber jet roared overhead on cue, they lowered the casket into the ground, we took turns dropping our EOD badges into the awaiting hole. I had nearly forgotten mine, but before I left, I dug in the basement and found the silver badge I had last worn on active duty. I hoped it would be sufficient to lie with Matt for what's left of eternity.

How much did we just put in the ground?

That was only my first question: Is his bottom half in the casket? By then, I had a hundred more.

WHEN I GOT home, I sat down at my computer, Googled Afghanistan, and pulled up the satellite map. I zoomed in on Camp Leatherneck, Matt's last home. It sits at the bottom of the loop, just south of the highway ring road that ostensibly connects the country, Kandahar to Kabul to Mazer-e-Sharif to Herat and back. But there was nothing to learn from this wide view. Zoom in once, the runway and living areas just come into focus. Zoom in again and the base disappears completely, a mirage in the desert.

I shifted the satellite image slightly to the east, to Kandahar, and found the airbase on the southeast side of the city. I zoomed in further. First, just sand and highway and tire-stained runway. Then details emerged, slowly and in blocks, and though there was little to see in the bland square structures, I stared anyway.

Soon a digital artifact revealed itself, a north-south line of clarity that split the airbase. C-130s and Marine Ospreys and Chinook helicopters and fabric shelters appeared in high definition on the west side of the base, yet on the eastern side the blur remained, no matter how I cropped and zoomed. The smudge stifled my attempts to learn more.

In eight years in the military and three tours in the Middle East, I had been to Afghanistan for a total of two days and one night, barely long enough to smell the place. I spent more time flying over the country than awake on the ground, and in my daily journal, I wrote little more than this:

"We are six hours ahead of Zulu. Eastern time is [then another] four hours back, sometimes five. We are further away from England than England is from Michigan. I am literally on the other side of the world from my wife. And I can feel it."

Disappearing Camp Leatherneck, the smear across Kandahar. Google reinforced that distance, rather than bridge it.

I had been to that blur, though, in 2005. On my sole day in Kandahar, I walked through it when it was still an active construction project: a parking ramp and hangars and taxiway extension for a new unit of Predator drones, now surely hunting along Matt's last patrol route.

Outside of Kandahar, Google confidently lays out highways that IEDs and mines have long since made impassable, and it misses the donkey paths that actually carry the traffic. From the air, the villages are bichromatic: brown huts and fields, green trees lining the canals. Each farm appears to be the model of orderly symmetry, every row precisely tilled, as if we are looking not from a satellite but through a microscope at a series of ribbed mitochondria.

With my mind's eye, I followed those dirt roads west, back toward Matt's final mission, and found the Reg desert and Mushan and Taloqan in the Horn of Panjwe, where Dan Fye lost a leg, and then farther toward Sangin and beyond, where Matt lost it all. Add up the last few years, I knew, and my comrades had left a few dozen arms, legs, hands, and eyes in that stretch of country.

When your comrades are coming home in pieces, I had always been taught, as an EOD officer, to focus back on the device. Adjust your tactics, disarm the next one. But I was out of the military and could no longer fight my way through, vent my frustration on a physical thing. And Matt's death cut so close; he was on my list of brothers I couldn't lose. I felt compelled to do something more, so I turned the tables and asked a different question.

Not what killed Matt, but who.

Who set the bomb on that road? More importantly, who built it, who designed it, who taught the grunts to use it? By 2012, nearly every roadside bomb was tailored for a specific purpose; to know whether Matt's death was random or the result of a deliberate scheme, I needed to learn more about this builder, designer, teacher. The master tailor.

I opened a new window, searched for recent war news, and discovered that Predators had been busy in Pakistan while I was driving to and from snowy Michigan. Two strikes on successive days had killed fourteen jihadists. Those killed on the second day may have been traveling to the funeral of those killed on the first. The dead included three Arab operatives associated with Al Qaeda. What does "associated" mean? What do they do? Who are these men? In the media they are always "organizers" or "planners." Anyone can hand out money; who actually engineered the bomb?

Yes, that's it. Who is the engineer who killed my friend?

It was a question I had never really asked, not with any specificity, and it consumed me.

I reconsidered everything I already knew about this man, including this possibility: could it be one of the same bomb designers, the same old hands from Iraq, the same minds I faced years before?

4 · CAT VS. CAT

WE ALWAYS CALLED HIM THE Bomber, and this is the first part we got wrong. It was useful shorthand, widespread in the media, and so even though we knew it was incorrect, we repeated it anyway. How did the IED get to the donkey path? The Bomber put it there. Why are there six artillery rounds hidden in the courtyard of this mud-walled *qalat*? This is where the Bomber lives. Who did we just shoot digging on the side of the road? Must be the Bomber.

We in the EOD community understood the imprecision, but the lazy figure of speech persisted, especially in our conversations with the uninitiated infantry and armor commanders who ran our sectors. So words guided thought, and thought guided action, and we spent many years chasing and killing men called the Bomber who were, in fact, no such thing.

The truth is harder and more specific. If the Bomber is the person responsible for an explosive device's existence, the ultimate guilty party, then mostly we know who the Bomber is not.

The Bomber is not the average foot soldier, the unemployable Afghan with a battered Kalashnikov and a literacy that does not extend beyond the Koran, nor, eventually in 2015, the disaffected middle-class British youth traveling to Syria to join the Islamic State. The gunman is a tool and a trend, not a leader.

The Bomber also is not the man who hides the weapons cache and then places the explosives in the ground. This job is too dangerous, exposed, and menial to be done by someone with the expertise to build the thing. Better to pay a desperate, out-of-work father to do it instead.

The Bomber is not the cell leader organizing the attack. Many of these men are extremely clever, but their cleverness is in camouflage and hiding the device and choosing advantageous terrain, not in the design of the bomb's firing circuit.

So too the Bomber is not the spotter waiting for an American convoy to approach, or the triggerman with his thumb ready to key the radio to set off the device. Once made, bombs are often placed by gun-toters in the service of an ambush. Despite the stereotype and the historic Western examples to the contrary, in Iraq and Afghanistan the designer of the bomb was almost always not the employer of the bomb. The Unabomber may have fought a one-man war against the American system, but jihadists fight collectively in groups.

The Bomber is not the one wearing the suicide vest. So much education squandered, so many future devices left unbuilt, it makes no sense to blow one's load on a single binge, no matter how high-profile the target.

The Bomber is not the courier, though such conflation proves tempting. When Hassan Ghul, an Al Qaeda agent, was captured entering Iraq in 2004, he was toting schematic diagrams for IED triggers. This caused quite a stir, but why would the circuit's designer carry such incriminating physical evidence and risk capture when the plans were also in his head? Ghul was a trusted confidant, but no scientist.

The Bomber may not even be the one mixing the homemade explosives by hand or, occasionally, constructing the devices in a rote assembly line in the basement of a concrete apartment building. Even these men and boys, in the end, are only skilled technicians. They can do, but know not why.

No, the Bomber was none of these people. Behind this manufacture and implementation system and web of insurgency lay a director, the real threat, the learned mind that actually understands how the bomb works and teaches others to build it. The Bomber's false title glosses over the nuance of the network, but it inadvertently expressed this truth: there was an original ultimate source of these electronic and explosive devices, even if our overgeneralization revealed that we didn't really know who it was.

Since the Bomber as a name is meaningless, colloquially referring to everyone and no one, I will stop using it here and now.

To establish a new and more precise name, I'll instead use the tradition of the Arabic-speaking people he comes from, and refer to him by his nom de guerre honorific. Invoking a *hadith*, a saying attributed to the Prophet Muhammed, Al Qaeda prescribed that its operatives should always use an alias of a *kunya* and hometown. A *kunya* is a nickname, normally *Abu*, meaning "Father of," followed by the name of the oldest son. Among his followers, Osama bin Laden was known as the Sheik, but also as Abu Abdullah. The second half of the alias, the hometown portion, is often mistaken by Westerners for a last name. Al-Asiri, on the FBI's Most Wanted list, is simply the Syrian. Abu Mansoor al-Amriki, a former commander of al-Shabaab in Somalia and a similar FBI listee, is the Father of Mansoor the American.

But among the mujahideen themselves, the noms de guerre are more than an alias meant to trip up intelligence agencies, and the larger tradition predates Al Qaeda. When an honorific is used, it can supplant an original name and come to completely define a person. Two famous leaders in Chechnya in the 1990s were al-Walid and al-Khattab, the Young Man and the Narrator. Saddam Hussein's chief chemical weapons specialist, "Chemical Ali," earned the surname al-Kimyai, or the Chemist. Even Hussein himself, no Al Qaeda operative in search on anonymity, was al-Tikriti, our man from Tikrit. Was there really any question where he would hide and ultimately be found?

To the average Westerner, the names are nothing but strings of similar syllables, but among jihadists and militants, such brevity is the reward for notoriety. We misunderstand that the names are great describers, distant cousins to Red Cloud and Sitting Bull. The names have meaning in a way John or Nancy or Edward or Dorothy no longer do.

So what will we call the bomb builder? This anonymous intellect, the electronic architect and resourceful originator of each new bomb design, the man who killed Matt Schwartz, is al-Muhandis, the Engineer.

Who is this man?

At the start of the war, we had almost no idea. Even now, he is still a shade to those who pursue him. He is a necessary box on an organizational chart, the inevitable solution of an intel analyst's continuously computed probability equation. His proof of life photo is a burning, bombed-out Humvee. He doesn't grant interviews. He doesn't issue fatwas. He doesn't make promotional videos. He is the true quiet professional, and for good reason. When similar men are caught in the United States—Eric Rudolph, Ramzi Yousef, Terry Nichols, Ted Kaczynski—we send them straight to Supermax. In 1996, a Palestinian bomb designer named Yahya Ayyash briefly became the most wanted man in Israel, until he was killed by security forces. Occasionally, one or two terrorist bomb makers garner worldwide media headlines, not to mention the NSA's attention, for crafting shoe bombs and underwear bombs for US-bound airplanes. They fail, and meanwhile al-Muhandis simply gathers kills in Iraq and Afghanistan and Syria, thousands over the last fifteen years.

Before I began my investigation, I reviewed the little I already knew, every intelligence report, news article, translated Arab novel and short story, memoir of Islamic militants, academic paper, conventional history of the Middle East, and bit of jihadist promotional literature I had ever read, every documentary and YouTube and LiveLeak and Ogrish and Brown Moses video I had ever seen, every conversation I had ever had with intel spooks and wonks, and every bomb of his I had ever dismantled, circuit design I had studied, and employment tactic I had taught. This is what I concluded.

At first, the only thing I knew for sure about the Engineer was how he killed, all of the ways we died at his hand. The war was a chess match, and al-Muhandis always went first. First, he built the bomb. Then we would try to take it apart.

THE *WASHINGTON POST* says the first IED in Iraq was a car bomb detonated on March 29, 2003. Maybe. It's hard to tell where these things start. Did it start with the booby-trapped bunkers and oil facilities and military headquarters left by Saddam's fleeing army? Did it start with the elegant "spider devices" in Afghanistan, radio transmitter/receivers soldered together from scratch? Or in the 1980s, when US agents taught Afghans to build the precursors of those spider devices because the mujahideen were killing Soviet invaders and not us?

Nothing is new under the sun, including IEDs. Ask what makes the wars in Iraq and Afghanistan unique, and an incorrect superficial analysis might conclude the IED, the greatest casualty-maker of the last fifteen years. But the IED is just an insurgent's weapon, not a tactic or strategy in and of itself, and the US military has fought many booby trap–laden counterinsurgencies over the last hundred years, from the *bundok* Philippines to Vietnam. The IED was not the difference. No, the innovation of this conflict was the method by which the IED was developed, how it was manufactured and emplaced, how quickly it evolved in reaction to our defenses, and, most significantly, the anonymity of the intellect behind the design. The average soldier could not say who they were really fighting.

History can rarely indicate precisely where anything begins, and no one knows where the IED trend leads in the future. But we collected enough data during the wars in Iraq and Afghanistan to know what happened then, and so while both ends of the "IED Incidents" chart are hazy, we can be fairly certain of the middle.

The evolution and taxonomy of IEDs proceeded thus:

The first IEDs in Iraq were rare, simple, and small. They consisted of common household items, wireless doorbells or garage door openers or transmitters from cheap Chinese radio-controlled cars or electromechanical timers we called washing-machine timers, though their origin was unclear. All these components were used to create separation, to allow the triggerman to be physically removed from his target. There was no sophisticated importation network yet, so the Engineer used what he had.

Those initial roadside bombs worked famously well against unarmored Humvees, and so they didn't stay rare for long. Yet as late as December of 2004, the Army was still teaching soldiers to run convoys in stripped-down trucks—no doors, no windows, no coverings, no armor—with sandbags in the floorboards and every passenger facing sideways, rifle out, feet dangling, chest plate toward the incoming small arms fire. In theater, soldiers knew better and were welding on every spare bit of sheet metal they could find—"hillbilly armor" we called it—to turn our rolling death traps into, well, something only slightly less than death traps. Still, some of those trucks were driven long past their shelf life; the ones that had never been hit were deemed lucky, and soldiers wouldn't leave them.

Armor became more plentiful in 2005, as bolt-on kits made flimsy trucks hard. The increase in armor prompted a reaction, and the main explosive charge in IEDs grew larger, more focused, or, though only rarely, both. At the same time, the triggers of IEDs were developing very quickly, though not in response to armor. The countermeasure that forced the IED to blossom into its full potential was our electronic jammer.

Why buy one when you can buy two at twice the price? This apocryphal rule of government spending proved useful: when the military needed a system to counter the Engineer's devices that operated via radio waves, it already had two sitting on the proverbial shelf. The Army had an older system, called Warlock, originally designed to turn off the sophisticated fuzes of incoming Soviet mortars. The Navy had a newer system, called Channel, developed after the bombing of the USS *Cole* to stop attacks by small boats in harbors. The Department of Defense bought as many of both as it could, boxed them up and shipped them to Iraq without so much as an instruction manual, and the resulting mix of models and manufacturers was nearly as varied as the IEDs they were shielding against.

The Engineer's principle design concern, more than target or camouflage or size of blast, is control. How to make sure the bomb goes off neither too early (killing the emplacer) nor too late (killing the wrong target). Wireless doorbells provided sufficient control until the first generation of American jammers drowned out their low end of the radio spectrum. Thus began a race to the top. The Engineer would choose a transmitter/receiver combination just outside of the spectrum of the jammer, and then the latest generation of American equipment would be fielded or tweaked to blot out the threat. This iterative summing process occurred weekly; twenty years of Northern Ireland Troubles IED development swept through Iraq in only three. Every consumer product that contained a switch and an antenna got a turn: toy cars, garage door openers, cordless telephone units, car alarms, handheld mobile radios of various powers, telemetry modules, air cards used in factories to remotely control manufacturing processes, WiFi. There were no mice in this game, only cats.

When cell phones finally appeared in IEDs, as we knew they would once the tower network infrastructure had been laid, a special kind of fear radiated. Cell phones are designed to cut through interference, to latch on to the weakest of signals, to filter out a thousand other cell phone users operating in the same space and still get the message through. Many died before we jammed them right.

The Engineer devised other ways to overcome the jammer—long command-wires, suicide attacks, pressure devices known as "Christmas tree lights"—but in Iraq those options never diverged into the varied art forms achieved by the radio-controlled triggers.

There were other, nontechnical IED development factors at work. After Sunni Al Qaeda affiliates bombed the Shia Al-Askari "Golden Mosque" in February of 2006, an entire violent branch was added to the IED family tree. Now Sunni and Shia, the Engineer and his counterparts in the Iranian Quds Force, killed each other with a lust they had previously saved for Americans. A pocket of pent-up bomb-making creativity was unleashed on the Iraqi police and representative militias of each group, US soldiers often caught in the middle.

So it was that by the end of the Iraq War, only the peak species on each side survived. The variety of the Jurassic had given way to the highly specialized of the Cretaceous. Evolution was done trying interesting combinations and now focused exclusively on effectiveness. The only trucks that remained on the road bore the best jammers and were the most armored, V-hulled MRAPs and Buffalos with front bumper–mounted kick-brooms and the occasional Humvee with multiple layers of bolt-on armor and horned projections on the nose. The only IEDs worth planting were large enough to overturn twenty-ton trucks or pierce armor with molten slugs, and used multiple arming and firing systems to defeat the few weak points in the jamming sequence. At the peak of the worst operations in Sadr City and Baghdad and Samarra and Baqubah, bomb technicians in the toughest trucks would clear a dozen IEDs a day, each one uniquely tailored to kill their vehicle based upon its particular inherent vulnerability. It was a bloodbath. The crescendo had been reached.

Then the meteor struck, a new president was elected, the United States declared the war over, and we all went home.

Well, some of us went home. The rest went to the war most had forgotten about.

Afghanistan remained a primordial soup. The war there began with rifles and landmines and the occasional suicide vest or car bomb. Following the initial blaze of the 2001 invasion, the fire began to burn itself out, ran low on fuel and dimmed, charcoal glowing red and cooling. The war in Iraq was a clarion call for foreign mujahideen, and the Engineer concentrated his efforts there. Iraq-style IEDs were almost nonexistent. Landmines, yes. Dud-fired rockets and RPGs, yes. Gunfights for sure. "I got more confirmed kills in Afghanistan than IED ops," was a usual sentiment from those American EOD techs deployed as late as 2007, when the mission was to drive the few roads and get shot at and clear the occasional command wire. At that time there were 25,000 US troops in Afghanistan, a country the size of Texas. Meanwhile, in the real state of Texas, there were nearly 54,000 police officers.

But war itself can be elemental, consumed with its own self-perpetuation, and below the ash the coals never quite extinguished. As Anand Gopal describes in *No Good Men Among the Living*, in those years the small American force regrew a native insurgency by propping up unpopular government officials and choosing sides in tribal conflicts. That these actions were done in good faith mattered little. By the time the Iraq War wrapped up, American soldiers were quashing a rebellion across southern and eastern Afghanistan.

The Engineer was back, and the IED-lite days were over. Afghanistan lacked the infrastructure—cell phone towers, reliable electricity, highways, domestic manufacturing—to fight a technologically sophisticated IED war. But when the battleground shifted to the steep valleys, winding donkey paths, and hilltops where only helicopters could fly, the Engineer gained the advantage. Al-Muhandis could provide reliable hidden booby traps with local materials. The development of Afghan IEDs accelerated quickly, with as many varieties of pressure plates—devices that function when you step on them—as there had been radio-controlled bombs in Iraq.

The total number of IEDs in Afghanistan doubled between April 2006 and April 2007. Then doubled again by April 2008, then again by the following spring, an 800 percent increase in three years. The president added more forces, to push to new territories previously unpatrolled, and the number of IEDs increased yet further.

The more rocky trails the soldiers walked, the more *qalats* they searched, the more IEDs grew like some hidden fungus spreading underground. That's where the devices were now, buried in the dirt and mud. Every footfall became suspect.

IEDs had devolved back to the simple, perfectly suited for the terrain and target. It was an ecosystem dominated by a single life form, but a species that existed in an infinite variety of permutations, adapted for the geology, soil type, available hardware, weather, time of year, and latest poppy crop. In the rainy season, soldiers saw different models of pressure plates than during the dry. In rocky soil versus dirt. In the desert versus muddy roads. Where wood was plentiful, planks formed the support pieces for the opposing contacts. When landmines were available, they were used as the trigger for an even larger main charge. And just as the jammer drove IED evolution in Iraq, the soldier's handheld metal detector inspired new pressure plate designs. When American basic landmine sweepers discovered hidden steel ordnance, the mujahideen switched to homemade explosives and put it in plastic jugs. When those metal detectors were tuned so they could still find the wires of the pressure plate, the Engineer developed devices that used carbon rods invisible to American scanners.

During those times of peak IED growth—in Iraq from 2003 to 2007, in Afghanistan from 2007 to 2010—the trend lines in both theaters were clear. Seventy-five percent of all fatalities and injuries in Iraq and Afghanistan were due to explosions. Every day the war got a little deadlier. The rate of casualties on both sides rose. The number of IEDs rose. The number of patrols and Predator sorties and air strikes and named operations and suicide attacks rose. Like adjusting the brightness and contrast on your television, the picture stayed the same, but every day the colors deepened and became more pronounced. Far back in October of 2003, the US Secretary of Defense, Donald Rumsfeld, asked if we were making more enemies every day than we killed. For years, in both theaters, the answer was yes.

We needed to do something different. And so in Iraq in early 2007, and in Afghanistan in late 2009, we implemented a new strategy. We decided to focus on people, protecting the population and hunting men like the Engineer, and we called this the Surge.

ON AUGUST 6, 1896, the parliament in Paris declared Madagascar a French colony and immediately dispatched forty-seven-year-old colonial counterinsurgency veteran Général de Division Joseph-Simon Gallieni to the island to put down the insurrection that was sure to follow. Gallieni had experience fighting the native people of lands known today as Mali and Vietnam and was well-armed with a tested theory of how to beat back such uprisings. He set up a central administration with a Malagasy face that determined national policy and then broke the island into seven *cercles* (circles), further divided into *secteurs* (sectors) and *sous-secteurs* (subsectors). French officers were given great autonomy to conduct operations in each *sous-secteur*, commanding both French and indigenous forces, as long as none of their policies contradicted the will of the titular central administration.

Gallieni's network prevailed, thanks to the initiative of his commanders and the co-opting of local tribal chieftains, and the monarchist rebels were pushed to the margins. The territory's pacification advanced "slowly from the center to the periphery, according to the method of the oil slick," wrote Gallieni in 1908. By then, one of Gallieni's lieutenants, Hubert Lyautey, had taken the *tache d'huile*, the oil slick, to Morocco to quash further colonial rebellion. The French toted it to Algeria and Indochina in the 1950s, the British used oil spots in Malay the same decade, and American Marine Lieutenant General Victor Krulak called for ink blots in Vietnam in 1964.

Appropriately enough, they would be called oil spots again when other American generals were "clearing" and "holding" towns and villages in Iraq and Afghanistan during each war's respective Surges in the late 2000s. Announce the intention to reclaim Fallujah or Marjah or Sadr City, allow the civilian populace to flee, kill every insurgent left inside the town, bring back the population, and the newly free town will ooze stability and commerce radially. Create enough oil spots, and their edges start to merge, the surface tension breaking as one success blends with another, and eventually Iraq and Afghanistan are left with a pleasing oily sheen.

But this was only half of the Surge strategy. Upon reflection, American generals and think-tankers realized that this model could be applied in two different ways. The oil spots they were seeking to establish were the mirror image of the insurgent networks they were trying to crush. Terrorist cells could be described as oil spots as well, and this insight provided a theoretical framework on which to hang new ideas about how to fight insurrections that, after half a dozen years of war, were still resolutely refusing to die, or, in some cases, still growing.

In numerical fact, five or ten million military-age males lived in Iraq and Afghanistan. But in practical terms, each contained an infinite number of potential trigger pullers. The democratically elected United States government, exercising the will of the American people, could not fight a war of attrition that condoned the elimination of two generations of boys and men. Killing the average insurgent eventually became counterproductive; one man inclined to help the militias became eight, as his previously unaffiliated brothers, cousins, and sons took up arms. Would you kill those eight? The sixty-four that followed? The village? The valley? The clan? The United States could not kill its way out of either country.

Enter a new oil spot method, where Gallieni is turned inside out, and every terrorist network is modeled as an oil spill three rings deep. With the photo negative flipped, now insurgent influence is to be curbed, rather than stability spread. The central daub of petroleum, Gallieni's administration, the impetus for expansion, is the core of ideological zealots and financiers. The next, intermediate level would be the fixers and cell leaders, the weapons stockpilers and smuggler kingpins, the enablers who were sometimes family members of the innermost core. The outer ring was the general population of either country, the poor farmer who fell easy prey to the lure of ten dollars to tote a gun or place a bomb, an unemployed (and unemployable) youth who was nine years old when the towers fell and had lost half of his cousins to a childhood of gunfights. Both sets of oil spots—insurgents and stability—need this outer ring to grow, which is why any public policy debate about the relative efficacy of the protection of local populations versus the hunting of terrorists—counterinsurgency versus counterterrorism, or COIN vs CT, in the military's jargon—missed the point. Not only would we do both in the Surge, spread our own oil spots while undermining the opposition's, but each effort was the yin to the other's yang.

The first ring provided the money and policy. The second ring organized and taught and equipped. The third did the dirty work. There would always be more dirty work, and so killing the doers of it did little to stop the spread of the stain. Ask any American soldier to describe their country's new Surge strategy in one sentence, and he or she would have responded with this catchphrase: "The people are the prize." Killing the poor and desperate alone ends no modern war.

The central core of the insurgency was in hiding, hard to find, and so needed to be lured into the open to be caught. Thus it was in the identifying and killing of the second level where success lay. Relatively few know how to design a bomb, few know the right proportions with which to mix homemade explosives, are trusted to buy the guns for the smugglers, to acquire mortar tubes, to plan the rocket attacks on lonely American outposts. Kill the second level, kill the Engineer, kill the nephews of the fatwa issuers, and the ideologues are cut off from the general population. They will eventually have to show themselves to recruit more, putting their own neck on the headman's block, and when they emerge, a Predator will find them.

Everyone thinks war is dehumanizing, but they're wrong. War is personal, deeply personal. Every soldier at some point realizes, "They're trying to kill *me*." But in modern war, rather than kill any person, we kill *that* person. That particular person, but not another. War has always been personal, but now it is individual, specific to the associated alias and photo and fingerprint and DNA sample and dossier.

The point is this: some people are worth killing more than others.

TO SPREAD GALLIENI's oil spots, to implement the first part of the new strategy, the generals said we needed to walk around. A simple order but a problem, because before the Iraqi Surge, there was a saying. "Death before dismount." Not everybody said it, but enough, across divisions and units of all types and around the country, and this is what we meant: I'd rather die than get out of this truck.

The conflict in Iraq was—and is, in the fight against the Islamic State—primarily an urban war. The resistance was spawned in the cities, the sectarian conflict pitted neighborhood against neighborhood, and some of the fiercest fighting occurred house-to-house, in small farm towns dotted like rest stops along the infamous MSR Tampa, main Highway 1. The IED construction cells largely kept to the blacktop, and we were happy to accommodate them. A war is more convenient when one can drive to it; not only do you arrive armored, but you can bring all the guns and explosives and robots you want.

By the time the Surge began, the IEDs and small arms and mortar fire had grown so thick that survival meant minimizing exposure to the outside world. For a mission to clear a car bomb, the average Iraqi would often see six gun-trucks arrive. Jammed inside those vehicles would be twenty or twenty-five men and women. But many times that local civilian would only see the helmets of four of those US soldiers, the poor gunners stuck in the turrets. No one would get out. The soldiers were hidden behind a wall of laminated glass, and as far as any local could tell, as robotic as the one-armed bomb-defusing machines they employed.

The Iraq Surge upended that model. For those in combat, the Surge was never so much about numbers as methods. Out of the trucks, out of the main-hub Forward Operating Bases, the FOBs, on foot patrols to little posts established in back alleys. Even if the average solider could drive through a neighborhood, it was better to walk, to meet the locals, know their concerns and loyalties, hear what happens at 0300, gain their trust, build a relationship beyond once-a-week tea-drinking sessions and visits for car bomb detonation investigations.

The generals said to get out of the truck. So we did, and it worked, but at a price. In 2007, during the main thrust of the Iraq Surge, 904 US soldiers, sailors, airmen, and Marines died, a 10 percent jump and the highest yearly tally for the war.

In contrast, Afghanistan was never an urban war. The few main cities were seized and pacified quickly, but President Hamid Karzai was derided as the Mayor of Kabul because peace barely extended to the suburbs. The fight was always in the mountains and across poppy fields and in clusters of mud hovels that appeared on no maps.

Iraq was dangerous, but when considering the basic structures of society—roads, buildings, government, utilities, attitudes, culture—it was fundamentally Western. In comparison, using those metrics, Afghanistan might as well be the far side of the moon and accessible only by time machine.

And so every aspect of the Afghan Surge was comparable but magnified in challenge and complexity. It focused on going to the parts of the country US and NATO forces had never been. But they had never gone because they couldn't get there: no roads, treacherous flying, long humps on the trail. The solution was to go once and stay, establish tiny fire bases throughout the frontier. IEDs followed.

The number of casualties produced by the Afghan Surge's mass movement of soldiers out of armored trucks was staggering, and proportionally far worse than Iraq. By mid-July 2008, after almost seven years of war and before the Surge, Afghanistan had claimed five hundred American lives. The Surge began a year later, and by May 2010 the total death toll was at a thousand. That number doubled in the next twenty-seven months, the two-thousandth death coming in August of 2012, just before the Surge officially ended. Seven years to lose five hundred. A loss of fifteen hundred in a three-year Surge. The killed-in-action rate, per capita, was double that of Iraq and equal to the Vietnam War overall.

A similar death toll would play out in the EOD community, and for reasons related to the second aspect of the new Surge policy. To get inside the insurgent oil spot and find the Engineer, JIEDDO said we needed to move "Left of Boom." JIEDDO, the Joint IED Defeat Organization, was a Washington bureaucracy charged with demystifying the IED and killing it, and their theory, moving left of boom, provided us the tools to make the war individual.

Envision a timeline where the past stretches to the left and the future to the right. Now place an IED on that timeline. In its normal life cycle, as time moves forward to the right, the IED will detonate and sow havoc and chaos. If a US soldier or local civilian finds the device before it detonates, we may be able to stop it, but our actions are still clustered chronologically around the placement of this bomb.

But imagine the chain of events that led to the placement of that IED. Someone had to put it under the bridge. Someone had to build it in a secret factory. Someone had to purchase the circuit board. Someone had to raise the money to buy the materials. Further and further left of boom we go. If we could interrupt the chain, if we could stop the Engineer from designing new bombs or teaching others to make them, then the device would never get out to the roadside in the first place.

And so this is how we would come to know the Engineer, by his bombs and the little they left behind. The first step in moving left of boom is to collect all of the forensic evidence of the IEDs themselves, and to do that, initially we used robots.

Two main platforms dominated: the Talon and the Packbot. The Talon was a shoddy, indestructible tank, a bedraggled hobo of black plastic and rubber wrapped in a worn felt carpet. Its arm operated via a bike chain and lacked the sophistication to break regularly. In contrast, the Packbot was half the weight and twice as sleek, a delicate vision with Apple-esque curves. It was thin and silver, and its arm came from a space alien, an extra joint and a camera at the elbow. The Packbot's manufacturer, iRobot, was a robotics company first and a defense contractor second; style was as important as substance. The Talon shrugged and pressed grimly on, rammed IEDs until they fell apart.

Those robots were our champions. We named them after porn stars and UFC fighters. We covered them in flags and posters and pinup girls. We loved them like a gambler loves a lucky pair of dice, kissed before rolling craps, and treated them with a mix of superstition and respect. They searched dark culverts and basements. They reached inside car bombs. They were impervious to nightmare and disease and fear. EOD and al-Muhandis, each of us sent our anointed surrogate into the arena to fight in single combat for a human master hundreds or thousands of meters away.

The Talon and Packbot were too large to lug any great distance, and so in Iraq we stayed mounted, encased in the best armor, carrying our technological counterpart to battle in a 47,000-pound chariot. But in Afghanistan, we had run out of roads, and so EOD techs were finally forced to abandon their trucks in large numbers and fight a war on foot in the mountains. Robots could no longer be our first and greatest shield.

The Surges were deadly for the average soldier, and within the EOD community, an equally grim tally played out. The initial years after 9/11 were relatively easy. We didn't lose a Marine EOD technician until 2004, a Navy or Air Force one until 2006. But that was the year—in the midst of the arms race up the spectrum between IEDs and jammers, when more and more robots were fielded, when new armor was only starting to be widely available—that the death toll started to mount. Fifteen in 2006, then eighteen at the height of Iraq Surge in 2007. We got a break in 2008, when the Iraq War started to wind down and the Afghanistan Surge had not yet begun, but then it increased again in earnest. Fourteen in 2009, seventeen in 2010, fifteen in 2011, sixteen in 2012. More deaths between 2009 and 2012 than the previous eight years combined.

WHEN MATT SCHWARTZ arrived in Camp Leatherneck in Helmand province in October of 2011, it was a red-hot cauldron that had long ago reached full boil. The IED and casualty statistics would not have been news. His eyes were wide open, and he knew the score of the game. He had even seen this coming, noted the danger increasing on each of his deployments, but still he went back. Why?

Sure, for the money, for the job security, because he was ordered to at some point. But he could have found a new military job. Could have faked an injury. Could have told the mental health counselor he was crazy, and it might have even been true. He could have done many things that would have kept him off that Afghan road on January 5, 2012. Why be there?

Roughly eight billion people ate and drank and slept and breathed and loved and did the best they could on the planet Earth the bright Afghan morning that Matt died. And out of those eight billion people, the three EOD technicians sitting in that JERRV that day were the best qualified to be on that route clearance mission, to perform that particular task at that particular moment, to clear that road, at that time, of all of the bombs that lay before them.

After more than a decade of war, the American military boasted the best trained and equipped EOD force yet produced by any nation at any time in history. Schwartz and Seidler and Bell had been in-country for months. They knew the road they drove. They knew the Engineer worked their sector, and they had learned his preferred tactics. They knew each other and worked as a team. They were in the toughest truck available for bomb clearance work. And unlike their brothers humping the Hindu Kush on a foot patrol, they had every robot and bomb suit and type of explosive they wanted. So many ways to die, but they had every advantage possible and they knew it; such confidence allows you to slip into your body armor every day.

The obligation of competence provides purpose and drives action. When eight billion people would be more at risk, how do you not get in the truck and go to work?

Which is why, the more I thought about it, the more Matt Schwartz's death seemed such an anomaly.

All we knew so far was that Matt died in a truck, the biggest, meanest truck we had. It was a shock, so anachronistically out of step. It had been years since a group of EOD techs had died like this, because the Afghan Surge had changed the war so drastically. Why not tell me Matt and Bell and Seidler fell on Hamburger Hill? That their ship sank after a kamikaze attack? Were overcome by the Spanish flu of 1918?

Yes, in that truck, Matt died midsentence. But I bet he never felt safer than the moment before the detonation.

I knew nothing else about how Matt died, but the one detail we did have nagged at me like the itch of a mending leg inside an old-fashioned plaster cast, inaccessible and ever more insistent.

There was more to this story. I was sure of it.

IN MY TIME in Iraq, I never caught the Engineer. More than that, I didn't know anyone else who did, either.

So before I got serious about this inquiry, I had to ask myself again, and not for the last time: Am I sure the Engineer even really exists?

This man. Not the gunman, not the emplacer, not the mixer, not the spotter. No videos of him. No statements issued. Slipping unseen from Afghanistan to Iraq and back, the lone educated scientist, everywhere and nowhere. Is he just a bogeyman? An unsolvable koan, or the center of an infinite series of Russian nesting dolls? Does there even have to be a prime mover, or could IED knowledge simply coalesce organically as the inevitable sum of enough authorless Internet sites? This isn't Oz: there doesn't have to be a wizard behind the curtain. In the real world, there can simply be another curtain.

The farsighted Isaac Asimov considered this question in his mirrored way in 1962, in a short story titled "The Machine That Won the War." Earth has just survived a long interstellar war with Deneb, all thanks to the Multivac, the great computer. The Multivac guided all battle decisions, all troop movements, all crop production and resource management. Data was fed into the machine, a program churned, and a decision was made. But in the glow of victory, three key men admit to one another that it is all sham. The data collector never trusted field reports and altered the input numbers. The programmer didn't have reliable parts, and the Multivac had not processed information correctly in years. And the supreme leader ignored the report outputs and made his decisions with the flip of a coin.

The Machine was really a coin flip. What is the Engineer?

I have come to believe that the Engineer is both a battlefield phenomenon and a very few flesh-and-blood individuals, probably less than a dozen, though I doubt anyone knows for sure. He is the aspirational target for a generation of special ops intel analysts and a specific man responsible for the device that killed Matt. As a member of a very, very small club, he's a solo artist within any particular region or organization, like an apex predator that hunts a vast range alone. Anyone who interacts with him—from jihadists allies to American counterterrorism forces—would call him "the Engineer." They would likely only ever know a single one.

When al-Muhandis appears in print, it is solitary, accidental, and fleeting. Abu Ahmed Rahman al-Muhajir ("the Foreigner"), the Al Qaeda builder of the bombs that hit the US embassies in Africa in 1998, is offhandedly mentioned only a handful of times in *The Black Banners*, former FBI agent Ali Soufan's definitive 562-page brick of a book about the days after 9/11. Early in *The Outpost*, Jake Tapper refers to a Nuristani bomb builder (even called an engineer by local tribesmen) twice in passing before moving on. The 2004

Duelfer Report on Weapons of Mass Destruction briefly mentions the Al Ghafiqi Project of the Iraqi Intelligence Services, a directorate attempting to build James Bond–esque assassination IEDs in "books, briefcases, belts, vests, thermoses, car seats, floor mats, and facial tissue boxes," but it does not name a single design engineer. Gopal mentions the Engineer only once: when the local Taliban commander wishes more advanced bombs, his superior called contacts in Al Qaeda, and "arranged for a visitor from Pakistan, a bespectacled, clean-shaven Arab in his twenties."

The most thorough description of the Engineer in recent publications may be found in *Voices from Iraq*, a compendium of first-hand accounts compiled by Mark Kukis in a Studs Terkel–style. In the book an Iraqi academic, using the non-*kunya* alias Omar Yousef Hussein, describes the process of joining the resistance in Baghdad in 2003. His cell wants to build an IED, but despite the fact that they had money and weapons and vehicles and the support of Iraqi generals, they don't know how.

"None of us had experience in explosives," he says. "So we had to be taught how to make the device. There was an Egyptian from Al Qaeda who showed us how. He had come from Afghanistan, through Pakistan and Iran to Iraq. From our group we dedicated an engineer who took lessons from this Egyptian."

An Al Qaeda explosives expert, a traveling contractor, already in Baghdad in 2003.

Omar Yousef Hussein continues to describe how this Egyptian taught them, how he planted a seed so they could make future bombs of the same style on their own, how he left so they could prepare the bomb using a hand drill to bore through the steel of an old artillery shell and insert old Iraqi blasting caps, how they carried it out of the mosque and planted it on the road and a Humvee came by and they detonated it and every American who left the scene did so on a stretcher.

So, no, the bomb that killed Matt Schwartz did not spontaneously appear because of an accumulation of information on the

Internet. There had to be a man, like the Egyptian Al Qaeda *muja-hid,* who taught someone to build that device. The hit man pulls the trigger, but someone has to design the gun.

THE WEEK AFTER the funeral, I stood at the stove making dinner, adding chunks of whitefish to a tomato and vegetable soup. Jessie walked up the adjacent basement stairs, a hamper full of clean laundry on her hip. My back was turned, so I only felt her enter the room, didn't see her red eyes, swollen from crying. She paused before she spoke.

"Thank you for not dying in Iraq," she said quietly.

I turned. "I'm glad I didn't die too," I said. "I don't know why I didn't."

"All the important people we knew in our twenties," she said, "the ones we spent the most time with, stationed in all those little towns in the middle of nowhere, all those people are dead now. Our friends are dead."

But that's not true. They're not all dead. Some survived.

The Afghan Surge was often deadly, but it was also dismembering. It sent too many of our friends home alive, but as a portion of their former selves. Mourn the dead, but don't forget those, who but for the grace of God . . .

When a bomb detonates in the midst of your EOD team, you do three things. You tend the wounded immediately, rescue and assess and transport. Then, when everyone is patched up, you collect the forensic evidence from the scene. Finally, using the three-ring oil spot theory, the intelligence apparatus figures out who did it, in order to hunt him down and kill him.

There was only so much I could learn about the Engineer from reading books, so the next day I started on step one and booked a plane ticket to see Dan Fye. Months before he had left a leg in Doab, just down the road from Matt Schwartz's last patrol. Fye had survived. He could teach me more about this Afghan War I had never fought, and he was intimate with the Engineer in a timely and personal way.

Matt Schwartz was dead and so was his whole team. I wanted to know if it was bad luck or if they were targeted, and late at night I lay in bed and asked Matt but he never answered.

So I sought out the wounded. I needed to talk to someone who had looked the Engineer's latest champion in the eye and lived.

PART II
TEND THE WOUNDED

"I wonder if a soldier ever does mend a bullet hole in his coat?"

—Clara Barton

5 · One Hour to Kandahar

DAN FYE HAS A BODY part that I don't have. You probably don't have one either. It's called a nubbin. It itches and grows hair in weird places. It has muscles that sometimes flex but usually lay limp. It points and twirls and gets tired by the end of the day.

Dan's body part that you don't have has a biological process that you don't endure. The skin on his nubbin folds and puckers and sweats, creating boring abscesses that tunnel beneath fatty flaps and stink. Vagination, he calls it, as he rubs yeast infection cream around the worst areas. The bones inside his nubbin continue to grow, sharp prongs pushing up through the skin from underneath. Heterotropic Ossification, HO, he calls this process, and when the ache finally intensifies to a stabbing peak, surgery is required to put the bones back in check.

The nubbin wears a sock most days, but it comes out to play when Dan's children are insistent enough. One of the skin folds looks like a jack-o-lantern's grin, and the kids laugh as Dan and his nubbin make funny faces. They dress it up and put oversize sunglasses on it and take pictures and post them on Facebook. This is the only way I knew the nubbin. I had not seen it in person when I rang the front doorbell of Dan's brick ranch-style house in the rolling highlands outside of San Antonio.

Dan answered the door himself and gave me a hug. I hugged him back and rubbed his stubbly head and told him that he looked great because he did. His smile was wide and his eyes were sharp. I expected more drug-induced haze and was grateful not to find it. He invited me inside but didn't offer to get me anything to drink, and I didn't ask. We headed back to the living room, and Dan and his nubbin eased into a wide, soft recliner where they obviously spend a large part of their day. The chair was surrounded by water bottles and pill bottles and children's milk bottles, and three giggling girls ran around and in between my legs as I made my way to the couch. Dan reached out with two meaty hands and used the armrests to shift his weight in the chair again, flopping the nubbin over one padded side.

We settled in then for a long talk, the kind of talk that long-separated brothers have. I didn't stare at the nubbin, but I didn't have to, to wonder, to mourn, to thank what may reside above.

How unpredictable the ties that bind. Neither Dan nor I nor Matt disarm bombs anymore, yet the shared identity remains. Dan and I had been stationed together once, but that was five years ago and our paths had diverged. He and Matt had moved on to the war in Afghanistan, the place about which I needed to learn so much more.

"Tell me a story, Fye," I asked. "What happened to you?"

Dan scratched at his nubbin and I leaned back in the couch, and though neither of us recall the specifics of the past as well as we'd like, we found that one memory would stir another, and a long-forgotten name on his lips prompted a story from mine, and my tour in Saudi Arabia rekindled his, and his helicopter-borne tale transported me to my own, and in this way we discovered that we remembered enough, so that bit by bit and moment by moment and shot by shot we took account of all that had happened since we were last together.

The Engineer had taken Dan's left leg and given him a nubbin instead, and among brothers, such a story inevitably begins with the last deployment.

WHEN DAN FYE arrived at the dirt-walled outpost in Mushan, a mealy apple hanging from the last twig on the longest branch in the canopy of that country's stunted tree, he knew he had finally entered combat. It was April of 2011, and in the meat of the Surge NATO was still expanding into new territory; Fye's team was establishing a permanent EOD team presence at Mushan for the first time. He arrived in a JERRV, the same kind of truck in which Matt died, and it was stuffed with every tool of the trade, every battery and robot and block of C-4 he might need for months. This was the last stop on the train, and Fye might not be resupplied for some time; he wasn't going to take any chances on his first real trip to Indian Country.

Mushan lies at the tip of the Horn of Panjwe, a curving and narrowing wedge of land that thrusts between the forks of the Dori and Arghandab Rivers like the business end of a charging rhino. It was the farthest edge of continuous American occupation from the main hub in Kandahar, a full day's worth of driving down cratered dirt roads. Beyond this last outpost lay only the empty Reg desert and the sparse highways where Matt would die seven months later.

Dan Fye had waited for years to arrive at this desolate end of the long road. On 9/11, Fye was already married and had a job with his father as a mechanic's apprentice at a machine shop in a suburb east of Oakland, California. He listened to Howard Stern on the radio on the drive to work and thought the idea of planes hitting the towers was the most disturbing joke he had ever heard. Later that week, he lost his job when the plant shut down his division. Then his wife, Nicole, told him she thought she was pregnant. Fye had previously considered joining the military, but these events, combined with 9/11, looked like all but a sign. He tried to enlist immediately, but the recruiter told him he was too fat, so he lost eighty pounds before Christmas and was a muscled six-foot-two, two-oh-five at basic training in March of 2002.

But until he went to Mushan, Fye had spent his military career playing the final garbage-time minutes of meaningless football games. When Iraq was busy, he fought boredom guarding the barracks at Eskan Village, outside Riyadh in Saudi Arabia. When Iraq was winding down, he did hoax calls in Kirkuk and sat bored at Tallil Air Base, a sleepy outpost south of Baghdad. And once he finally made it to Afghanistan at the height of the Surge, his explosives had been gathering dust rather than creating it while he was stuck guarding the airfield at Kandahar during a particularly quiet lull.

But now Fye had finally left behind the big base routine and was at Mushan, in the heart of the suck, just as harvest season was ending and fighting season was about to begin, his first taste of real combat in a ten-year military career.

He would never fire his weapon. He was bleeding out in the back of a helicopter a month later, clinging to one thought and one thought only, running in a continuous Times Square news ticker across the front of his oxygen-starved brain:

One hour. If I can get back to Kandahar in one hour, I'll live. One hour, and I'll live. That's what they say. You'll make it if you can get back to the hospital in one hour. Jesus Jesus Jesus, my Lord and Savior, please get me back in one hour.

"YOU WANT TO know how this happened?" asked Fye, and pointed to his nubbin.

I nodded.

"It actually starts on the twenty-sixth. Because, um, we got the call . . ." Fye said, and trailed off.

"We were told we could go on that mission. Because, um, actually, it starts earlier than that. But what happened is, um, um . . ." Fye tried again, and lost his train of thought again, and looked down, rubbing, rubbing, rubbing his single shin, searching for words, as if they might be hidden in the scarred folds of his remaining hamburger leg.

"They had intel of guys planting IEDs in a place called the Taliban Bazaar, out by Doab, on the Horn of Panjwe. They saw the guys putting them in. A Pred or a helicopter or something. And that's why we went. They saw the IEDs and knew they were there." Fye got it out in a rush, and the rest of the story followed.

It's that chess match. And the Engineer goes first.

DO YOU HAVE the required materials? the Engineer may have asked.

Yes, *agha sahib,* the young man said. My cousin drives a . . . a . . . —here he spread his arms and formed a large boxy shape with his hands before giving up and retreating briefly to Pashto—*laarey* at the *kuffar* base in Kandahar. He brought what you asked for.

His Arabic was barely passable, ignorant of any word that wasn't found in the Holy Book. But he was somewhat reliable otherwise, and opened a rice bag full of nails and wooden planks broken off shipping pallets.

Good. I will only be here the day, so we will work quickly, al-Muhandis may have said, and then he began unpacking long spools of wire and worn pliers and a shabby box of Chinese batteries out of a saddlebag and placed them on the table in front of him. A huddle of bare-cheeked mujahideen gathered around him as he spread out his tools and props. They were more fascinated than wary, a dangerous proportion.

Sunlight streamed in the open windows and onto the pale walls and brightly colored rugs that were dotted about the floor like a huge *ifranjiah* game board. The dry breeze blew in, and the heat was not yet oppressive. A suitable place to teach; the cameras on America's drones could not yet see through walls, he surmised.

In the back of the room near the door, a young boy and two older men waited tentatively. The boy was curious, clearly, but the two old men chewed on the tar of the poppy and cast scowls.

Salaam, he said to them. Thank you for your shelter and hospitality, *baba.*

They said nothing, wisely, and turned and left and moved into the courtyard to tend their chickens as their own similarly ignorant grandfathers had.

He turned to the only youth of the group who spoke Arabic.

You will translate for me. Slowly, and every word just as I say it. I will teach you to make these, he said, and held up a device made of two bits of lumber and crisscrossed wires, complete except for the final explosive primer.

You lay these in the road for the large and heavy armored *laareys*, he said. And I will teach you to use others to attack the *kuffar* who come on foot.

Now he carefully pulled from his bag a small, round container, plastic and rubber with a hole in the side. Even these simple *mujahid* knew it was a landmine, but how to arm it? And how best to use it? How to combine it with the pieces they built themselves? He showed them how to screw in the fuze housing, release the locking collar with the detent pin. The youth struggled with the technical nomenclature, but the demonstration was clear enough.

Many times, he said, the *kuffar* walk now, without their *laareys*. But you must think, where will he walk? And how long do I have to work? Not long, before they see you from the sky. Dig one hole, set one bomb, then go back to hiding and wait. Do not be greedy. Be slow. Patience. Persistence.

The young man had more trouble translating these last two words, but al-Muhandis ignored it. He was distracted, having just noticed a stack of yellow plastic jugs, grimy with the crusted spillage of indelicate preparation and piled up in a corner.

And you have mixed those as we discussed last time? he may have asked.

The youths looked at each other. No one was eager to claim ownership.

This is important, he repeated. It is not to simply combine the ingredients. It must be done thoroughly, carefully mixed, so the *albuyah nasiffah* detonates correctly. You have done this?

Inshallah it is so, *malem,* the young man said.

The young boy hiding at the door could take it no longer, and when the group was focused on the jugs and the Arab's back was turned, he crept up to the table and began inspecting the various fantastic implements he found there. The Engineer caught him but did not scold.

When you are older, you will fight jihad like your *lala*, al-Muhandis said to the boy, holding his shoulder.

Will not the *kuffar* be gone by then? the young man said.

I read the Western papers, al-Muhandis said, and here the group gave a disapproving murmur that should have been stifled. He rubbed the head of the boy affectionately.

They say that this incursion cannot last, the Engineer went on, but if it not here, then there will be *kuffar* to fight somewhere else. The Great Satan is always searching for a new land of the *ummah* to invade.

THE CANADIANS CONTROLLED the sector, and even though they insisted on speaking only French on the radio ("it was some strict military rule, they said") and wouldn't use his normal EOD call sign (using *déminage* for "demining" or a variant thereof), Fye enjoyed working for them. Their vehicles were tough, they went on patrol every day, and they fought like dogs in one of the worst IED hotspots in Afghanistan.

But soon after Fye arrived, the Canadians announced they were pulling out, ceding to political pressures to bring their troops back to North American soil. They would be home within months. The US Army was taking over, and as part of the president's Surge strategy, fresh soldiers would push out even farther into areas that hadn't seen a regular NATO presence. Ever.

Though he had not been in Mushan long, Fye knew well the threat details. He'd spent hours doing his own research, reading the reports and studying photos. Most of the IEDs were pressure plates, balls of tape and wood scraps and rusting saw blades buried in the ground that completed the simplest of electrical circuits when stepped on. The average main charge was a forty-pound slurry of homemade explosives. Manufacturing the explosives involved multiple steps of drying and sifting and mixing, and then they'd pour the concoction in a plastic container that began life as a jug of motor oil. Forty pounds is enough to kill the guy who steps on it and his buddy next to him. Some main charges were as large as ninety pounds; those killed more, or knocked out unarmored Afghan Army pickup trucks. The month before Fye arrived at Mushan, a Special Forces guy from the local Operational Detachment-Alpha (ODA) team had stepped on one at the Taliban Bazaar, killing him and his interpreter. The ODA team called in airstrikes after that and leveled it.

How does such a place earn a name like the Taliban Bazaar? Be a dense nest in the cradle of the twenty-year-old Taliban movement. Host regular meetings of the group for a decade under the nose of an orbiting Predator.

Before leaving, the Canadians provided intel on one particularly ugly stretch of donkey track that led to the Taliban Bazaar. "They"— Canadians or Americans or NATO, it was hard to tell sometimes— had allowed the IEDs to be placed along that dusty walking path, watching them all the time from above. "They"—Taliban or Hakami or pissed-off local tribesmen, it was hard to tell sometimes—had dug in six or eight IEDs before an attack helicopter or fast mover had taken them out. Judging from the size of the crater on the imagery, Fye guessed it was probably the second, a five-hundred-pound JDAM smart bomb from an F-16 or F-18. Either way, a Predator or helo or UAV of some type (it was hard to tell sometimes) had taken photos a week ago, and there they were, plain as day, intact IEDs untouched by the bomb that killed their emplacers.

Killed the emplacers, not the Engineer. Again. Some Surge lessons took longer than others to stick.

"So what do you think?" asked the American intel guy who handed Fye the overheads. The Army wanted to start patrolling Doab, and the bazaar lay right along the key route.

"I think we don't go searching for IEDs," Fye said, "but if you want to work out there now, and since we know that the IEDs are in these spots, then we could go clear them. Tell the company commander we should go out there. I think it's good if we go clear the knowns."

Which was how Fye found himself at nearby Combat Outpost Robinson on May 26, prepping his team for several days of continuous operations. Mushan was physically large, a few acres of farmer's field that the Army had encircled with dirt-filled HESCO-barriers, but it had little infrastructure and few troops, only one platoon of US Army infantry, plus some Canadians and Afghan Army stragglers and an ODA team. COP Robinson, on the other hand, while just a tiny old Afghan police station in the hamlet of Taloqan, had showers and laundry and hot meals and, in a fit of necessity-as-mother-of-invention ingenuity, a pool made out of a water tank cut in half. Even more importantly, though, Robinson had lots of US soldiers. So Fye stopped for one quick overnight to pick up new security and extra firepower for his excursion to the Taliban Bazaar and beyond.

Fye's two team members were Dove and Harry. Dove was Fye's reliable right-hand man. He was older than Fye and outranked him, but had cross-trained into EOD halfway into his Air Force career. While he had plenty of leadership experience, he was still learning the technical aspect of the job. Harry was the youngest member of the team, smiley, everyone's kid brother. Dove and Harry worked well together: Dove handled all of the logistics and comm and equipment issues; Harry drove the JERRV and served as a safety backup. Fye trusted both of them completely.

When they got to COP Robinson, they had hoped to finally bathe, but the line was so long they instead spent the evening cleaning and inventorying the armored truck, killing time before the next day's mission. Fye studied ISR-provided imagery of the days to come. First they needed to clear out the remaining IEDs and collect any available evidence scattered about the Taliban Bazaar. Then the next day their patrol could push farther into Taliban-controlled lands, farther from the safety of the FOB than Fye had ever yet traveled, into wastes that had a reputation for being more dangerous than anything he had yet seen.

But on that day, before their first missions, as they sat beneath the camo netting and waited and could do nothing but wait at Robinson, they got news.

That morning, several hundred kilometers away, three members of Fye's EOD unit—Solesbee, Hamski, and Mirabal—had hopped out of a 101st Airborne Division helo in the remote mountain village of Shorabak. The target of their raid was a secluded trailer at the top of a low rise, an enclosed mysterious container discovered by Army Pathfinders and believed to be full of homemade explosives. No robot, no bomb suit can be brought along when riding to battle in a helicopter, so, armored in vest and helmet alone, Solesbee approached the trailer. To give him a better view, Hamski and a small fire team moved up and took cover along a berm just down the hill from the trailer. Hamski put his magnified rifle scope to his right eye, brought Solesbee's cautious form close, and watched his team leader take the long walk alone.

When the trailer detonated, Solesbee all but disappeared. The force of the blast flattened the security along the dirt berm, drove the optical sight of Hamski's rifle backward. It broke his face like a ballpeen hammer on an overripe melon, lodged the optics in his brain. As Mirabal scrambled to get up and render first aid and clear a safe path to the victims, a second IED detonated, then a third, then more. Chaos reigned on the remote hill.

Solesbee and Hamski and six Pathfinders from Fox Company, 4th Battalion, 101st Aviation Regiment, 159th Combat Aviation Brigade, 101st Airborne Division, died that day. Eight Americans dead total. There were few days in the Afghan War worse for the United States than that one.

Fye got the call at Robinson. Two of your bros are dead. But you're still going to the Taliban Bazaar tomorrow.

This would not necessarily be the case. Traditional EOD command policy stated that any unit that suffers a casualty, either killed or seriously wounded, will stand down and not conduct operations. Another EOD unit, often of another branch of the service, will backfill their area of responsibility and conduct missions in their stead until all safety investigations are complete and the unit grieves. When you put your brother in a box and load him on a States-bound C-130, your head isn't in the game. And on a tactical level, if an enemy method evolved, if a serious mistake was made, if al-Muhandis had built a new device, if there was a new way to die, that information needed to be broadcast to other EOD units as quickly as possible. Otherwise, casualties mount. EOD forces had been taking safety stand-downs since 2005, when we began dying in bunches. They were near mandatory in Iraq and were done in Afghanistan as often as possible, though the limits of transportation, manning, and the vast size of the country made it challenging.

"Why didn't you guys stand down?" I asked Fye.

"I don't know."

"Should you have been on that mission at all?" I pressed, gently to him, more firmly to myself. The small part of me that was still a military officer needed to adjudicate.

"It wouldn't have made a difference," Fye said. "The IED that got me was so well hidden, the amount of metal in it so little, I don't know if the detector beeped. I don't know if I would have found it. And if wasn't me, it just would have gotten someone else. I'd feel worse if someone else got hurt."

On the morning of May 27, Fye loaded up in the JERRV with Dove and Harry, drove to Afghan Army Checkpoint Number 22, and began work on an IED for the last time.

"THIS ISN'T WORKING!" Fye called out to the platoon sergeant.

Fye looked across the line of soldiers stretching from one side of the road to the other. They were packed not quite shoulder-to-shoulder, each with their backs to him, each sweeping a small section of the path with their own handheld metal detector. For weeks Fye had tried to train his security on how to use the Valon mine detectors, but they had continually rebuffed his efforts, citing the lack of time and need to be on patrol and simple exhaustion when finally back at the COP. Now that they were out on the road, the paucity of skill was painfully apparent and thoroughly bogging down operations.

"My objective is not this road," Fye said to the platoon sergeant. "My objective is the IEDs we know about at the Taliban Bazaar."

So far Fye's first multiday operation had not gone as he imagined. They woke early at COP Robinson, but as they loaded up into the JERRV and got ready to leave, the routine began to deviate almost immediately.

"Hey, guys, let's be safe out there and watch each other's backs and everyone comes home," Fye said. He said these words, in this order, without fail, every time they went on a mission. But then something new happened. Harry piped up.

"Dove's going to be fine. Ask him about his dream," Harry said.

"What does that mean, Dove? What's he talking about?" Fye asked.

"I had a dream I came back alive and unhurt," Dove said.

"Well, what about me and Harry?"

"I said *I* came back okay," Dove answered sheepishly, and Harry giggled a bit as he drove the armored truck out of the gate.

Fye and his security convoyed to the last Afghan checkpoint and dismounted according to the plan. With so many hidden pressure-actuated IEDs it was unsafe to drive on unswept roads. No, not roads, Fye thought. Dirt trails less substantial than the average four-wheeler route back in California, a herd path of pedestrian and donkey and motorcycle traffic. So they decided to patrol on foot, clearing a path first to the Taliban Bazaar, then to the impact crater of the bomb that had killed the emplacers, then to the nearby IEDs identified on the ISR imagery, until finally pushing the next day into Indian Country.

Instead, after thirty minutes of sweeping, thirty minutes of checking (by hand, with a knife-tip in the ground) every tiny fragment of metal, every screw and nail and scrap of discarded pig iron and piece of mortar left from decades of war, thirty minutes of chasing beeps from the mine detectors in the hands of the untrained soldiers, they had made it a total of one hundred feet from the Afghan checkpoint. Fye could turn around and wave at the Afghan soldiers and police.

They probably think we look ridiculous, Fye thought, inching forward from their checkpoint as if a mine was hidden under every speck of dust.

"Get on the radio with your TOC. We need to skip the road and just cut across the poppy field. We'll maneuver around the road and just hit the Taliban Bazaar from the side," said Fye.

The platoon sergeant agreed—let the engineers sweep the road, his job was shooting and moving, not standing in an execution line—and was grabbing his radio to inform his command when a shout came from the perimeter. Fye turned to see his outer security pointing down the baked-mud road. A vehicle was approaching from behind them, slowly but deliberately, kicking up a cloud of dust.

The platoon sergeant called for his men to take cover and rifles came up and Fye looked for Dove and Harry to tell them to get down in case it was a car bomb. But the vehicle stopped. And a boy got out. And the vehicle sped away, back down the dirt track from where it had come.

The boy was typical of Afghanistan in every way: dirty, sandaled, dark-haired and light-eyed, American T-shirt, scrawny in an unfed sort of way. *Shorter than my son*, Fye thought, *though I bet they're the same age.*

"Mista mista, boom boom!" the boy yelled as he fearlessly ran up to the line of American soldiers.

"Hey, go get the terp," the platoon sergeant called to his men, using the common slang for interpreter.

"Boom boom!" the boy repeated, pointing in the direction of the Taliban Bazaar. The terp was slow to arrive, and in the meantime the boy's singular English was more effective than any of the soldiers' Pashto.

"They're trying to draw us in," Fye said to the platoon sergeant. "Who would just drive up and drop off their kid? This isn't right."

"Maybe not," he replied, "but he's pointing to where we think the IEDs are anyway. Let's go. He can come with us a little way, at least."

The rainy season was long since past, and so the field through which Fye and his security tromped more closely resembled a weedy brick obstacle course than any farmer's plot in the San Joaquin Valley near Fye's childhood home. They patrolled through shin-high cut poppy, harvested only weeks before but already as parched and woody and shrunken as the boy who led them, always pointing, always repeating his assertion that booms lay ahead. Fye and Dove and Harry and their security hopped over a low wall that separated the poor farmer's swath from another donkey trail, moved in a staggered line down this new path briefly, and then, still led by the boy, approached two elderly gentleman squatting in the midday heat.

Only here in Afghanistan, Fye thought, *would this make sense. We're in the middle of nowhere, fields and the occasional mud hut, two men sitting outside to pass the day smoking, a boy leading us.*

Fye pulled out a printout of the latest ISR imagery and figured they were about halfway to the bazaar. He looked down, the Predator pointed at the bombs. He looked up, the boy pointed at the bombs.

The terp was more helpful now, and an animated discussion began with the older bearded men. Yes, they could confirm that there were bombs down the road at the Taliban Bazaar. Yes, there was a detonation that killed the men placing them. But the Americans must leave now, stop speaking to them and leave them be, because the Taliban wanted to ambush the Americans. The longer they spoke to the soldiers, the greater chance someone would see them doing it, and then they would die a much more painful death than that delivered by a missile from the sky.

But before the patrol could push on, the platoon sergeant's radio lit up again. Cross-intel from another unit that the elderly men's fears were well-founded. The spooks were listening to the Taliban ICOM radio chatter in real time, and they were rallying right then to ambush a patrol.

There was no way to know if the Taliban were waiting for them at the bazaar or along another patrol route, but either way, there was only one American unit in the area. The day before, Fye's security had gotten popped in a firefight—or a TIC, Troops in Contact, as everyone called it now—and they weren't eager to get caught again. He and his team needed to get to the IEDs and clear them quickly, or he'd be doing it while ducking bullets.

"What were you thinking then," I asked Fye, "knowing an ambush was coming right when you were about to start working on these IEDs?"

"Man, I was stoked!" said Fye. "I thought, after ten years, I finally get a chance to do something."

FIRST, THERE IS usually a simple flash of light. Fireballs are mostly for movies. Then, after the detonation, there is always a cloud, sometimes deceptively light and gray and sometimes oily and black. An explosion is nothing more than an instantaneous chemical reaction, and the cloud contains the toxic gases violently released. The cloud contains the vaporized bits of packaging that had surrounded the explosives. It contains the vaporized bits of whatever person or thing was unfortunate enough to be kissed up against the main charge.

After the cloud comes the debris. Counterintuitively, the largest chunks are thrown the farthest, up and out, and so as the cloud hangs still a moment the steel and clods of dirt and concrete and heads and hands and feet start falling on top of you. "Frontal *and* overhead cover," the Army field manual warns, is needed to bunker against a blast.

And after the debris comes the screaming. There is an audible pause between detonation and the cry of pain. The human body requires some brief but measurable time for the nervous system to send the correct signals from the body to the brain, to inform the cortex that a previously attached arm is now missing, a lung is filling with blood, bowels feel a breath of outside air for the first time.

Fye had been watching this cloud of dust on television for a decade. On 9/11, the first two clouds were black and filled with jet fuel. The second two clouds were chalk white, glass shards and concrete dust. The cloud in Madrid was fiery, then thick and dark. The same in London. Fye saw videos of the Oklahoma City bombing in EOD school. In a time before ubiquitous cell phone cameras, the clouds he saw at the Murrah Federal Buildings were from secondary fires started later, in the rubble of the structure's face.

First there is a cloud and then the debris and then the screaming and then, finally, the charge of responders. The wounded try to crawl out. The firefighters and police and medical workers rush in. Fye had also watched them for a decade, sitting at home on a couch while others ascended World Trade Center steps, pulled children from train wreckage. Despite his years of service, despite deployments to Kuwait and Iraq, Fye felt that he was always an observer. He had taken apart a few IEDs so far in his time in Mushan, but he had never pointed his weapon at the enemy, never done a terrible post-blast while the fires burned, never was the first volunteer to the scene. Not until he entered the Taliban Bazaar in May of 2011, expecting to be disarming bombs under direct fire.

It was finally his chance to run into the cloud.

THE CRATER SAID: Five hundred pound bomb. You won't find any pieces of the men killed here.

The smaller shot holes said: That aerial bomb's blast wave was so big, the shock functioned our hair-trigger pressure plates.

The mounds of fresh dirt said: We still hide death.

Only a fool walks directly up to that, Fye thought. *I need another way around.*

They had left the boy with the two old men, patrolled down the path and to the Taliban Bazaar. After the ODA-directed airstrikes, it was little more than a cluster of low walls, debris, and drainage ditches. Fye stayed along the outer edge, reconned the devastation from afar.

There was almost no cover, only hard-packed mud and occasional bushes that obscured their line of sight. Still, he found an area for Dove and Harry to set up, to unload their packs, and build explosive charges and bunker down against the IEDs ahead and the possible ambush behind. He also cleared an area for the rest of the patrol to dig in as they could, to survey the fields for gunmen approaching.

He couldn't know that this space would serve as a landing zone for his medevac helicopter in less than an hour. *I cleared my own LZ*, he would later think. *At least I know it's safe to put the helo down.*

Fye cleared all of this land with an expandable metal detector called a MIMID, a subdued green box that looks like a cross between a musician's microphone stand and a transforming robotic children's toy. It folded to a manageable size so he could stuff it in his backpack, but it also unwrapped and telescoped to a sufficient length so he could stand erect, strap it to his arm, and swing the flat oblong head across the dirt and listen for the telltale beeps of metal in soil. And there was a lot of metal, the artifacts of decades of war, plus new frag from the bombs just recently dropped. With a dial he reduced the sensitivity of the detector so it didn't beep with every sweep, checking this new setting by swiping it over his foot. A beep for the ringlets and cams on his boot. Silence over the earth. Such a delicate balance of complacency and paranoia, finely tuned anew on each mission.

Once everyone was set, he was finally ready to approach the bazaar alone.

At an airfield at Kandahar sat thousands of soldiers and airmen and armored trucks and countersniper teams and mortar platoons and computer servers full of IED data and trend software and Fye's battalion headquarters and four dining halls and the Predators and the attack helicopters who found the bombs. Fye left those behind and moved to Mushan and Robinson, and then left them to drive in his JERRV, full of bomb suits and robots and hundreds of pounds of explosives, to an Afghan checkpoint so he could leave it behind as well. He had put on a rucksack containing as little as possible—"Ounces are pounds," the men on patrol always say—radio and rope and food and a little water and a couple of blocks of explosives. And now, at the sticking point, he left the pack too, and, armed only with what was strapped to his body and lashed to his hand—his rifle and pistol and nine magazines, helmet and vest, unfolded metal detector—he made one last safety check with Dove and then began sweeping the path that led to the first confirmed IED.

This clash between EOD and al-Muhandis in Afghanistan was a decade old, but now the odds had tipped. The Engineer could still send his champion into battle, but Fye did not have a surrogate. No, in fact he had become one.

Fye skirted the main path, looked for a novel track to the known "booms," as the boy had call them. At the edge of the bazaar, a dry canal bed separated him from the objective, and beside the gully a mud-walled *qalat*. It rose like a knobby mole off the back of some pocked and pitted giant, a growth in the dirt-scape of the same stuff Fye kicked up with his boots. Fye thought it would provide temporary cover if the ambush hit quickly.

He moved up to the hut, looked down along the ditch more closely, and spotted a small footbridge surrounded by tall green stalks. The dirt and cement canal was shallow at this point, only three or four feet deep, and the rickety bridge was small, maybe two feet by eight feet. The whole scene was somehow familiar.

I've seen this before, Fye thought. *This footbridge. On a previous mission, there had been an IED at one end of it. Plus, this is where the Canadians got hit last time.*

The Canadians drive armored vehicles called Badgers, a tracked tank with a backhoe and a grenade launcher and a bulldozer blade and a machine gun and crane. A pressure plate had blown a track off the Badger and left it for dead, an impressive feat against such a large target.

This is good, thought Fye. *This area may be IED saturated, but it's been recently swept after the Badger hit. If my mine detector goes off, it's probably something bad.*

He approached the footbridge, used one arm to brush aside the tall green plants shading it like a grape trellis. Marijuana plants, he could see now, taller than he. In the middle of the bridge was a bag. Hanging out of the bag were two pressure plates and what could only be a fat landmine.

"Hey, Dove," Fye called back. "I found a bag left by the guys who got smoked!" He laughed quietly, in spite of himself.

They would leave their gear on the footbridge, Fye guessed, hide it in the pot plants, take out one IED and go put it in the road, and then retreat to cover before they could be spotted by passing Preds. Except they were spotted, and their spare setups were left behind.

Fye now left the bag and bridge—too obvious, too suspicious— and outflanked them by crossing the low, dry canal via the embankments, making his way for the first time into the bazaar. Rubble and dry bushes were everywhere. The ground was all compact mud, hardened and untrammeled, an artifact of the rains that come and liquefy the country before the heat and parch return and encrust a shell over the earth. Anything hidden here should be months old, at least, Fye thought. Still, the metal detector silently checked each footfall.

Fye was approaching a spot along a low mud wall that looked suspicious, still on his way to the first known "boom," when he heard the sounds of a moped or motorbike and shouts from behind him, maybe shouts in Pashto, maybe between local men and the patrol, or the terp and the locals, and as they got louder and angrier, Fye knew that the "booms" didn't matter anymore.

This is it, thought Fye. *This is the ambush. The Taliban ride dirt bikes. They're coming. I need to shoot back. Here we go. This is it this is it this is it.*

The *qalat* wall and a large pile of dry harvested poppy stalks blocked his way. He couldn't see. He was a sitting duck. The shouts got louder. His rifle cinched close, his mine detector in his right hand, Fye scrambled to get a better view.

As Fye put his foot down, he thought of the ambush about to strike. He thought about the silence from the metal detector. He thought of his bros, Solesbee and Hamski. And in the back of his mind, the tall pot plants, the boy the age of his son running around where he could get hurt, the truly dangerous operations in Indian Country he had to do the next day.

All of that, yes, but reflecting on it later, Fye realized he wasn't thinking about the very dirt under his feet, or whether the mud crust where he put his boot down was freshly disturbed. He would never know.

Fye's world erupted, and he found himself sitting in a hole.

"Dove!" he yelled. "Somebody's been hit!"

6 · A Child's Pride

ON APRIL 25, FYE PUT a picture of himself on Facebook that he knew would be trouble. He's standing against a shoulder-high mud wall, dusty multicam uniform with the sleeves rolled up, armored vest dripping ammo and explosives, checkered keffiyeh scarf around his neck, right gloved hand cocked on his rifle, finger outside the guard, no helmet, beard, cool-guy wraparound sunglasses. Several months of time in-country had made him tan and thin, broad-chested, with muscular forearms. He looks off into the distance. In a previous generation, the photo could sell war bonds.

"I knew I was screwed, as soon as that went up," Fye told me. "That's the kind of picture they put on your casket."

Thirty-one days later, he was counting the minutes to get to Kandahar.

FYE WAS ON the ground. His ears rang. Dirt was everywhere. Small fires smoldered about him. His MIMID was still in his hand. If shots were being fired, Fye couldn't hear them. He couldn't hear anything.

Someone's been hit, Fye thought. *But I'm on the ground. That means I got hit.*

"Hey, Dove, dude, I think I got hit!" Fye called out.

If Dove answered, Fye couldn't hear. *He can't see me*, Fye thought. *He probably thinks I'm pink mist. But I'm not. I need to yell, to tell him I'm alive.*

Fye looked down into the crater, saw his left leg tucked under his right, saw odd bumps and projections through the tan uniform. No more looking down. He scanned back to the path he had used and saw Dove start to approach. To bring first aid, Fye realized, to him.

"No, man, stop!" Fye said, all business. "I got no metal hit. There's no metal signature. There was a PMN in the bag. I think there are more PMNs out here!"

The PMN looks like a Tupperware container, complete with molded rubber lid. In the 1950s, the Soviets designed this landmine to produce a specific combination of objective thoughts and adrenaline-fueled feelings in the mind of a NATO battlefield trauma medic. The thought is this: the femoral artery has been cut. The feeling is this: holy fuck, this man is going to bleed out, we all need to do everything possible to evacuate him right now.

The PMN is large for an antipersonnel mine. It was engineered to remove not just feet but legs as well, to kill not just the shin but also the knee, to bite into the main blood line that runs through the groin, to increase the chance that a young man's heart might try to fill the Danube via the newly exposed spigot. When this geography proved unlikely, the landmine found new markets and has been scattered from Africa to Southeast Asia, copied by satellite states and knockoff artists, the Bulgarians for use in the Baltics and the Pakistanis for use in Afghanistan.

This was probably the source of Fye's PMN. The Pakistanis shaved down the Russian firing pin to make an already hard-to-find landmine even more difficult to locate with a standard metal detector. The PMN was a lump of plastic and cast TNT, but a tiny sliver of essential metal remained to start the detonation, and before he went on that mission, Fye was sure he could find it. He had practiced with a recovered PMN and his MIMID before he left Kandahar. He had done his homework.

Fye would consider the genealogy of the landmine later. At that moment, Fye simply sat in the crater, devoid of insight, all complicated thought blown away in the blast, ears flattened and bits of homemade explosive gently burning about him. Dove swept the embankment with his own metal detector and rechecked the path down and up the ditch sidewalls and across the baked mud. When Dove finally made it, Fye looked up at his wide-eyed face.

"Damn, dude. That hurt a hell of a lot more than I thought it would," Fye said.

EVERY SOLDIER ON patrol carries two tourniquets. One for them-selves and one for their brother. The tourniquets fold up into a rigid and compressed package, a black nylon band of Velcro and lash and a cylinder that feels like a stout pen. They are stuck in gear flaps and against body armor and forgotten until the moment Dove reached for his.

Dove put the tourniquet on Fye's right leg because that was the only one that looked injured. An injured leg has bones sticking out. An injured leg is wet and dark and smells of a vital funk. Fye's right leg matched that description. His left was simply tucked under-neath, like Fye was sitting Indian-style at grade school.

Dove leaned Fye back against the crater in which he was wedged and made him comfortable. Fye still gripped the MIMID but his gloved hand was bleeding freely now, his face was bleeding, his nose and chin, but the metal detector was a twisted wreck, and had clearly caught blast and fragments that could have done far worse damage.

Dove shifted Fye's right leg to increase pressure with the tourni-quet, moved his left leg out of the way, tried to pull it from under-neath but it flopped in a heap.

At that moment the medic, Pete Hopkins, arrived. He had been in-country less than a month, green as newly mown grass.

"No one's holding pressure," Hopkins said in surprise. He threw open his aid bag, slipped on a condom, and fist-fucked Fye's left thigh with his gloved hands. He buried his fingers in the wounds and twisted them around until he found the femoral and stopped the worst of the hemorrhage.

Dove kept twisting his tourniquet and Hopkins held pressure. Someone called about a problem with the medevac and Hopkins held pressure. They pulled new tourniquets from Hopkins's bag and put one on Fye's left leg, and a second on his right, and another again on the left, and Hopkins held pressure, and still Fye kept bleeding.

Now there was a crowd of soldiers around, all working on Fye. They cranked again and again on the tourniquets. They pushed their hands into his legs and needles into his arms.

They said things, terrible terrible things.

They said: "Your wife loves you so much." Though they had never met his wife.

They said: "Your children will be so proud of you." They said this so many times Fye nearly asked them to stop.

They said: "I can't stop the bleeding." This was Hopkins. He said it to his squad leader, but when Fye heard it now for the first time, he was truly scared, and wondered if he should look and risk going into shock to see what was about to kill him.

Fye felt nothing, sensed a flurry of movement below his waist with no nervous system feedback. He stared at the sky, never braved a glance down, as Hopkins and Dove constantly tightened his tourniquets and moved them ever farther up his legs. The farther up they went, the more leg he would lose. *Well, plenty is lost already*, Fye thought.

They worked on Fye a long time, and the longer they worked, the more anxious Fye got about the precious minutes slipping away. "I don't hear the bird," he said, over and over. They wrote the time of the tourniquet application on the white headband Fye wore under his helmet. Hopkins pushed morphine into his veins.

And just like that, life wasn't so bad anymore.

Hopkins, though, kept checking the sky. It was silent and time had stopped.

Fye and Hopkins had not met before, and they wouldn't meet again afterward; waiting for the medevac was the sum of their moments together. They chatted of wives and kids, but soon Fye's talk started to slide again to darkness.

Eventually, an eon since Hopkins arrived but only twenty-five minutes after the blast, the hyperactive *thump* of helo blades cutting air slowly emerged in the distance. While it may have been the morphine talking, Fye thought it was the most wonderful sound he had ever heard. They were at the extreme limit of the NATO footprint, and so it was a sixty-kilometer flight to the main hospital at Kandahar. If they moved quickly, Fye would just make it in the magic golden hour.

Hopkins kept working, but Fye said, "If the bird is here, just get me on it, get me the hell on it." They brought an expandable litter to the hole in which Fye still lay and loaded him on it. Once he was strapped in place, six soldiers carried Fye to the landing zone. Hopkins cinched down tighter on the tourniquets and wiped off the blood and repacked the wound and applied another layer of QuikClot dressings but dark blood kept flowing and Fye dripped like an unwrung rag all the way down the ditch and back up again and out into the open field where the helo waited.

As Fye was carried on the litter, he decided that he was finally willing to look below his waist.

"Dove," he asked, "where's my leg? Is it gone?"

"No, it's not gone. It's right there, in the bag," Dove said, and he pointed to a plastic mound at the end of his left leg. The oversize sandwich bag wasn't fully sealed because a strip of flesh still linked the lump to his haggard knee, a bone-in steak dangling via fat and gristle.

My foot is in a bag, Fye thought. It was bare, the boot blown off. *They can't save that*, he thought. *Yeah, that's lost, that's gone.*

They arrived at the LZ, and Dove knelt with Fye as Hopkins gave the medical report to the flight crew. "Hey, Fye, remember that dream I had? Remember that dream I had?" Dove said, and they laughed an impossible laugh.

With a heft they slid his stretcher into the helo, and Fye's view changed from open blue sky to enclosed black sheet-metal and rivets. Fye had heard stories about the superstars that work the long-run medevac missions, that pluck wounded soldiers out of hot-zones while under fire, but instead of some Air Force Pararescue cool guys with beards and wrap sunglasses and enormous wristwatches, he got two baby-faced Army Privates First Class that barely acknowledged his presence. Fye was high on morphine and talkative, and they ignored him. Hopkins handed over the IV bags, and they dutifully tossed them on the stretcher before going back to their flight checks. They didn't take Fye's vitals. They didn't finger-fuck his legs. They didn't speak to him. They didn't do anything.

Great, he thought. *I got two PFC robots! Our porn star and martial arts EOD 'bots have more personality. This is the worst medevac I've ever seen.*

The engine of the helicopter started to roar, the fuselage began to shake as the pilots got ready to launch, and Fye's mind already started to drift, the oxygen slowly draining. Hopkins finished up his report to the PFCs and patted Fye on the arm. He barely noticed.

Logic and reason had fled, and so, despite his primary concerns just before detonation, in that moment, as the bird was about to take off, Fye never asked himself this basic question: how was the helo able to land in the middle of a firefight? Where was the ambush? How come they weren't getting shot at?

The answer was that there had been no Taliban ambush. The patrol was just shouting at some local guy on a motorbike.

"DID IT HURT?" I asked Fye from the safety of his couch. I had to ask. I couldn't believe that he hadn't mentioned it, other than his offhand joke to Dove. How was it that he hadn't focused solely on the pain?

"It hurt," he said, "but it wasn't screaming hurt. It was dull. It was a dull ache and throbbing. The thirst was worse. You aren't supposed to give water to a trauma victim. I could have drank three gallons of water just sitting in that hole."

"Didn't you pass out at some point?"

"It's not like surgery in a hospital, where you kinda go in and out," Fye said. "I was awake the whole time, from when I got hit all the way to the hospital where they put me out."

"So what were you thinking?"

"Ninety-nine percent live if they make it to KAF, just get to KAF."

Fye paused and considered.

"I was so blessed that day," he started, and then trailed off.

He clearly wanted to say more, but he had a look on his face like every thought was present but a bit out of order. He rubbed his knobby leg, and when he finally started again, he pulled water from a very deep well.

"The only reason I think it's kinda hard to remember exactly now is because, it's such a traumatic event my mind is trying to get rid of it, but I don't want it to. I don't ever want to forget it. It's one of those events in your life that makes me who I am. I don't want to forget it. I'm not ashamed of anything I did on it. I'm proud of it. I know I cried out to God on it."

FYE SPUN IN a morphine dream of swirling and vibrating wind. The rotor wash pummeled him with engine exhaust. The robots never spoke. The overhead view never changed, but the narcotics kept him company in his time machine of delirium. He wasn't counting minutes anymore. He was just surviving an endless now.

Fye had always liked watching the medevac Blackhawk helicopters practicing their dust-off procedures near an open plain near his base. In the Horn of Panjwe, DUSTOFF—the code name for aerial medevac for decades—was literally a dustup, the rotor blades turning daytime into orange twilight. Now Fye was the beneficiary of those practice runs, screaming across the brick-red Reg Desert bisected by green river valleys full of pomegranate groves and grapevines and poppy fields.

Poppies, pink poppies. Attractive to the eye and soothing to the smell. Poppies, poppies will put Fye to sleep. Sleep.

But Fye couldn't sleep. The robots ignored him, the landscape rolled, Fye endured.

You're out of the woods, you're out of the dark, you're out of the night.

No, not yet he wasn't. He fell further into his narcotic stupor. On his farewell tour across Afghanistan, Fye stared like a junkie at a gun-metal ceiling.

The NATO Role 3 hospital at the Kandahar Airfield is no Korea-era, tent-bound MASH unit. The plywood floors and ratty fabric-framed structures of the early Afghan war were long gone, and in their place stood a brick bunker surrounded by concrete blast walls. Once inside, though, the setting could be confused for a slightly skewed version of a medical center in Des Moines, Iowa. The floors were made of some blue plasticized substance impervious to fluids. There were white sectioned drop ceilings and pale Sheetrock walls. The staff wore camo scrubs, but the monitors and surgical equipment were the most modern available anywhere in the world.

Fye noticed none of this, of course. Fye dreamed a morphine dream.

Until a woman snapped him out of it. *I must have landed*, he realized. She was at his bedside, as his cart was wheeled into the emergency room. He never got her name, never heard if she was a doctor or nurse or medic, but she smiled at him said, "You're going to be okay," and a wave of peace rolled over him.

The relief was temporary. A much rougher voice suddenly said, "Okay, dude, this is going to be uncomfortable."

Through the haze, Fye managed to think, *What could be more uncomfortable than getting your leg blown off?* before the doc, without further preface or preparation, flipped him over and stuck a finger up his ass.

"You could have at least bought me dinner first!" shouted Fye at the doctor, who laughed at his morphine joke as he checked for internal bleeding. The latexed digit he pulled out was full of shit, not blood. Good news.

The anesthesiologist arrived and pushed more meds. Fye slipped from a chatty, carefree reality to full hallucination, started fighting the staff as sense and meaning slipped away. The drug cocktail was transcendent, moved him body and soul into another world. The

MRI machine became a Portal from the video-game of the same name, and Fye screamed that he didn't want to be sucked into another dimension, that he wasn't a puzzle-solving white rat that would dance for some machine's amusement. The Portal players on the medical staff chuckled, the rest were just confused. The doc hit him with another roofie, and Fye's fight was over.

When Fye awoke—hours later, days later, no counting minutes in a morphine dream—his ears were ringing, his body throbbed, his stomach was empty, but his mind, for a minute, was clear. Clear long enough to embed this picture on his brain: his left leg gone below the knee. Blessedly below the knee. His right leg was bandaged but present, even his foot, somehow his foot. Surrounding his right lower leg was a shrink-wrap clear plastic bag and a mechanical apparatus. Two steel pins the size of his thumb pierced the meaty mush near the top of his shin, two more were inserted above his ankle. They were linked by two rings and a long rod. Fye wouldn't find out what those rings and pins were until later. All he knew now was that they itched, already. They itched and itched, and then he realized he could feel the itching.

I'm alive, he thought.

The picture that was taken soon after the incident shows Fye with an ear-to-ear, shit-eating grin. He is in a sterile hospital, an array of medical equipment behind him, and clearly high as a kite. He is giving two thumbs up, exposing his hands. The right is bandaged—the blast shot a piece of his foot through the meaty palm and flayed it open to the tendons—and on his left index finger sits a blood/oxygen monitor. He is aping for the camera, and on either side of him, replacing the PFC robots, are two of his EOD brothers. They look almost as happy as him.

And why not? That same day they had put Hamski and Solesbee on a C-130. A ramp ceremony, as Jenny Schwartz would learn the term six months later. They had stood in the sun in formation and saluted as the honor guard carried the two flag-draped coffins across the tarmac and into the waiting shade of the cargo plane's interior. Hamski and Solesbee were headed for the morgue in Delaware, to their awaiting families, to funerals in Ottumwa, Iowa, and Arlington, Virginia, to rest.

As soon as he was stable, Fye was sent to the major theater hospital at Bagram, where he had another surgery and a general gave him a Purple Heart. Then to Landstuhl, Germany, for another round of treatments. Those days are a blur, except for this: at each stop his EOD bros would visit him at his bedside.

Fye was no longer capable of counting the minutes; that task had been taken up by his wife, Nicole. The proof-of-life picture had been sent to her long before the rest of us saw it. She had gotten the knock, had seen the sea of blue hats, had heard the news, but with that picture she could be sure, absolutely sure, that her husband was still alive and would soon be home.

NICOLE FYE IS a shy woman. Her hair and makeup are always just so, in an I-want-to-make-a-good-impression sort of way. Her first instinct is to look away when addressed. She is generous and courteous and in constant motion at your peripheral vision, doing an art project with a young daughter, helping the eldest son with homework, teaching and dressing and cleaning and baking cookies for an after-dinner treat. All out of sight, while her husband and I talked about the war in the living room.

The house was new. The city was new. The nubbin was new. All of these facts were related; the family's home was Seattle, where they had been stationed at McChord Air Force Base, but Dan's long-term treatment would be in San Antonio. And so they moved, for an amount of time still to be determined.

Nicole stayed some distance away at first, but as Dan got to talking of the doctors and hospitals, as her part of the story approached, her orbits shrank, she drifted closer with each pass, and eventually she sat on the couch a polite distance away to hear what she had doubtlessly already heard dozens of time.

"She got the knock on the door. She's been through that. Do you understand what that means?" Dan pleaded with me. But how can I ever understand? The war will never take my spouse, right? In the beginning, after 9/11, wasn't that the point of the war, that it take us soldiers instead of our wives and kids at home? It was hard to tell anymore.

"I can never do that to Nicole again," Dan said. "Even if I could go back, I can't do that to her again."

"What were you thinking when you got the news?" I asked Nicole. "Did you have any idea this was coming?"

Nicole sat up and turned to me. This bashful woman, who had spent the rest of the day demurring, now looked me directly in the eye, and her gaze never wavered.

"I believe in the LORD. And I believe He prepares you for these things."

7 ⋅ THE ROBOT HAS A NAME

NICOLE FYE MADE A VIDEO of Dan's homecoming with the camera on her phone and posted it to Facebook soon after. In the video, Nicole drives her family's SUV to the airfield to meet Dan's plane. She is chatty, giddy even. She whoops and celebrates with her children. Her smile fills the cab of the truck.

As the clip continues, Nicole drives across the small taxiway, nearly up to the plane itself, hopping out with her children to lead them in a fit of exaggerated waving. Dan was flown to San Antonio in a special aircraft, a Learjet converted for medical use. It is a tiny thing, and when the side hatch opens, Dan fills the interior, bandaged legs awkwardly stuck in front of him. Dan waves to his wife and children. They hoot and holler and wave back. The relief is palpable, and joy exudes from each digital frame.

The Nicole and Dan Fye that sat with me in their San Antonio living room nine months later bore little resemblance to their not-too-distant selves. Nicole was tired from caring for four small children, from being separated from an extended family, and from holding everything together while her husband recovered. Her smile had waned in proportion to the exhaustion that followed that happy reunion.

Fye too had changed. The beard was gone. The head of dark hair had been shaved clean. Thin and tough Fye was replaced by a balloon-animal version of himself, a round head twisted on a round chest and belly, round arms, round thighs. For months, Fye had been sitting in the same reclining easy chair, flopping his nubbin over the same armrest, and it was taking a toll.

FYE FLEW FROM Germany to Walter Reed in Washington, but he didn't stay there long. Almost immediately, he was transferred to Brooke Army Medical Center (BAMC, pronounced "Bam-see") in San Antonio. Fye was gaining more lucidity, and on the flight across country the mid-America summer humidity drove him to distraction as the sweat dripped from his head and stung his wounds. He sweated like . . . like what? A camel in the jungle? A whore in church? A snake's ass in a wagon rut? After two decades of deployments to the Middle East, soldiers have invented many colorful analogies for relative heat, and my favorite has always been "hotter than two rats fucking in a wool sock."

Immediately after Nicole and his children met him on the airfield in Texas, he was rushed into surgery again. The doctors made a number of final fixes to Fye's battered body. They repackaged his nubbin, scraped off some sharp bits of bone and folded good hairy skin over the end. They checked smaller holes in his upper thighs, ass, and lower back; small pieces of plastic and metal had shot through him but missed major nerves or blood vessels. They peeled off the soaked bandage on his right hand and discovered that no one had examined it since it was wrapped up in Kandahar. The wound—the skin and muscle were missing down to the extensor indicis tendons—was still full of the Reg Desert's rust-colored sand, made muddy from blood and lymphatic fluid. As they scrubbed and cleaned and rebandaged, small bits of Afghanistan fell on the Texas operating room floor.

Every one of those fixes was minor compared to their prime installation. The day Fye landed in San Antonio, the orthopedic surgeons made a philosophical decision: they would try to save his right leg. To do it, they installed a Taylor Spatial Frame, the upgraded version of the ring-and-pin device Fye discovered encircling his leg upon waking up in Afghanistan.

Orthopedics is a dimensional discipline, more like carpentry than pop-a-pill medicine. It involves pins and screws, saws and hammers, sanding of rough surfaces. The orthopedic surgeon walks into a house where the structural members are rotting and determines how to reframe it from inside, except with this twist: the wooden two-by-fours are still alive and keep growing.

When a bone breaks, the body starts creating soft tissues immediately in the affected area. Gradually, over time, those tissues mineralize, forming a new solid piece that connects the two fragments. But this works best when the two bone pieces are flush against each other. Fye's right tibia wasn't so much broken as shattered. Soft bone tissues won't reconnect fragments stretched over far distances, and the chasms between Fye's potentially healthy bone segments were too large for the body to fill correctly. So to recreate Fye's tibia, the small part of it that remained would need to be broken and then stretched. As it regrew, as it expanded from the freshly broken end, it would eventually be close enough to bond with the small portions reaching from Fye's ankle.

This was the purpose of the Taylor Spatial Frame installed around Fye's right leg. The frame evolved from the torture devices of the Spanish Inquisition, kin to the head box of rats or a metal chair put over a fire. It stretches your leg like the rack, except internally, and over the course of months. The calibration knobs on the pins could be subtly adjusted each day via a computerized algorithm, to slowly spread the bone fragments apart. Open the gap too quickly, and only fibrous scar tissues fill the abhorred vacuum. Open the gap too slowly, and the bone solidifies and needs to be rebroken. To be his old height, Fye needed to regrow 12.7 centimeters of bone. On average, surgeons typically attempt to grow back only 5.6 centimeters.

There is a certain mad horror in seeing your skin grow up and around metal pegs erupting from your body, stretchy hairy cuticles that must occasionally be pushed back in place. But there are also a number of medical complications to the frame's use, including pin tract infection that causes general patient sepsis. A pile of pamphlets teaches one how to spot it: pus, dense or discolored drainages, red, inflamed skin (more inflamed than normal? What is normal anymore?), loose pins, and pain. Always more pain, so how to tell the difference?

Fortunately, the staff at BAMC had significant experience with the Taylor Spatial Frame by the time Fye landed there. The changing Afghan War had made them very skilled at the game of lost and salvaged limbs.

In mid-2011, BAMC was surviving a statistical bubble, and the medical staff could tell something was wrong. Emergency room nurses the world over joke that waiting rooms fill during full moons, but BAMC's lunar event was going on eighteen months. Surgeons were so inundated with patients that they researched the trend and published their results in the *Journal of Trauma and Acute Care Surgery*. They discovered that in only two years, the rate of amputations as a percentage of war injuries had quadrupled, and that the rate at which the average soldier was losing a limb had leapt 700 percent.

That the exponential rise in amputations would correspond exactly with the Afghan Surge was no accident. When a soldier leaves his armored truck behind, it is easier to access remote villages, collect evidence and intelligence, interact with the locals. It is also easier to lose a leg.

Compared to Iraq, the average American soldier in Afghanistan had roughly double the chance of losing a limb. By January of 2013, 696 arms and legs had been blown off in Afghanistan. Only sixty-seven were lost between 9/11 and the end of 2008; the rest, 629 of them, came in the four years that followed. German researchers found that the amputation rate had grown to double that of Vietnam.

At the height of the fighting seasons in the Surge years of 2010 and 2011, an amputee was created, on average, every twenty-four hours.

Better to count amputations than the dead, and in previous wars many of these soldiers would never have seen BAMC. As helicopter medevacs became speedier and more reliable, as armor reduced the severity of injuries, as access to quality battlefield medical care increased, so did the survival rates of the injured. The wounded to killed ratio in World War II was 2.1. It climbed to 2.7 in Korea and 3.3 in Vietnam. But then the revolution in medical technology and individual body armor pushed it to an astounding 8.1 in Afghanistan and 9.1 in Iraq. To put it another way, if our soldiers were killed in action in the same ratios in the Iraq War as they were in World War II, our country would be mourning over 14,000 dead instead of 4,500.

But brutal statistical logic also predicts that as survival rates increase, so do the scope of amputations as well. In World War II, 7.0 percent of soldiers with amputations had multiple limbs lost. That rate increased to 16.8 percent in Vietnam. In Iraq fewer soldiers lost limbs, since we could stay mounted in armored vehicles in the city. But in Afghanistan, the Engineer's pressure-plates hidden in the dirt were very effective. The survival rate of those that made it to Kandahar was up to 99 percent, but the multiple amputation rate also jumped to 30 percent.

Fye lost his leg in May of 2011 because that's when it seemed like everyone lost a leg. The greatest percentage of amputations, 42 percent of the total, were simple transtibial losses, a lop-off at the shin. Fye might not have known it at the time, and his doctors may not have identified him as such, but Fye was the typical case in every way. The height of the Surge, landmine–actuated, one leg, below the knee, and a fight to save the other.

WHEN HE ARRIVED in San Antonio and underwent his first surgeries, Fye was so pumped with medications that he was racked by hallucinations. Dwarves walking around his hospital room. A guy with a large afro jumping outside his window, even though Fye was on an upper floor. Streetlights turning into people and then back. A small part of his brain knew that such things could not be real, and so if the doctors gave him enough painkillers that he saw them, then he must be in rough shape.

They gave him an Alzheimer's medication for the pain. He never got the name of it, but when that didn't work, they put him on methadone, a synthetic heroin used to treat junkies. As the worst of the pain receded, he backed off the high before he could get hooked, and gradually, ever so gradually, the hallucinations passed. Fye's teeth hurt, because he had clenched his jaw when the blast hit. His vision was blurred, and his ears rang for weeks.

Fye spent nearly three months as a patient in the hospital, far longer than the average stay at BAMC. The Center for the Intrepid in San Antonio specializes in out-patient orthopedic and rehabilitation services, not long-term in-patient hospital care, so he received a demoralizing parade of short-term roommates arriving fresh from theater. They came at all hours, sometimes in a rush, sometimes silently materializing in the middle of the night, woozy from surgery and combat. One leg gone, one arm gone, maybe two legs clean. A unit flag tacked to the wall, a stream of well-wishers and first sergeants and family and cards and flowers and then, all of sudden, discharged while their stitches were still pink and tight, off to rehab, quick to a prosthetic and learning to walk. The young men and visitors came and went, the old men with bad hips stuck around, and still Fye lay in his bed with his dwarves and dancing streetlights.

Fye never got used to the hospital. He never got used to shitting in a bedpan; visitors always walked around the curtain at the worst time. It took him two months to get a shower. It was all unsatisfying sponge baths until a nurse remembered that there was an old roll-in shower on another floor that had been turned into a closet. The staff unpacked it, and it had a bench you could sit on, and when Fye finally got under the water he realized it was his first shower since Kandahar. No shower at Walter Reed, no shower in Germany or the KAF Role 3 hospital, no shower at COP Robinson, only a solar bag in a wooden box at Mushan.

There were other trials to endure. The blast that took his leg had scrambled his thoughts, but Fye had not been officially diagnosed with a Traumatic Brain Injury, and he wasn't sure he ever would be.

Until he was off pain medication, testing him would prove little, and in any case, he didn't need a test to know how bad his short-term memory was; every day the nurse would ask if he had had a bowel movement, and he'd have to check the bedpan to know the answer.

The EOD warrior, the invincible bomb defuser qualified to take on the Engineer, reduced to overcoming the hurdles of bedpans and handicapped showers.

Even when he moved into the one-floor home Nicole had purchased in a nearby suburb, Fye never felt like he was making progress at his daily appointments. Only surgery yielded obvious results, and so he found himself settling into a pattern: two months of painful grueling stasis, surgery on a foot plate or his nubbin, a marked jump in ability, followed by more disheartening months of fruitless therapy until he went under the knife again.

Fye's body fought him every step of the way. Phantom pains in his missing leg, or "zingers," as the doctors called them, shocked down his leg and shook his body. He developed Heterotopic Ossification, the disruptive and unhelpful formation of bone at sites of massive trauma, on the nubbin on his left leg and on his ankle and tibia on his right. HO is frustrating because it is haphazard; either new hard bone spontaneously erupts in the middle of soft tissues or the fractured bone grows painful spikes that push into surrounding nerves and muscles. For reasons that doctors do not fully understand, HO is more prevalent in patients who experience brain trauma at the time of their amputative injury, and so HO has been the particular scourge of combat veterans since World War I. The government and media have dubbed Traumatic Brain Injury the "signature wound" of the post-9/11 wars, but IEDs have created epidemics of other afflictions as well. HO was previously classified as "infrequent," but the latest research shows that it affects over 60 percent of amputees from Iraq and Afghanistan. The interior barnacles on Fye's nubbin made it painful to wear a prosthetic leg, and an eruption of tiny needles poking through the skin of his right shin were sharp to the touch. He knew he was lucky, though. One fellow soldier at BAMC had HO growing around his femoral artery; his X-ray looked like a flowering tree in full bloom.

And at least the HO was caused by an actual physical phenomenon. No, the worst were the uncanny sensations that had no name.

"They're bizarre," Fye told me.

"What do you mean?" I asked him.

At this Fye visibly shrank into his chair and paused and looked away.

"I don't really want to do it because I'll probably get it back now," he said. "I don't even want to talk about it really."

"What could be so awful?" I said. I didn't mean to press, but I had no frame of reference to even know what he was alluding to.

"You know when your toes get crossed?"—here he demonstrated with the index and middle finger of his right hand, binding them up—"I could feel that. I can't see it, but I could feel my muscles, in my mind. I could feel there was a foot there. It was so weird. I could feel it, and I couldn't get my toes uncrossed. It was weird, it was so weird, and it would last like that for a whole day at a time.

"So you just do this," he said, and tapped the end of his nubbin with some urgency. "You tell your body, this is as far as it goes, you train your mind, tell it, 'I can't feel my crossed toes because this is all there is.' And I can feel everything. The nub is awesome."

But sometimes that didn't work. Once the toes on Fye's right foot could move, he hoped to do mirror therapy to fix the uncanny feeling. The medical techs could put his right foot in a mirrored box, and he would watch as they crossed and uncrossed his toes, and finally, he heard, relief would spring from the ether on his left. Hopefully, some day.

A certain family-wide cabin fever set in: Nicole had no time for outside work and home-schooled the four children. Dan left the house only for BAMC. The tedious grind, every day the same struggle, was like a never-ending deployment. At least when he went to Iraq or Afghanistan, his family knew they only had to endure until a specific date marked on the calendar. Now Fye fought the effects of the Engineer every day, no relief in sight.

Cut off from his old unit and the EOD brotherhood and daily rhythm of the war, he spent much of his time on Facebook, watching videos of other men's tours, desperate for news from those who were still at Kandahar and Robinson. He discovered that the Engineer had been busy, and the next three EOD team leaders at Mushan—his replacement, a second Air Force tech, then a Navy guy—all got blown up themselves and had to be medevac'd. He stayed in touch with some of the Special Forces guys from the task force, and he stayed in touch with Pete Hopkins, the medic who first attended to him, started the tourniquets, bagged his leg.

Fye was Hopkins's first real trauma. Over the next year, Hopkins would do over a hundred more.

FROM MUSHAN TO Taloqan to Perotsi, Pete Hopkins was a traveling medicine man.

He was first trained as an emergency medical technician—an EMT like a firefighter or ambulance runner back in the United States—at Fort Sam Houston, adjacent to BAMC.

But he became more than that. He started IVs and pushed fluids and morphine and fentanyl, and his scope of practice grew as the Army docs taught him new skills. Cricothyrotomies, better known as crikes, better known as an emergency definitive airway, often confused with a trake and the movie *Playing God,* where David Duchovny pokes a ballpoint pen through the guy's throat right below the Adam's apple. Needle chest decompressions, also known as NCDs, better known as that scene in *Three Kings* where Ice Cube and George Clooney fix Mark Wahlberg's sucking chest wound by sticking a release valve in his rib cage.

Not that Hopkins got those valves; he always had to improvise with a catheter.

He was allowed to do crikes and NCDs and more, things that would make a stateside EMT jealous, but his skills were still focused on combat trauma. So when he arrived at the village and treated locals in the interest of spreading some of those Gallieni oil spots of stability, it never proved sufficient for the Afghans or provided closure for him.

He was supposed to do simple work within a limited scope of practice, but reality never cooperated. Kids would show him infected chai burns, or a young man would pull up his *kameez* and reveal that an IED had blown off a leg and the tip of his penis, or the old man of the village would come to him and say, "I think my hip is broken," and point to a desiccated compress prescribed by a local medicine man attached to the side of his ass. Hopkins may have been limited, but the medicine man was a charlatan, and Hopkins would unglue the cloth cast and find lesions or maggots or worse. And parents would bring their children and say, "He broke his wrist five years ago," and the boy would still be wearing a cast made out of pink fiberglass insulation and a T-shirt from some American cancer awareness 5K run. By then, the wrist would be fused and discolored and as crooked as a mesquite tree. Hopkins couldn't break it and reset it, and the only Taylor Spatial Frames were at KAF, so he did nothing. But he still thinks about it sometimes.

Hopkins also thinks about the old man and his son. The old man had an abscess on the back of his head, and Hopkins cleaned it and packed it with gauze and started an IV. The physician's assistant Hopkins worked with called for an antibiotic called Rocephin, and it had to be given every twelve hours. So Hopkins told the son to bring his father back twice a day, to get the abscess cleaned and receive more antibiotics. The son returned with his father for a day or two, but then not again for over a month. By the time they did come back to see him, the old man was hallucinating. Hopkins took off the bandage, the same dressing he had applied a month before, and saw rotting tissue falling away from the man's white skull. The abscess had dug an open-pit mine from crown to neck. Hopkins was helpless, and the young man was furious that the Americans refused to heal his father. The Gallieni oil spot spread no more in that village.

Sometimes the Afghans came to him at COP Robinson. Local laws and culture said that as a man, Hopkins could treat the men and the boys and the prepubescent girls but not the women. At his tiny fire base in Mushan and Taloqan there were three female soldiers: a cook, a psychological operations spook, and an EOD technician. None of them could treat, so the men and children had their chai burns cleaned and dressed, and the women watched and went home with unknown ailments hidden under their robes. One day, a husband and wife arrived with massive injuries. The man had taken shrapnel to the abdomen, and the wife was hemorrhaging on the ground. But the husband would not let Hopkins near her, so while he was treated and flown out on a medevac, relatives drove his bleeding wife to Kandahar. The trip would have taken all day. Hopkins thinks about them too.

At a local madrassa was a unit of Afghan National Civil Order Police (ANCOP) commandoes. ANCOP was organized to be a more reliable, literate, and disciplined national police force, and this unit was to be the elite of the elite. Hopkins treated innumerable stabbings and gunshot wounds in the unit, all either self-inflicted or one cop stabbing another, shooting another. In the foot, in the hip, in the jaw where the bullet settled in the upper cheek. They were always friends who shot each other, he was assured.

One day Hopkins was patrolling through a village, and they saw an old man baking naan at the ANCOP School Checkpoint, the same checkpoint from which Fye launched his last mission. They called it the School Checkpoint because NATO had built a beautiful modern school there a few years before but it had been converted into a military compound. There was a fire pit off to the side, and the man built the fire in the dirt and then pulled his bowl out of the dirt and mixed the bread dough and then put it on the fire. Hopkins knew too much about germ theory and transmission of disease, and he saw that the dough and the dust were one. *They might as well be kneading it with their feet*, Hopkins thought. At that moment he swore he would never eat it again, not the naan nor the local meat that hung on hooks in the open air of the bazaar for days, nor anything else that he had not seen grown and washed and cooked. But then a few days later, when chasing a gunman through a village, they burst into a house and interrupted a family at dinner. The patriarch invited them in to eat, and they had to stay, because it was polite, and because of Gallieni's oil spots. So Hopkins and his platoon leader and the gunner sat and drank tea and ate a roasted sheep and naan bread, kneaded in dirt that was full of nothing but infection and disease and bullet lead.

After four decades of conflict, war is just part of this culture, Hopkins thought, *down to the dust on the ground.*

He took a doxycycline antibiotic every day after that.

Hopkins eventually got wise to the cycle. A new American unit would arrive, and the locals would ask for anything and everything, to test the new group. Then the Americans would set up KLEs, Key Leader Engagements, to see what they could do for the tribes in the interest of raising their own internal statistical metrics, to show leaders back home that the Surge was working. And then the Afghans set up their own KLEs, to agree on what wells and crop assistance and medical aid they could get from the Americans. Everyone got what they wanted, money and Surge metrics, and then the war continued.

Hopkins learned other lessons about Afghans the hard way. He eventually realized he had to ask what medications they were already taking, since the medicine man at the local bazaar prescribed everything from daily vitamins to Viagra.

He learned from his physician's assistant how to use Narcan, an opioid antagonist, to block the effects of heroin. Unlike the long-term management drug methadone, Narcan is a way to immediately interdict narcotics in the bloodstream. The Afghan cops ate poppy on patrol, picking the buds off stalks as they walked by, and they took opiates to celebrate after every battle. Hopkins would recognize the pinpoint pupils and push Narcan on them, and afterward they got violent as they came down.

And he learned that gratitude for his work would never trump safety; one day at COP Robinson he would save a child's life, the next he would see the family in the market and they would not acknowledge his existence. The privacy of the aid station allowed a gratefulness not possible in a public space with unknown eyes watching.

Hopkins learned things about himself as well. He was a trim and focused thirty-year-old in Afghanistan, but military service was never a foregone conclusion. A childhood bone disease had destroyed his knees, and when he was fourteen he had extensive surgery to rebuild them with plates and screws. Over the course of a decade, before 9/11 and after, he tried three times to enlist. But the Army didn't want him. Those rebuilt knees disqualified him, they said. By the late 2000s, though, the Army had trouble meeting their recruitment goals and they lowered their standards. So Hopkins snuck in on his fourth try, an armful of medical data in hand saying he was fit for duty. Eventually, after Afghanistan, he would run a marathon.

Hopkins would come to decide that it was Fye's injury that solidified the new course of his life. In his twenties he worked as a debt collector at a call center in Buffalo and bartended on the side. He was going nowhere, and he knew it, but saving Fye validated all those attempts to enlist. *You never really know what you can do until you do it*, he thought. Fye's injury was his first chance to prove that he wouldn't freeze up, that he could do emergency medicine.

It was different than EMT training. They are always unresponsive in training, Hopkins realized, but in real life they talk to you. They're alert, rational, as if they aren't lying in pieces in a smoking crater.

When Fye got hurt, it was the first time he had ever heard the "Medic!" call. It was only a few weeks into his tour, so he had never before left his place of relative safety between the platoon leader and the machine gunner and sprinted into the dust cloud. Like a relay race, running from man to man, checkpoint to checkpoint, along the single path clear of IEDs to reach the patient.

And he learned things about his fellow soldiers. He learned that wars are fought by children. It wasn't like the movies. He was thirty, and the average infantry soldier was a decade younger. They looked more like Zack Efron than Mark Wahlberg, he thought. When they were injured, he could gauge how much pain they were in from their talkativeness, where their mind went.

At first it was all business. But then, the more pain, the more they talk about their wives and kids or high-school girlfriends. That's when you want to get the morphine onboard. Because eventually they stop talking. That's the worst, except when they never start talking at all; those are the ones you lose.

After Fye's incident was over and he was safely home, Hopkins learned how close they had come to not transporting him to Kandahar at all. The medevac took so long to arrive because of a miscommunication. Over multiple radio calls between Hopkins's platoon and the rescue operations center, his report of "bilateral amputation" had been converted, telephone-game style, into "bilateral lacerations." The medical operations center had actually turned the rescue mission off; helos don't fly for scraped knees. The bird that eventually picked up Fye wasn't even a real medevac bird. That's why the robotic flight crew ignored him, didn't treat his wounds as they went. They weren't medics. The helo pilots had just been in the air and happened to overhear the radio traffic, including the original call for help. They understood the mistake and had disobeyed orders to go get Fye. If the human pilot of that bird had been less stubborn, the golden hour would have been long past by the time Fye made it to KAF, and he could well have been one of the 1 percent.

Hopkins's worst day came in the front half of his tour, during his company's assault on Perotsi. It took an entire day of fighting to get into the city. First platoon and ANCOP went ahead, and the sappers fired MICLICs, the giant landmine–breaching rockets, down the streets, each dirt road detonating linearly to clear the hidden IEDs. Hopkins was with the company headquarters in reserve, but then the medic assigned to first platoon got hit himself. By the time Hopkins got to him, soldiers had already placed tourniquets, so Hopkins packaged him for medevac and bandaged the head of the Afghan cop who was next to him, and suddenly he was the medic for first platoon.

The sappers kept firing the MICLICs, and Hopkins and the rest of the platoon crept forward behind them, taking ground as it was pulverized. MICLICs look like a long rope, of the type you had to climb in gym class, except with C-4 at every knot. They were designed to clear Soviet minefields and usually the massive charges obliterate everything in their path. But then, unexpectedly, they saw the pad of a pressure plate revealed in the road nearby. It was a piece of an IED, and as the road thundered and the ANCOP bunkered down, the platoon sergeant pointed to the pressure plate, called to a specialist and machine gunner to run to get it. The clear sky rained dirt on their heads, and the platoon inched forward under the fire of the sappers, and they knew that the pressure plate was evidence, that this is what was different about the Surge, that JIEDDO said to win the war they needed to move Left of Boom, and the specialist and gunner broke off and ran to get the pressure plate, and they retrieved it and had it in their hands and on their way back to the line the specialist stepped on another and blew their world to shreds.

The specialist died quick. When they die, they die fast. They don't talk. Their brains can't run the program. The mechanical pumps the red on the ground, but the computer crashes and the microchip memory fades like a dimming LED. The specialist was dead and quiet.

But the machine gunner talked him through every moment. The bomb took his two legs and an arm and threw him clear, and as Hopkins worked on him, it was all business. After Fye, Hopkins had changed the type of tourniquets he carried. The new model, with the metal friction adapters and windlasses and locking screws, looked fancy but they never stopped Fye's bleeding. So now Hopkins ratcheted on six of the older but tested conventional type. The gunner was in shock and had morphine onboard, but he was present like a Buddhist monk. He talked about the bomb. He talked about drinking Jack Daniel's and eating a steak dinner. He talked about the bird. Just like Fye had.

Of all the ways to die, this is the worst, Hopkins decided. To be rational and coherent. To understand. To know you are dying and talk through it and see the black corners creep in as the blood leaks out. To know every second what's happening and be powerless to stop it.

But Hopkins also knew that if they were talking, there was still hope. The quiet ones died. The gunner was all business. There was still a chance he might make it. And he did. Hopkins sealed him up tight and he made it. Triple amp, one of the 629 soldiers who lost at least one limb in the Surge.

Hopkins didn't know about the Engineer, didn't know where the bombs came from, only knew that the soldiers went in on foot and came out on stretchers, that he cranked tourniquets and packed holes and waited for the QuikClot chemical reaction to burn and bind while the rescue helicopters ran the circuit. Soon after that day, the company commander said that, despite the Surge guidance, they were done with foot patrols. They all remounted their Strykers, and the casualty ratio improved immediately.

Hopkins also didn't know the numbers, that in Afghanistan eight guys are supposed to make it for every one that dies. On his worst day, did he only manage three to one? The first platoon medic and the Afghan cop and the machine gunner against the specialist who died quick? No, the number crunchers wouldn't even cede him that. The Afghans don't count. Only two to one for the record books.

After they had all got back in their armored trucks, Hopkins's company had another day, a bloody day throughout the province. Sixteen medevacs later, they almost made the average, fourteen hurt and two killed. Then they had another day, and another day, and another day, and enough other days that the medal he got at the end of his tour said he did over a hundred traumas. He has no idea who did the counting.

If you were an Afghan, it was easy to die in your own country: infection, gunshots, malnutrition, stabbings, detonations. But if you were an American soldier, it got harder and harder to die every day.

Eight to one. But that one.

It had never been so hard for an American to die in honest-to-goodness, help-me-sweet-Jesus combat. But Matt Schwartz had. He was one of the quiet ones. He died midsentence.

JENNY SCHWARTZ KEEPS the autopsy report in a manila envelope on the top of her coffee table with the TV remote and her daughters' homework. The report is a thick sheaf of white printer paper densely packed with strings of medical terms. Jenny was enrolled in the local community college and had recently taken gross anatomy, but that only decoded half of the words. So my wife, Jessie, the former emergency room nurse, helped her through the hematomas and edemas and contusions and cardiovascular failures.

The autopsy said Matt died from a herniated brain. The volume inside of the main cavity of the skull is fixed and packed with three substances: brain, cerebral spinal fluid, and blood. When Matt's skull hit the ceiling of his armored truck, it caused a flooding hemorrhage, and as his brain bled it filled the cavity. Via simple physics, the constant pressure of the fluid pushed his cerebellum and brain stem down and out of the bottom of his cranium like a half-shit turd. Brain death is immediate.

The autopsy said Matt died from overwhelming blast injury to his lungs. The armor of his truck failed, and the main blast vented immediately to Matt's left. The compression wave travels through the body with a tremendous shearing force, and each air sack in Matt's lungs, each delicate structure evolved to transfer oxygen to blood, burst from the shock. Matt bled out from the inside and drowned.

The autopsy said Matt died from a cut spinal cord. The impact of his head on the steel truck ceiling broke his top two cervical vertebra, the atlas and axis, C1 and C2. An injury so high, where brain stem becomes cord, causes immediate paralysis. His brain stopped telling his lungs to breathe. But his brain was already herniated, and his lungs a red rag.

The autopsy said Matt died from generalized trauma throughout his body. He wasn't wearing his seat belt and combat harness, perhaps because they had just remounted after clearing an IED, perhaps because he hated it and had nightmares and didn't want to get trapped in a burning truck. Whatever the reason, the collision of his body on the ceiling broke half his ribs, fractured his pelvis, and disconnected his internal organs from one another. In 2004, in Kuwait, a bullet shot through Matt's foot. In 2012, every one of the bones in both of his feet were liquefied, and bags of mush filled his boots.

Matt died four times.

It has never been so hard to die in a war, and Matt died four times. At least he didn't know he was dying, but he died four times. He had boots, so I finally had one answer from the funeral: the casket was full, and we put all of him in the ground. Of all the ways to die, thank God it was such a good death and at least he didn't die in a fire, but he died four times. He died midsentence, but he also may have died before the truck hit the ground.

"They told me it bent the JERRV," Jenny said to me.

"What?"

"The JERRV. Their big truck. The truck you guys always tell me is so tough nothing can hurt it. Yeah, the blast from the detonation bent it. Broke the truck's spine. That's what they told me."

Big enough to break the truck's spine. This is the work of the Engineer, and it would be my first piece of forensic evidence.

IN THOSE DAYS I spent with the Fye family, Dan rubbed his right leg incessantly. He absentmindedly scratched it with the nails on his right hand. He would lean forward to knead the shin with both thumbs. He pushed on the skin that grew up around each structural pin of the frame, swamp moss enveloping a tree trunk. He would tug and pull and rub, seem satisfied, lean back, and then, before he was even settled, be forward again, poking.

"Does it itch?" I asked. "I can only imagine."

"No, I rub it because I can't feel it. Right here"—he pointed to one spot, smooth skin and fine leg hair—"I can feel. But most of it, no."

There is a lump of scar tissue protruding from the top of his calf like a softball in a tube sock; he constantly rubs it to break it up. The alligator pattern dominating the front of the leg is the skin graft, the large swath that came off his ass. The injuries on his lower back, back of his legs and torso, blobs of scar tissue where chunks of dirt and plastic entered and exited, don't itch so much. But he says the scars on his lower left ass-cheek feel like they are liquid-filled.

And this is all on the parts of him that survived.

"Actually, I should let this air out. It can smell," he said, and took the latex sock off his nubbin. He'd had the covering on all day, so it had been sweating on itself, vaginating, stinking like an unwashed crotch.

But the nubbin was fully healed compared to his right leg, and it was finally getting rid of the Taylor Spatial Frame that dominated his thoughts.

"I won't have the frame holding me back anymore. I pray that the leg isn't in bad shape," he said, as though the leg were not his, as if it were not attached and lying in front of him to be examined. Fye talked of his right leg like a car that he had dropped off at the auto mechanic, and he was ignorant and helpless until the repair bill arrived.

But then he added, to reassure himself and me, "I have faith. I really think it's going to turn out okay."

Near the end of my visit, I came into the living room to see Fye and his young children all watching the movie *How to Train Your Dragon*. It was at the very end, and the main character, who had lost a leg in battle, was getting it replaced with a specialized, yet still medieval, prosthetic.

Fye didn't wear his own prosthetic very often, but he had plans to get his motorcycle retrofitted with buttons on the handlebars and a special brace for the foot pedals. In the movie, the main character had a similar set-up for his dragon's harness. It was clear that the movie was on fairly constant rotation in the Fye home, and so I had to ask the obvious question.

"Your kids are young," I said to him, "do they make the association here, between the movie and you?"

"Oh yeah," he said. "They love it." And then, switching genres in a moment:

"They call this my robot leg," he said, pointing to the metal prosthetic propped near him. "I'm robot Daddy."

I thought of all of our Talons and Packbots back in Iraq, covered in martial arts posters and porn stars. The robot has a name again.

"What was the worst part of all this?" I asked Fye.

"Watching guys come in after you and leave before you, already walking on their new legs," he said. "I'm still in the hospital, and I haven't really walked yet, but after only a month or two, they're already running around."

"How does that happen?" I asked.

"Well, if they're a double, they have two new prosthetic legs, and it's easier. Nicole and I talk about it. Is it worth it to keep the leg? Maybe we should just cut it off, so I can walk again."

I had never considered this before. From the moment Fye stepped on the PMN, every medical professional—Pete Hopkins, the emergency room staff in Kandahar, his surgeon, all the unnamed nurses and anesthesiologists and physical therapists—had been trying to save as much of him as possible. When you've lost so much, why wish to have lost more? When is the flesh no longer preferable, the robotics superior?

Fye had already taught me about the foot-patrol war in Afghanistan, and I had more questions, about the kind of device that got him, and whether the Engineer was personally involved, but I was so amazed and surprised by this idea I couldn't help asking:

"Can you even do that? Cut off your own leg?"

"Oh, sure. You should talk to Chris Frost. He cut his leg off. Never been happier."

8 · Breached Hulls

THE LORD'S SLEDGEHAMMER HIT THE bottom of their tin can and the bell rang so loudly the world went silent. Dust leapt from every surface and for a moment hung suspended in the air. The tin can started to rotate. Wilson tumbled down into Frost's lap, and then the side wall of the can rose to meet them and Frost's back and head were slammed into the plating as Wilson's shoulder drove into Frost's gut.

Frost lay stunned on his back. Wilson was on top of him and not moving. It stank like acrid cordite and black powder. Sunlight streamed in through the back hatch, and every tumbling dust mote twinkled.

That was big, Frost thought. *That was real big. Bigger than the others, a few 130s maybe. Artillery rounds. Yeah, a big one that they were saving.*

Frost checked himself. Nothing hurt. Wilson was lying across his legs and hadn't even groaned yet.

He felt movement to his left, and saw the lieutenant and driver scramble out of the gunner's hatch. The gunner was already gone. *They must not have been able to open the armored door from the inside*, Frost thought. *Too heavy. We're laying on our side. On our side, and Wilson isn't moving.*

Now figures to his right, casting shadows from the hatchway. Anxious, purposeful movement, and groans and whimpers and shouts and a scream and now blood all over the exit. The heavy figures pulled the top half of Haunert out. Frost could see Max yell, and his legs were gone and the figures yanked him clear too.

Silence inside the can.

Frost patted himself down. Wilson still hadn't moved. His rifle was at his shoulder and the stock and ACOG optical sight were covered with blood. He reached up and felt his split chin, felt a little higher and found a softness about his right eye. If he pushed on the outer orbital, the bone sunk in. He stopped pushing.

More silence in the can, a greatly muffled shouting outside the back hatch. Wilson was getting heavy.

He's sleeping, Frost thought. *Lazy, malingering son of a bitch.*

"Come on, wake the hell up and get off of me," he may have mumbled, may have shouted, but either way, he barely heard his own words.

Frost lay like that—on his back, face covered in blood, Wilson in his lap, wedged against his seat—for an eternity before he saw it. There, just out of reach, dangling above him, hanging by a single nylon strap, was a two-hundred-pound steel tow bar. The pig normally would have been stowed under the bench seat, a small bit of cord barely keeping it from shifting during normal driving. Now the cab was on its side, the seat was broken away, its former occupant Wilson was pinning him, and the massive rod hung six feet over his head.

Frost started to squirm but found he couldn't move. He yelled and pushed. The steel bar loomed. Wilson lay there. Desperate, Frost took off his helmet and threw it out the back of the truck, and the Tow Bar of Damocles stared down at him.

A moment, then shouts from outside. "Hey, there are still guys in there!"

One of the Navy EOD techs stuck his head in and saw Wilson and Frost and yelled for the medic and his other teammate. They grabbed Wilson by the strap on the back of his body armor and hauled him out the back hatch.

Good, thought Frost, *now I can get out. I'll just slide myself out. Now I can move because Wilson is finally off of me.*

He tried to move, but a bandolier of linked 7.62mm ammo hung in his way. He pushed the belt and the butt of the M240B to the side, and then he tried to move again, but his feet stayed where they were. He tried again to pull himself along the side wall, but once more his feet stayed.

Suddenly, arms grabbed him about the armpits and started to pull him backward toward the hatch. For one sickening moment his feet did not move with him; they just lay there, in a pile, until, eventually, they too followed, bouncing along the steel flooring like a soup can on a string. Frost tried to stop his rescuers, tell them what was wrong, but he couldn't get the words out and then he was out of the vehicle and in the sunshine and his feet flopped out of the door all by themselves, up over the lip of the armor and into the dust of the unpaved road.

He felt it now. Out of the truck, out from under the tow bar, now he was wide awake, and he knew exactly what was wrong. His feet hurt like he had stuck them in a wood chipper, and they would not stop hurting for years. Somehow, though, he wasn't bleeding too badly. He realized the swelling in the lower limbs, his body's natural response to trauma, must be constricting the blood vessels.

We're built well, he managed to think, *somewhat resilient, if you look at us like machines.*

Frost took his first look around. He saw medics and the Navy EOD guys working on Max and Haunert. He saw a hole under his truck and the second axle gone and the V-hull twisted and tossed aside. He couldn't see the Army EOD Battalion Commander, the lieutenant colonel who at the last minute had tagged along on the ride. Frost had given up his normal seat for the boss, and there, at the rear of the column, idled his regular truck, undamaged.

Four guys on litters lay in a line waiting for the bird. His four guys? They lost four? No, that's not right. It must be four guys from another truck, maybe from the route clearance convoy that had already been hit, the one they were responding to. Soldiers were everywhere, watching a sector from a canal bank, marking the LZ for the helo, talking on the radio, starting IVs.

"What was it?" he heard one of the soldiers ask another.

"It was probably a command wire," Frost called to them, all business, answering reflexively even though they weren't speaking to him.

"What?"

"Yeah, it must have been a command wire. They hit us when we pulled up. And it was big. Maybe military ordnance. We get a lot of that here. A couple of 122s or 130s from ASP 3. But there is no frag, so maybe HME instead. From the size of the crater, it would have to be a ton, and—"

"Hey, man, don't worry about that now," his medic said. "The helo's already on its way."

So lucky, Frost thought, so lucky to be hit on a day that flights were not grounded, so lucky they had already radioed for a bird. Only thirty miles from the main theater hospital, but thirty miles of RPGs and surface-to-air missiles that often kept them on the deck.

Max was awake, and they were cinching down the tourniquets around his thighs since there was nothing lower. Branden Haunert had crumpled, he had crumbled fast, quiet, and his body armor was blown open and his chin was on his chest and the stumps of his legs had stopped dripping.

Thirty minutes or less or your pizza is free, and the helo arrived right on time. They loaded him on the bird but forgot his helmet. Too bad. It was his favorite one, and he wouldn't get it back. Well, he'd never need it again anyway.

It was May 18, 2008, almost three years to the day before Fye lost his leg, three and half years before Matt died in a similar truck. Technical Sergeant Christopher Frost was on a medevac helo, a one-way ticket out of Iraq, and his war was over.

FROST'S FIRST STOP was a regional trauma center at FOB Speicher, a miserable moon dust–laden base in Saddam's hometown of Tikrit.

There the doctors declared Frost's right foot to be unsalvageable—"soup in a boot" Frost would later call it—but they would try to save the left, so they knocked him out and sent him to the main military hospital at Balad Air Base, where he woke up the next day.

The hospitals at Balad and Kandahar were roughly analogous; both were on the second-largest base in their respective countries, both had world-class trauma capabilities, both had survival percentage rates in the high 90s. In personality and feel, however, they diverged. The Role 3 hospital at Kandahar was multicultural, run by a succession of branches of the US military and a variety of NATO countries cooperatively and with an integrated staff. The Level 1 Trauma Center and theater hospital at Balad, on the other hand, had been run by the Air Force alone from its inception and served as a vital deployment outlet for that service's vast fleet of stateside doctors and nurses. The hospital was a focal point and source of pride for the Air Force, especially on a base known for its abundance of brass and comparatively cushy lifestyle. Kandahar was big but, compared to Kabul, still provincial. Balad, on the other hand, could feel like Baghdad's safer exurb, and the eponymous base was a back-office logistical hub. Balad was an important airfield and warehouse and truck stop, but clogged with American-style traffic and fattening food and the most notorious poolside office pukes and rear-echelon motherfuckers and fobbits in country.

It is a testament to airmen generally, though, that many such desk dwellers appreciated their good fortune. After typing away at emails all day, many volunteered at the hospital evenings and overnights, as stretcher bearers and aides. Like a catch basin with a single drain, the hospital accumulated all of the lost blood of each day's combat, conducted by helos and casevac Humvees and funneled through the small entrance known as the Hero's Highway. Via that tiny walkway, a tent frame skinned in an American flag, administrative clerks and cooks bore each wounded soldier from the landing pad to a stainless steel table in a just-sprayed-down operating room, and so the hospital gathered a country's worth of pain and suffering to itself through the labors of the dismissed and despised.

Frost woke up at Balad just long enough to acknowledge visitors; like a band of bearded candy stripers, the EOD brotherhood had gotten good at making hospital room calls. Soon, though, Frost was back in his drug haze, off to Germany for another round of surgeries, and then bound for the United States.

The armor of Frost's truck failed spectacularly, but not directly under him, and so he was fortunate to avoid some of the worst effects of the detonation. Unlike Fye, he didn't take frag from head to toe, or suffer a Traumatic Brain Injury. And unlike Matt, who absorbed the full vented explosive force and died four times, Frost had no organ damage or internal bleeding, only minor face trauma that would ultimately be repaired with a metal plate around his eye. No, the main damage was to his lower legs, and after years of explaining his mechanism of injury, he has found that the only guys who really understand it are old WWII Navy sailors who have been on a ship that has been torpedoed.

When an old Japanese Type 93 hit one of our floating steel tubs, it didn't just leave a hole at the waterline. It threw the whole ship upward, the plating violently colliding with the boots of the men standing on each deck. It was not blast that crushed the feet and lower legs, then, but blunt trauma. The flooring of the armored truck beneath Frost's seat reacted much the same way; he could have received the same damage by taking a heavy steel beam across the shins.

Surgeons at FOB Speicher amputated his right leg fairly high, right below the knee, because the tibia and fibula were pulverized into gritty oatmeal nearly to the joint. It would have been significantly worse at or through the knee, however, and the surgeon did Frost a lifetime favor by saving as much as he could.

The left leg was more complicated. Some combination of forces split his foot nearly in half, wrenching both his heel and toes upward and leaving his ankle bone exposed. His Achilles had retracted like a bungee cord and pulled his heel backward, but the toes randomly splayed forward and could probably have touched his knee before they were sewn back in. The surgeon folded back each layer of muscle and tendon and wired together the bones of the foot and installed a plate on the fibula with ten screws and then stapled it all closed in the correct general shape, but it only grossly resembled the foot it was. Frost's lone shoe size grew from 10 Regular to 13 Wide.

Frost would spend the next two and half years trying to save that left foot, and he did it as a professional patient at Walter Reed Army Medical Center in Washington, DC, a hospital beset by scandal and in the process of shutting down.

CATHY HAD SEEN him at the bottom of the hill before, but she had never asked if he needed help. It's rude, she knew, to assume the guy in the wheelchair needs someone to push him up the hill. But she had seen him around—on the porch reading in the sunshine, on the way to and from appointments—and she had been looking for an excuse to talk to him.

He is pretty gimptastic, she thought, *but so are all these guys. And anyway, I'm pretty jacked up myself.*

Cathy was a nineteen-year-old Army Private installing fiber optic cables for computer networks at Camp Victory in Iraq when she was told she had six months to live. She wasn't injured in combat, and her abdominal pains weren't due to bad food at the chow hall. No, the doctor told her it was pancreatic cancer, and she was rushed to Walter Reed for a Whipple surgery, the only treatment that offered a five-year survival rate out of the single digits.

Whipples were first performed in Europe in the nineteenth century, and the procedure retains a certain excessive thoroughness that characterized premodern medicine. During the operation, not only is the cancerous half of the pancreas removed but so are the gall bladder, bile duct, half the stomach, and two thirds of the small intestine. The remaining portion of the stomach is then plugged back into the end of the intestine, and a few juice ducts are rerouted so the right chemicals from the pancreas can still make it to ingested food. Months after the surgery Cathy was still recovering, and would be for some time. She would ultimately spend a year at Walter Reed as her remaining organs and the massive chop across her midsection healed.

Cathy was out for her regular walk, but when she saw him again at the bottom of the hill, she realized she finally had an opening. His arms were full of boxes, and he couldn't roll himself and hold them at the same time.

Ha, ha, I've got him now, she thought, and confidence filled her steps.

"Can I help you carry those?" she asked. He looked up at her. His head was clean-shaven, and cool-guy sunglasses hid bruising around his eyes.

"Sure," he mumbled, and looked away, and handed over a few boxes. They were heavier than she thought.

"What is all this?" she asked.

"Donated books from the quilting group at church."

"Do you read a lot?" She already knew the answer from watching him on the porch, but that started the conversation, about Terry Goodkind and Garth Nix, history and architecture, throw-away space operas and spy thrillers, and before long, Cathy and Frost had each found a partner to navigate the insular and utterly unique institutional culture of the Patient Mafia at a military hospital.

The military is full of mafias. The Air Force's Bomber Mafia, propagated by men like General Curtis LeMay at Strategic Air Command, shaped policy for decades until the Fighter Mafia took control in the 1970s. The Corporal Mafias of the Army and Marine Corps are famous for breaking every rule—especially the ones that involve the lawful acquisition of supplies and materials—to outfit their units for missions. The Patient Mafia, particular to the hospital, more closely resembles the Corporal system and is the inevitable result when medical, military, and quasi-penitentiary cultures are combined.

The old Walter Reed Army Medical Center occupied the northernmost point of the District of Columbia, a compound surrounded by a wrought-iron fence and squeezed between a forested public park and the middle class suburb of Silver Spring, Maryland. Closed in the summer of 2011 to be redeveloped into a modern mix of apartments, offices, and shopping, the main hospital consisted of an old columned redbrick colonial structure built in 1909 with a sort-of 1970s concrete spaceship campus perched on top. Very few of the patients seen at Walter Reed occupied in-patient hospital beds, though, so surrounding the main structure were a mix of commandeered hotels and dormitories that housed the legions receiving outpatient physical therapy. In these buildings the Patient Mafia thrived.

Each of the four services imposed a separate command structure, to maintain control and combat the cliques that would naturally form among patients who received care together. The Army had daily 0900 formations of wheelchairs and crutches, every soldier in some sort of uniform. The Navy and Marine Corps had few patients at Walter Reed, but to Frost it seemed they assigned two or three staff members to watch over each one. The Air Force wanted its airmen, without irony, to answer daily emails.

The Patient Mafia existed to beat this system. Like a thousand Reds from *Shawshank Redemption*, it consisted of nothing but troops who knew how to get things. If a soldier missed formation, four contradictory alibis would be volunteered by his squadmates. If an airman wanted a new pain medication, he would receive advice on which doctor would prescribe it. If a sailor wanted a higher disability rating, she would learn what to say to her shrink. If a soldier wanted to go on a sponsored fishing trip, he would learn how to ask so he wasn't saddled with fire watch on top of it. If you're healthy enough to fish, you must be healthy enough to go back to work . . .

Cathy lived in Abrams Hall, the best Army barracks she had ever seen. Frost lived in the Mologne House, a former high-end hotel. They were lucky in their accommodations. The Department of Defense had put Walter Reed on the closure list in 2005, but the wounded from the war kept coming, and so even as the medical center tried to shut down, it operated at full capacity, swollen by the fallout of the Iraq Surge. This tension proved impossible to balance. A 2007 *Washington Post* investigation revealed a system of overwhelmed, shabby, and neglected facilities, especially the infamous Building 18. The Surge was producing more than five hundred injuries a month, and the soldiers needed to go somewhere. The Fisher House, similar to the one Jenny Schwartz would stay in three years later at Dover, tried to always keep a room or two open for incoming families. It was not always successful.

Six months into her stay, the Patient Mafia and overcrowding collided at Cathy's front door. She was given a roommate and told to babysit. The girl had shot herself in the shoulder to leave Iraq. She screamed in her sleep. She lied and skipped every formation. She bought street drugs outside the hospital's main gate and hosted a threesome fueled by oxy and crack in her barracks room. One of the guys OD'd and died. Cathy called her the Black Widow.

FROST AND CATHY became inseparable, and when not surviving the Walter Reed mafia, they helped each other heal.

The injuries to Fye and Frost were remarkably similar, only mirrored: one amputated leg healing quickly, the remaining leg stubborn. Frost did not suffer from the painful random bone growth of HO, but he did wear a Taylor Spatial Frame. The pins propped apart his ankle bones and gave his fibula time to heal, keeping his toes from flopping onto his knee again. He wore the frame for only four months because it was misinstalled. The securing bolts were wildly unstable, only ten degrees apart, so if he bumped the frame at all it would rotate and twist the bones internally.

"Can't sue 'em!" Cathy would quip when Frost grew frustrated at the pain. She joked that the mistake was due to that fact that Walter Reed was not only a military hospital but a teaching one as well.

Once the frame was off, Frost's ankle became the focus of repeated surgeries and procedures. It was dying from lack of blood supply, a condition known as avascular necrosis. Bones constantly break down and are rejuvenated from normal use and circulation, but take that blood away and they grow brittle. Hidden away inside his bandaged foot, Frost's ankle resembled the skeletal remains of some cattle carcass lying exposed in the desert sun.

As a first step, doctors attempted an experimental surgery. They removed one of the extensor digitorum brevis muscles—the little muscles in the top of the foot—and stuffed it into a hollowed-out section of his ankle bone and sealed it with plugs. Blood flowed to the starved bone, but the rest of his foot suffered. Less than a year later, complications arose, and Frost received a subtalar fusion, a procedure normally reserved for geriatric patients. Eight bones in his foot were drilled out and bolted back together. He was left with a mass of scar tissue and a foot stuck in one orientation, never to be flexed again.

"Worst. Idea. Ever," said Cathy later, remembering the nightly massages to unbind the scar tissue, just so Frost could wiggle his toes. They were engaged by then and knew another fusing surgery would inevitably be required. During the day, when patients and staff innocently asked about the progress of his ankle, Frost provided inappropriately long and complaining answers. At night, during the foot massage, he and Cathy both asked whether they should consider other options.

Fifteen months after the blast, Frost was still trying new treatments, and he wondered why.

IN FROST'S OPINION, post-scandal Walter Reed Army Medical Center did not provide an ideal environment to rehabilitate and salvage his mangled left foot, so he sought to escape it nearly immediately. He successfully lobbied to be formally assigned to the EOD unit at nearby Andrews Air Force Base rather than the "patient squadron" at Walter Reed. He bought a condo in northern Virginia just to have an outside address. He reminded himself that his identity was not wrapped up in being a patient, and that, to use his words, he was "still an EOD superhero, just getting the tires changed on my car."

Frost felt that the hospital struggled to find meaningful activities for his generation. The older patients, National Guard guys with heart attacks and the ailments of middle age, were content to go sit on a barstool at a baseball game. Meanwhile, the younger and otherwise healthy soldiers were stuck fighting over the few opportunities to go sailing or rock climbing. He saw too many grow frustrated and take to the wheelchair instead. Always analytical, Frost watched other patients in physical therapy and saw that the sooner he could get out of his own wheelchair, the healthier he would be.

"You'll die in the chair," he realized.

So when a chance to get out of Walter Reed came, he took it. In the summer of 2010, two years after his injury and in the midst of recovering from the subtalar fusion, Chris Frost signed up for a cross-country bike ride.

The trip was sponsored by World TEAM Sports, an organization that plans trips for mixed groups of disabled and able-bodied. Frost had been a bit of a bike geek when he was younger, so he used the Patient Mafia to get all of his paperwork signed off and official permission to go. It was a second chance, a do-over, two months out of the hospital. He bought the stiffest shoes he could find and completed a few hundred-mile training days in preparation. He needed this.

The 3,500-mile ride attracted men and women of all backgrounds and abilities: veterans and not, support riders and college interns, guys paralyzed from the waist down using hand crank systems. Paul Bremer, the former head of the Coalition Provisional Authority in Iraq, rode along as the semiofficial grand marshal of the parade.

Frost completed the ride, but it was a misery, and he couldn't walk at the end of each day. His ankle had no cartilage, and his foot was tearing itself apart from the inside. The bones held up, but the tendons and ligaments were failing; his toes acted like the end of a long lever, and the front of his foot was shearing off the back. He took six tabs of oxycodone a day, just enough to make him functional but not so much that he wasn't lucid. Frost never liked pills, and he was afraid that if he took too many he'd forget to think or breathe.

On those long, painful days of riding, Frost spent a lot of time with a twenty-something kid named Chad Jukes. Jukes had a scruffy beard and flowing locks; Cathy called him Blond Jesus. In 2006, he nearly lost his leg in Iraq when his truck hit an IED. He too survived the Taylor Spatial Frame. He too had an ankle that died. But he quickly developed a severe infection, and the doctors said the leg should go. Jukes seemed unfazed.

"I'd rather be an amputee than a cripple," he decided.

So he cut off the leg. Now he's got a bike-riding prosthesis, and a special mountaineering prosthesis, and a special ice-climbing prosthesis with a line of crampon spikes that bite harder than anything you can strap to your boots. Several years after the World TEAM Sports ride, Jukes would go on to climb 20,075-foot Lobuche in Nepal's Himalaya with a team of wounded veterans, a tale told in *Outside* magazine and the documentary *High Ground*.

Should he be an amputee or a cripple? Frost looked at his legs. The prosthetic side was strong and tight and sore from success. The painful crippled thing on the other side was just in the way.

Cathy and Frost got married in August of 2010. In October he requested that his left leg be removed. By then he had endured over forty surgeries, and he knew that his good leg was the steel one.

There are two times, he realized, when it's easy to cut off a leg: right after the detonation, and after you've tried everything else.

ON HIS COMPUTER, Chris Frost keeps a series of photos of the crew of his armored truck. Their interpreter, Max, lost both legs and moved back to Jordan. His lieutenant, the platoon leader in the front seat, made captain and got selected for Special Forces. Corporal Kody Wilson was his roommate at the hospital. Private Branden Haunert, a kid from Cincinnati who had been in the Army less than a year, died before the helo landed.

He died quick, but unfortunately not as quick as Matt Schwartz.

Frost had photos of his wrecked truck too. It was a Caiman, a relative of the JERRV and very similar in design and capabilities; the back passenger compartment and hatch looked nearly identical. In Frost's digital photo, the effects of the blast were plain, one axle gone and the drivetrain exposed, fiberglass hood blown off, the interior decking broken loose from the floor joists. The device that destroyed his truck must have been large, hidden, center of the road, the product of years of armor-defeating intelligent design and development. I had not yet seen post-blast photos of Matt's truck, but from the little evidence I had—massive explosion, bent frame—the damage to his JERRV was surely comparable, if not worse. This was my next step, tracking the forensics that would tie Matt's IED to the Engineer.

Next to Frost's computer sat a series of complicated electronic clocks and weather stations that use old Soviet nixie tubes, a steampunkesque analog display that glows like a branding iron. Frost is a gear guy and a tinkerer, and he builds the contraptions in his spare time. Which is why I found it odd that his bionic leg was tossed in a corner of a spare bedroom, forgotten under a pile of knives and helmets and other accumulated military gear. He keeps the drop holsters and body armor just in case. He keeps the bionic leg because, well, he's not sure.

"Everybody has several legs," he said, "but there are only two that I really wear."

He has a set of ergonomic flexible arcs for running, but he has only worn them three or four times. His second set, his favorites, are even simpler: custom-molded carbon fiber encasements for each stump, a single metal shaft, a foot with natural flex. The legs are reliable and elegant, few parts to lose or break. The toes roll and the heel is shaped so there is a spring to his step. He buys the coolest most uncomfortable shoes available now, he said, purely for looks.

His gait is distinctive and a bit unnatural, but fluid and fast; with his pants on, it would be hard for a stranger to identify what was slightly off.

"Have you ever walked in ski boots?" he said. "It's like that."

"Walking in ski boots drives me nuts," I said.

"Unless you have no other option. And if you skied every day, you'd get used to it. See?"

And he put up his arms, flashed a set of jazz hands, and danced the Charleston right there in the kitchen.

I asked to see the bionic leg, and it took him a while to find it in the back of the closet under the stacks of cardboard boxes and black trunks. He found only one, and when he pulled it out, he made a show of blowing the dust off before handing it to me.

It looked like a movie prop. The outer encasement was shaped like the curved steel calf of a body builder. If the designers were going more for Robocop than mannequin, they achieved their goal. In the back of the lower leg, however, was an exposed green circuit board containing three microprocessors and a battery pack. The components were all choked with the grime usually found caked between the buttons of your computer keyboard. Just below the circuit boards, in the heel, was an electronically controlled actuator, meant to replace the Achilles and calf muscle. It reduces the effort needed to walk by pushing you along, but it also consumes a lot of power.

Frost checked the batteries, found they weren't charged, and apologized that he couldn't demonstrate how the leg worked. It would take a long time to get the legs functional again, and in fact, it was the batteries that convinced Frost to stop wearing them in the first place; a software upgrade reduced their usable life from four hours to two. The whole contraption was just past prototype. It didn't even have a cover to keep rain away from the electronics.

"Heavy fog is probably not good for it," Frost remarked drily.

"Are you frustrated that the development of arms has proceeded much faster than legs?" I asked. Every week the news reported on another robotic arm breakthrough, one that had five independent movements, then eight, all operated via electronic sensors stuck on the body. The holy grail for the industry was an implantable version that was connected directly to the nerves in the shoulder.

Frost shrugged.

"No. I don't need to pick things up with my toes."

And then Cathy walked in, home from an evening cooking class, and Frost met her with a kiss. They are certified foster-boarders for abandoned pets, and their current guests, two puppies and a kitten, all jumped up to receive attention. Cathy was pregnant and hugely so, and they talked about her latest ultrasound and what vegetables she chopped in class that night. She had beat every cancer survival rate projection, and Frost was beaming.

"Top three decisions I've made in life," he said, "volunteering for EOD, cutting off the leg, and saying yes when a pretty girl asked if I wanted to be rolled up the hill."

"You both won the jackpot," I offered to him.

"You're right," he said. "What do you call the guy with no legs?"

I thought it was a joke I had heard before, and I considered every variation and answer I knew, about Bob and Art and Phil and Matt, but none of them fit.

"I don't know. What do you call a guy with no legs?" I asked.

"Lucky," he said.

PART III
COLLECT
THE EVIDENCE

"And when he came unto Lehi, the Philistines shouted against him: and the Spirit of the LORD came mightily upon him, and the cords that were upon his arms became as flax that was burnt with fire, and his bands loosed from off his hands.

"And he found a new jawbone of an ass, and put forth his hand, and took it, and slew a thousand men therewith.

"And Samson said,

"With the jawbone of an ass, heaps upon heaps,
with the jaw of an ass have I slain a thousand men."

—Judges 15:14–16

9 ✦ BRAVE NEW WAR

IT IS A GREAT UNREPORTED irony that a force central to fighting the "Global War on Terrorism" was nearly decimated on the very morning the conflict began.

On September 11, 2001, hundreds of military EOD technicians were in downtown Manhattan, traveling via subway and taxi to the World Trade Center even before the planes struck the towers. The United Nations General Assembly was scheduled to open in two days, and the Secret Service was holding an initial planning meeting in Tower 7.

The once-a-year General Assembly is a massive gathering of presidents and diplomats, and it has always required extensive security. Quietly, and in civilian clothes, technical aspects of that security have long been provided by military EOD and K9 dog handlers. On the morning of 9/11, nearly 10 percent of the total active duty EOD force of all four services was scheduled to be at Ground Zero soon after the first tower was hit. Most never arrived at the meeting, and not a soul was lost, though the first medal for heroism earned by an EOD tech in these wars was won by Navy Petty Officer James Prewitt that morning, for rendering first aid to victims below WTC 2 even before the towers collapsed.

Chris Frost was not in New York City on 9/11. Several of his teammates were scheduled to work at the UN, but Frost himself was seventy miles south, at Fort Dix, New Jersey, sitting in a classroom and listening to a lecture titled "Emerging Threats of Global Terrorism." The class focused on the Red Brigade in Italy and the failed Millennium Bombing and the USS *Cole*, and when another instructor walked in and said the towers had been hit, Frost thought it was a dramatization. Instead, the course was canceled, and Frost and his fellow students received new orders. By that afternoon his class was sequestered, given vaccines, and put in Humvees to drive one hundred miles south to spend the next week and a half processing the remains from the Pentagon at the Air Force Morgue at Dover, Delaware.

The mortuary facility consisted of two main sections: a plush carpeted front filled with chapels and coffee cups, and a refrigerated back made up entirely of concrete floors and stainless steel. The day after Frost's arrival, a large briefing was held to explain the mortuary process to the many new faces that had arrived overnight to work this sudden surge. Frost was surprised how huge the undertaking was, in terms of both physical infrastructure and manpower. At that briefing were many "touchy feelies," as Frost thought of them, critical stress debriefers and psychologists and the like. But after the first day, he never saw them. The cold of the working section of the mortuary pushed out anyone not immediately processing remains. They fled up front, where the press briefings were held, and VIPs and dignitaries could visit, and free food from local restaurants piled up. If you worked in the back in scrubs or coveralls, you were not welcome up front. Frost didn't get any free food.

By the time Jenny Schwartz arrived to meet Matt eleven years later, that morgue had long since been torn down. A new mortuary building was constructed in 2003, the old one worn out from decades of use. In the new building, the front area is even larger, but Jenny never saw it or got free food either. She wasn't allowed in to see Matt after the dignified transfer outside on the tarmac.

The transfers from the Pentagon were a little different. The remains flew in body bags via helicopter directly to Dover. The workers unloaded the bags, put them on a truck, drove them to a separate facility, placed the remains in metal transfer cases, loaded them back on the truck, drove them to the flight line, placed them in the back of a static aircraft, draped flags over them, and only then an honor guard conducted a ramp ceremony to carry them inside the morgue.

Familiarity, Frost thought. *They're doing what they practiced, that last part anyway.*

Once inside the morgue, the first stop for the transfer cases—that is, for the 189 Pentagon dead and Matt Schwartz and the thousands who made the trip in between—is a large X-ray machine operated by an EOD tech. He or she is searching for anything hazardous that might harm a worker further down the assembly line. This initial step is a by-product of the First Gulf War, when workers discovered far too late that the first casualty they processed had a small but dangerous artillery round still lodged in the body, the delicate fuzing exposed, the striker primed and still ready to fire. Now the aluminum coffin is loaded inside an airport baggage screener, and two X-rays are taken.

Frost had some small background in the overall process. He was a biochemistry major in college, and his advisor was a forensic entomologist, so at least he had heard the technical terms used by the criminal experts at the mortuary. Two of those professionals sat with him as he worked the X-ray machine: on his right an FBI stenographer, and on his left Dr. Doug Owsley, a forensic anthropologist and current division head of physical anthropology at the Smithsonian Institution. Dr. Owsley had been the prime expert witness for a number of high-profile trials, from Jeffrey Dahmer to Waco.

The dead arrived in fits and starts, a swell very early in the morning and then occasional spurts the rest of the day. The first two men Frost processed were two Navy kids, twenty-one-year-old Matt Flocco and twenty-six-year-old Ed Earhart. They had probably died of smoke inhalation, Frost thought. Their uniforms were crisp and their name tags were easy to read. It would get worse after that, the bodies deteriorating in condition as the week went on. The fires at the Pentagon raged for days, and depending on when they were loaded, the remains were either crisp or water-logged. For years afterward Frost avoided BBQs and lighter fluid and cooked meat.

Frost doesn't think about those days very often, but when he does it's no longer about the smell. It's about Flocco and Earhart. He doesn't remember them because they were first. He remembers them because they looked like they were asleep.

Frost worked fourteen hours a day for ten days, and then he went home because the Pentagon was done providing dead. He found nothing explosive. He did find many magnetic signatures, and just like those discovered by Dan Fye's handheld mine detector years later, each one required a search. One such investigation led to the presumptive identification of Lieutenant General Timothy Maude, the Army's deputy chief of staff for personnel. Maude was a Vietnam veteran, the highest-ranking officer to die at the Pentagon on 9/11 and the highest-ranking officer to die from enemy action in fifty-six years. Frost identified him only because the three metal stars on his uniform gleamed brightly in the X-ray.

The mortuary would ultimately identify 179 of the 189 men, women, and children who died at the Pentagon. The remains of five of the victims were never found. Another five sets of remains could not be identified and are presumed to be those of the five hijackers of American Airlines Flight 77.

Frost didn't know it at the time, of course, but seven years later he would still be examining the evidence of war, picking through body parts until he provided some of his own.

"WHAT WAS THE worst part, about getting blown up?" I asked.

"That stupid tow bar, having it hang over my head," Chris Frost said, without a moment's hesitation.

He and I sat in his living room, going over the official evidence photos of his wrecked truck, and he pointed to where the tow bar would have been.

"I was looking up at this thing," he said, "and it's like something out of a movie, like *Saw* or some other really bad horror movie. And it's held by one strap, lowest bidder or some best value contract. It was absolutely the worst. Worse than getting blown up, it was worse than walking down on IEDs, it was worse than getting shot at, it was worse than all that."

Frost is an active typer and clicker, and soon he had shifted to photos of the rest of his tour, then videos of detonations, then the Great Mosque of Samarra that lay near his last base in Iraq. With its great twisting ramp, the mosque resembles Brueghel's *Tower of Babel*, though the country in which it sat often seemed more like a scene of hell, as painted by him or his mentor Bosch. A million tortures, a million ways to kill and die.

Samarra led to maps of Highway One, maps of Iraq, maps of Afghanistan, maps of Washington, where he and Cathy lived. While still on active duty but a full-time patient, Frost had parlayed his EOD experience into an internship at the Defense Intelligence Agency, or DIA. That temporary internship led to a permanent position once he was discharged, working on a branch of communications secret enough that he provided only the vaguest details.

Such hesitancy did not apply to Google Earth, however. Kandahar Air Field and Camp Bastion may have been concealed, but Frost happily pointed out every obvious DIA and CIA building in northern Virginia, in ugly strip malls and office parks and neighborhoods, making a lie of the satellite image again.

"What *were* you doing over there, when you lost your legs?" I asked.

"Weapons Intel," Frost said, almost offhandedly.

I was startled. Weapons Intel. Frost had been on the inside of the big secret intel machine, or as close as an EOD guy could get in the conventional military. In that veiled hierarchy, the first person to look at all of the evidence and try to make sense of it in sum, the Bruegel of the system, was a guy like Frost.

FORWARD OPERATING BASE Brassfield-Mora was a plowshare beaten into a sword, a massive complex of old grain storage silos commandeered into the main hub for the US Army in Samarra. The FOB was named for two Army Specialists, Artimus Brassfield of Flint, Michigan, and Jose Mora of Los Angeles County, California, who died within a day of each other in October of 2003. Mora was killed during a mortar attack on the base; Brassfield similarly, but while playing basketball. Back then we were just hunkered down, waiting for the war to end. When Frost arrived in December of 2007, it was under very different circumstances, as part of the main thrust of the Iraq Surge.

Samarra continued to resemble the Wild West long after other provinces had been pacified via their respective Sunni Awakenings or sectarian settlements. It would be easy to get caught up in that, Frost thought: *Shoot first, blow up every slightly out-of-place car, death before dismount.* But he prided himself on staying above it all, staying analytical even when his knotted gut said otherwise, taking no undue risks. Plus, he was there to change the culture in some way, to start a hunt for the Engineer that had been haphazard, to put it generously, until then.

The US Army is responsible for conducting technical intelligence on ground ordnance, and in 2003 they had one active duty battalion dedicated to the task. By 2004 those forces were burned out, and so the Army began rotating through backup plans, burning out their reservists in 2005 and volunteers in 2006. Those volunteers came from a variety of backgrounds: military police, administration, chemical corps. They received a crash course in evidence collection and intelligence analysis, and the quality of the work they did was spotty, ranging from exceptional to dangerous. In 2007, the Pentagon temporarily gave the Weapons Intelligence Team (or WIT, as it was known by then) mission to the Air Force, tasking them to provide over twenty teams to the Army and Marine Corps, one per brigade and expeditionary force. Similar, though not completely analogous, teams would appear in Afghanistan a year later.

The WIT mission was deceptively simple: investigate every IED attack in the entire country. At the height of the Iraq Surge, an average of 175 such incidents happened every day.

Each team consisted of an Office of Special Investigations detective or photographer, a machine gunner "tactical" expert, two intel guys, and an EOD tech to lead them. Frost found the spin-up training to be a review of the basics, but there was a steep learning curve for the intelligence analysts on his team. The Air Force sent intel wonks of all types to WIT, and Frost ended up with a Russian linguist and satellite imagery specialist. The team learned to do battlefield forensics, de-encrypt the call data on cell phone SIM cards (a process known as ripping), download laptops, and conduct sensitive site exploitations. This last part, searching a bomb factory without ruining the good evidence or killing yourself, is no light matter; half-assembled IEDs with dangling homemade blasting caps can be more dangerous than completed and emplaced devices.

"Battlefield forensics" sounds sophisticated, but the fundamentals of evidence collection are known to anyone who watches crime dramas on network television. The most dangerous part of the job was usually just getting to the blast site. Once safely on-scene, though, the work is almost pedestrian: Shoot photos from all cardinal directions, measure the size of the crater with an aluminum tape and record its precise grid location, interview witnesses, pick up smoking pieces of battery and shredded wire, gather bits of blood and bone for DNA analysis. The entire job can be done in five minutes by a competent team, faster if one is getting shot at.

Frost did learn a few new techniques. He could now poke a cotton swab in the ground and put it in a sealed test tube and send it for explosives residue testing at the Combined Explosives Exploitations Cell (CEXC, pronounced "sexy," of course) at Camp Victory. In a theoretical *CSI: Baghdad*, CEXC would serve as the central crime lab, and received an avalanche of reports and evidence every day from across the country.

Frost and his team of intel analysts were assigned to the First Brigade of the 101st Airborne Division. The brigade made its head-quarters in Tikrit, but Frost chose Samarra as his home base since it was centrally located, in the crotch of the Y between Baghdad and the cities of the north, Kirkuk and Mosul. It was a transit hub, and while his area of operations (AO) was geographically large, 120 miles by 90 miles, it felt like he could wrap his head around the whole thing. Baghdad had so many people and so many soldiers and so many fragmented AOs that no one could see the entire pic-ture. Everyone saw a little slice, and if the same IED was used on the opposite side of a brigade's boundary, even just a mile or two away, you would never hear about it. Not in Samarra. He could read the internal reports and trace the distribution network, watch the same type of device pop up first in the south, outside of Balad, and then work its way up the Tigris River Valley, along Highway 1, to Samarra and Bajji and then Tikrit and beyond.

Frost believed that in this role, as the chief of the WIT in Samarra, he had an opportunity. Not necessarily to do anything dif-ferently but to think about the IED problem in a new way. EOD techs had been collecting IED evidence for years and had been making no progress, caused no substantial reduction in the number of bombs placed or caught the Engineer. Frost decided that this was because they were spending so much time and energy taking the IEDs apart and keeping themselves alive, they had no time to study the evidence they collected in any detailed or systematic way. They always trusted someone else to do it—JIEDDO, CEXC, the counter-IED HQ in Baghdad known as Task Force Troy, the FBI's Terrorist Explosive Device Analytical Center (TEDAC) in the hills outside of DC—and assumed it would be done well, considering the billions of dollars spent and daily headlines at home.

But Frost had now looked behind the curtain. He had attended the intel school, had seen the inside of the great machine, and he knew it might just be Asimov's coin flip after all. The storage area at TEDAC looks like the warehouse from the end of *Raiders of the*

Lost Ark, and just as Bill Hailer had emailed TECHDIV for help on the rocket in 2004 and Matt Schwartz's foot was nearly blown off in response, Frost knew there was no smart analysis coming from higher up. Frost had shipped bags of IED evidence to CEXC in Baghdad, priority evidence from attacks that killed and maimed soldiers, only to discover it laying forgotten in a corner when he visited in person months later. Every trip to HQ left him disillusioned, filled with the sense that "shrimp and gristle night" at the chow hall was the most important thing in the lives of the civilians and contractors who worked at CEXC and in the marble palaces of Camp Victory.

He needed to do the analysis on his own. If he didn't, no one would, no one was looking. And now, unlike his EOD brothers still dismantling IEDs every day, he had no response team to run, no robot to fix, no bomb suit to clean, no explosives to inventory. He had space and room to step back, breathe, and just *think* about the IED problem from scratch. And this is what he came up with.

FROST WAS SICK of playing defense. EOD teams always reacted, waited to get a call to go disarm a device. The challenge in going on offense lay in predicting where that device would be placed.

As the Engineer undoubtedly taught his students, it is a truism among IED emplacers that it is only worth putting a bomb where someone is likely to travel. This may be obvious, but it also grants insight. Digging in a device is dangerous and exhausting work. A Predator can spot you. A soldier can shoot you. Your accomplice can rat on you. The safety mechanism on the bomb can fail. The cell leader can blame you if it fails to function. So much risk, so much can go wrong, why place a device where no one will ever tread?

On the micro level, there is a delicate balance to be struck in this question of where to place the bomb. American patrols long ago learned to avoid the most obvious funnels and routes. Never step in the entranceway of a house. Never walk in the center of the road. Never take the most well-worn donkey path unless you watch the locals take it first. But it is also dangerous to take the most difficult path. Once insurgents saw soldiers leap through a window instead of knocking down the door, landmines appeared in dirt floors beneath sashes and sills. The sheer cliff face was as likely to be booby-trapped as the labeled trail. What then is left?

The pendulum swung from one extreme to the other, until the war settled into a tenuous middle ambiguity. The direct route was both off-limits and probably free of hazards. The soldier shuns it, so the bomb placer does too. The most indirect route is likewise avoided by both under the same logic. The most obvious and least obvious are deadly. Safety lies in the random. The soldier walks anywhere between the extremes. The bomb is placed anywhere between the extremes. Round and round the mulberry bush it goes.

But now Frost wanted to answer the bomb-placement question more strategically. To do this, for years EOD units and brigade intel cells and Special Forces teams had been using a technique called Trend Analysis. It is a fancy term for pushing pins into a map, multicolored to discriminate the data most important to each community. EOD techs might use red for radio-controlled IEDs, blue for car bombs, yellow for suicides, black for command wire. This sorted by type but little else. The Army infantry brigades mapped for effectiveness, using different colors for the number of soldiers hurt and killed, trucks destroyed, attacks deemed "effective" or not. They would create a "heat map" to correlate the frequency of a certain type in a certain place at a certain time. When pins bunched up, they gave the place a name. Tactical Area of Interest (TAI) Tennessee. TAI Detroit. Named Area of Interest (NAI) Vicksburg. NAI Celtics. But the names were nothing more than another way of saying, "Here is where we die."

In his mind, Frost likened this whole process to pouring a giant jar of pennies all over a basketball court and then walking around and noting heads and tails. You could search the scattered pennies and mark every time three heads or three tails lay next to each other. Then the battalion intelligence officer could say, "Hey look, there might be something here, because there are three! There's a cluster, and there's a cluster, and there's a cluster." And Task Force Troy in Baghdad and JIEDDO in DC could write reports that said, "Hey, look, we see a cluster here." As late as the spring of 2008, Frost was still receiving such vapid reports for Samarra, as if his pushpin map didn't already say the same thing.

There is a cluster of pennies. So what?

Frost decided that pushpin-based Trend Analysis survived as a legitimate tracking method for as long as it did because it worked just well enough to get a unit to the end of its tour. It worked well enough to tell the brigade commander what street to patrol, where to put an observation post, which route to stop traveling at which times. It worked well enough to catch *a* guy and make everyone feel better. But they never caught *the* guy, and the Engineer labored on.

Frost started to run through the Big Data differently, and while he was far from the only one doing so in the spring of 2008—many of the twenty other WIT team leads assigned to other brigades in other parts of the country were starting a similar process—he knew he was the only one doing it for his area. As the leader of an intel cell, he was now plugged in to the massive intelligence apparatus in a new way and could use the network to pull reports. The main database, known as CIDNE (Combined Information Data Network Exchange, pronounced "Sydney"), provided great statistics but no analysis. In Frost's view, the military had long confused one for the other; CIDNE counted widgets, told him there were seven hundred car bombs, but data do not become intelligence until they are analyzed and filtered.

When he tackled the data, Frost did not sort IEDs by effectiveness or general category. Instead, he taxonomized them by how they were employed or by the very specific material of their construction. Sorting by employment allowed him to get into the tactical mind of the local leader. Sorting by material allowed him to track makes and models across wide geographic areas. Then, by combining the two data sets, he could identify IED cells and draw circles on the map that meant something. He named each cell by its leader: Directional Frag Asshole, Northside Dirtbag, Southside Dirtbag. Each time, he felt he could say, "This is really a cell," and not random penny clusters, because of the accumulation of data points. He knew that they used old military ordnance and thin-gauge command wire and a particular red switch as a safety and a particular white outlet box to contain the electronics and they always worked along Highway 1 on Saturdays after prayers.

Once the cell was identified with this specific signature, he could begin to analyze the pattern, ask smarter questions, draw conclusions. Where is the cell based? Where are they moving? Where do they build the devices? Have the devices changed, signaling that the Engineer had been near recently, teaching new skills to local thugs? Where do their materials come from? The answers to these rarely asked questions had always lain in the data, but hidden.

Frost wasn't doing rocket science, and his method wasn't novel, but he and the best of his fellow WIT leaders could apply a thoroughness and persistence to the analysis that had not been possible on previous tours on a brigade-wide scale. Frost was drawing circles on the map that actually meant something. He was drawing each cell's Gallieni oil spot.

Draw it, then dismantle it.

It was at this point that reality intruded upon theory.

THE BRITISH CALL their EOD operators ammunition technicians, or ATs, and in the Troubles in Northern Ireland they became famous for truly understanding their IRA opponent. Nervous citizens would call the local police about a suspicious package left at their door, and the AT would walk up and cut it open with a knife and toss the mail aside. How did they know? Because the ATs were fighting trustworthy professionals. They knew where the IRA would put a real bomb, and therefore a package anywhere else was a hoax or trash.

After months of trying to track the various cells in Samarra, Frost envied the AT's situation. The British techs had worked in a nearly homogenous population that they intuitively understood. The IRA built consistently identical bombs, so often repeated that the ATs would give them nomenclature, Type 4 and Type 19 and so on. Frost had neither advantage. Iraqi IED construction was varied, similar but not identical, occasionally sloppy and haphazard, and the population he worked in was foreign, mixed, sectarian, aggressive, and to him, unpredictable.

And he had so much to learn. Frost was trying to track very specific information, but there was little foundation for him to start with, very little institutional knowledge because no one in the US military consistently specialized in the habits of IED cells in Samarra. The Army did not send the same brigade back to Tikrit every other year. Same for EOD techs. Special Forces only began to send the same units back to the same Afghan villages in 2010, after the Iraq War was over. JIEDDO eventually tried to set up a "desk" system, similar to how the CIA and DIA organize their specialists, but by then the hour had grown late.

Frost wanted to do more than just gather information, though. He wanted to convince his brigade to do missions to catch the cells making the IEDs. The normal cycle for all intel-driven mission planning is roughly the same: collect, process, target, execute. It was WIT's job to collect and process, but absent regular support from Troy or JIEDDO, he took on the targeting role too, to get the Army to move.

Convincing the 101st Airborne he had enough information to justify a raid was a challenge, and Frost seemed to face a constant headwind. The backlog for fingerprint identification could be a year. Circuit and radio frequency spectrum analysis from CEXC was quicker but still too slow to plan a timely mission. He even seemed to be at odds with the Army brigade he was working for. Too many soldiers wanted their own "petting zoo," as he called them, a collection of bomb trophies kept under the bed. That was IED evidence he never saw and thus could not analyze. Out on patrol, or on the scene of a detonation, he felt like he was hiking in the wilderness and tying to enforce a Leave No Trace ethic: take only pictures, leave only footprints . . . but not in the middle of the crime scene, and not in that sandal print, I'm going to need a photo of that.

So Frost started working outside the system. When he couldn't get a report from a particular intelligence agency, he pulled the information from their classified online databases himself. He hung out with the infantry guys. In the Surge, it was now their job to stand on the same street corners every day. They knew who the good and bad guys were, but that information rarely worked itself into official intel channels because they simply weren't asked.

At one point in Frost's tour, IEDs in his AO suddenly started using military ordnance, long after most cells had converted to easier-to-hide homemade explosives. Frost had a hunch and organized a patrol to check on a massive ammunition supply point, ASP 3, in the desert west of Samarra. In 2003 and 2004, the Army Corps of Engineers had hired four private companies to destroy several Iraqi ASPs. In the case of ASP 3, it appeared to Frost that the contractors (many retired military EOD techs) simply got sick of piling up ordnance and disposing of it. So they just poured concrete over the bunkers and left it to dry. It looked as if no one had checked the bunkers in years, and when Frost arrived he found fresh digging and broken chunks of concrete. Within the cement chunks were cylindrical impressions that matched the diameter of the artillery rounds that were appearing in the IEDs. When Frost reported this to Task Force Troy, they assured him that ASP 3 was properly disposed of and could not possibly be the source of his munitions. Frost felt more like a quality assurance inspector than a spook, managing the fallout of a bad contract from years before.

Frost made headway, but never as much as he would have liked. He investigated a series of bombings against Iraqi Police checkpoints, IEDs that were unusual in construction and only detonated when no one was around. The culprit turned out to be the police captain, laying devices to ensure he and his men were seen as valuable and stayed employed. Another failed bomb maker turned out to be a sixteen-year-old kid who just liked the technical challenge. These two cases represented a tiny (but "non-zero," in Frost's words) fraction of the IEDs he saw, but they took valuable time to track down and were hugely disappointing finds.

Frost can point to a few successes. They found two "mother lode" weapons caches, and they caught nine definite leaders, second layer oil-spot guys, facilitators and planners. But in both cases, they found the mother lode because of an informant. It was rare to get a good source; anyone reliable got snatched up by Special Forces, and the leftover dregs usually just said enough to get paid or save their own skins. And in the case of the nine, two popped from DNA and seven from fingerprints, information kept in the big biometrics database that Frost was not allowed to access. One got caught when he applied for a job. Who applies for a job with the US when they've just been planning ambushes and IED attacks?

Despite his increased understanding of the IED cells, his tracking of their materials, and his drawing of Gallieni oil spots that far outpaced the old pushpin maps, Frost still found it hard to proactively move Left of Boom. His work mostly confirmed intel that had been gathered elsewhere. When a leader was caught, Frost could tie his fingerprints to a certain device. When an informant claimed a weapons cache was hidden in a certain district of Samarra, Frost could prove that was feasible, based on the types of IEDs seen nearby. But he couldn't put together all the pieces to identify the Engineer or, most importantly for convincing the Army to do a cordon and search, know precisely where he was.

So, like police forces all over the United States, he was stuck chasing lowlifes. He would rather have spent his time on the kingpins, but who has time for kingpins? That was the point of the Surge, but Frost worked across a wide AO for the conventional Army, not on a Special Forces task force or at a three-letter government agency, and so success was tenuous and incremental. No victory was definitive. Frost never got the Engineer.

He did learn one more important fact, though, from researching his Gallieni oil spots. After six months of analysis, Frost noticed an additional trend within the cells. They each had distinctive methods, distinctive materials, but some also had distinctive targets. Some tried to kill Iraqi policemen and assassinate politicians. Some only conducted nuisance attacks against the main oil refinery in Bajji. Some killed civilians, the more the merrier. Some neighborhoods tried to kill each other. Some killed American soldiers, any soldier. But a few, an ever growing number in fact, discriminated. They passed over one truck for another. They skipped security to focus on the package being secured.

They were targeting us just like we were targeting them.

10 · I'm Going to Kill You Bomb Man

IT WAS IN THE MIDST of the Surges, both in Iraq and Afghanistan, that I had a job as a contractor teaching EOD techs the skills they would need to survive al-Muhandis. In the worst of the years, sometimes even this limited aspiration seemed to be too lofty. Survival always came first, and often wholly defined success. But eventually, the message of the Surge—that there were a practically infinite number of potential bombs available, and so hunting the people who made them was our way out of the country—sank in, and the students understood that their long-term survival would be based on the short-term collection of evidence. Post-blast investigation was already part of our job description, but the effort was sporadic and opportunistic, and not a universally accepted and explicit priority until now. The setting for my classes may have been academic, but the students' relationship with the topic was not; the soldiers would run daily missions less than a month following our brief encounter.

So a Left of Boom paradigm shift was in order. The bomb in the road was no longer simply a dangerous obstacle to be breached. It was now an opportunity to understand the thinking of the insurgents, and, ultimately, the Engineer. The forensic evidence was necessary, but just the means to an end, nothing more than lumps of burned scrap unless combined with an analysis of the scene; the will behind the attack almost always more important than the bomb itself. Was the device indiscriminate, general chaos, meant for any poor soul? Or was it controlled, saved for a specific target? How do you know?

Or to put it another way, as I would ask myself later, were the bombs that got Fye, Frost, and Matt simply bad luck or meant for them?

To start this conversation, I always showed two videos to my students. Chosen to inspire reflection and discussion in the classroom, they were examples of their enemy collecting intelligence and evidence in reverse.

The first grainy video stream shows an American patrol of armored vehicles winding through an Afghan canyon. The camera is zoomed in. No ridgeline or sky is visible. The line of armored trucks slowly creeps along an impossibly narrow gravel track, left shoulder open to a steep ravine. No soldiers are visible, no gunners even poking their heads from rooftop turrets, only the great shuffling beasts, armored nose to armored tail. Then a cloud of smoke appears under the front tires of the lead vehicle. The convoy lurches to a halt. As is typical of such videos, popular Muslim prayer melodies sung by all-male choirs loop in the background; if the detonation was audible from the cameraman's vantage point, it was lost in postproduction. Nothing happens for several minutes, the camera stays fixed, the dust cloud blows away, the chanting continues, and then several tiny soldiers appear in the frame. They dismount and run up to the lead vehicle, pick up bits of armor and headlight and the front bumper that has been blown off, open up the rear hatch of the RG-31 MRAP, and toss them inside. A banner in Arabic scrolls across the top of the video, subtitled in English by the helpful intelligence agencies who passed on the tape: "The Americans hide the shame of their weakness."

The second video is more heavily edited and doctored. The target is the same: a line of knobby machines with nary a human in sight. But this time the armored patrol is close, partially obscured by a field of poppies. Two blasts hit this convoy, and a prolonged firefight ensues, the camera jumping wildly as the videographer takes cover. The same religious music plays in the background, but the sounds of the shots remain, the heartbeat thump of the incoming heavy machine gun fire, the clip and rack of the AK outgoing, the calls of *ALLAHU AKBAR* over and over and over again, the shouter's voice turning falsetto in the ecstatic throes of it. Then suddenly the scene breaks and jumps forward in time, and we see the driver's view as the ambushers travel the same road that the American patrol had just occupied. The camera pauses to focus on an enormous pile of jettisoned .50 cal brass and links, a stain on the sheets providing evidence of the American portion of the orgy. The camera stops at each blast crater along the road, the frame freezing as a clip art arrow from PowerPoint is sloppily superimposed over the hole, the words (again, helpfully translated) "The American Illusion" printed across the top of the screen. The short video ends with an inspection of evidence picked up from the scene: a pile of truck parts, the sharp teeth of a rear differential, the drive shaft and forked clamp, assorted nuts and bolts, and armored plates that could only come from the undercarriage of a Humvee. Now the title banner has changed: "The American Delusion."

Such videos are far more sophisticated than the standard camera phone clip of your daughter's dance recital. The graphic overlays resemble those of 1970s-era local news, but the editing and distribution network is slick, the work of established production companies that run credits at the front or back of each video. Shot by the teenage gunmen, uploaded to the Cloud, sliced and diced by the militia's own editing staff or an affiliate both sympathetic and savvy, then distributed via complex channels that mirror tribe and sect. The Islamic State would eventually master the art of such videos, producing a mix of propaganda and extortion. But the audience for these earlier incarnations was still primarily local, and the goal was inspiration and recruitment. Attached to emails and posted on bulletin boards, so that, in a matter of hours, crowds of young men would huddle in Middle Eastern Internet cafés and city squares, watching the flickering images on their cousin's cell phone.

"What's the illusion here, guys? What is the delusion this video is combatting?" I asked the soldiers sitting in my class.

My students instantly got it.

"The delusion is that with all of our armor we're invincible," they said. "The videos are proof we can be killed."

I LOOKED, BUT I never found a video of the attack that killed Matt Schwartz. I looked because I wanted to know if Matt was targeted. Watch enough of those videos on YouTube, and you can tell some are more than basic ambushes. You can tell they discovered this oil spot thing for themselves.

I don't know when they figured it out. I also don't know if it was al-Muhandis that first told them, but I suspect it. As a contractor, I have dug in far more IEDs than I have cleared, and I have played the Engineer far more often than the hero. The ratio isn't even close, and I know the first thing I always wanted to do when placing a bomb is kill the guy who's coming to take it apart. I don't think I'm projecting. I think it's human nature.

I served as a proxy al-Muhandis for years, testing, training, and fine-tuning portions of the military's IED detection capability. In Balad in 2005, the Predator pilots wanted to test their thermal and infrared cameras. How long does a heavy metal artillery shell retain the heat it collects all day, how long into the cooler evening can you spot it? So we placed devices along the runways, using real steel ordnance but fake triggers. We did the same in an old bomb dump in Kirkuk in 2006, for Predators and other aircraft. Again in Nevada in 2007, where the brand-new Predator pilots practice looking for the telltale signs: fresh dirt, changes in temperature, artificial lines and curves where there should be only natural jumble. The human eye has a remarkable ability to spot slight order in randomness, even when the eye and the Predator's camera are separated by seven thousand miles.

More often, I played the Engineer to train other EOD technicians. Thousands of IEDs it must be, over the years, that I've placed in bags on the side of the road, stuffed into the trunks of cars, slid into culverts and under asphalt roads, sifted into sand and loose gravel, packed into snowbanks, hidden in Hawaiian jungles and Alaskan tundra and Adirondack hills and Carolinian piney woods and the empty gullies and wadis of the Colorado uplands that look like an Afghan postcard.

When you build a device for another EOD tech, rather than a Predator, a higher level of precision is required. EOD techs are often taught, when searching for a bomb, to imagine "how they would do it," how they would booby-trap the area, where they would hide the device. But that's wrong. You have to imagine how your adversary would do it, get in his mind, synthesize every device you have ever disabled, and then apply that algorithm to your terrain and specific sector. If you get that wrong, your EOD students will know. So the IED construction has to be perfect, the placement genuine, the scenario legit. And after having trained the unit, spent time with the guys, there was an intimacy. I wasn't trying to kill an empty uniform. I was trying to kill Tom. I had seen Tom work. I knew where he would step, and so that's where I would put the bomb.

This kinship is not an artifact of the training environment. I once heard a story from a Marine unit out west, in Fallujah or Ramadi or similar enclave resisting Gallieni's oil spread. They did a raid, and in the rubbled basement of a bombed-out apartment building they found a weapons cache. It contained all the normal evidence, RPGs and remote triggers, but also, very unusually, a television and a VCR. Next to the VCR was a pile of tapes all labeled like this: Staff Sergeant Jones. Sergeant Perkins. Gunnery Sergeant Taylor. And they all look at each other because that's their names, the Marines doing the raid. And when Gunny Taylor put the tape in and watched—and this is the part that will make an EOD tech's blood run cold—it was hours of spliced-together video of every operation he had run for weeks. The Engineer had identified each man from the name stitched on his uniform. This wasn't propaganda meant for a general audience; al-Muhandis had been creating game film like a football scout. Perkins uses the robot, but Taylor skips it to outflank and do a visual recon. Jones always talks to security first, stands at the window of the platoon leader's MRAP. The Engineer had been stalking Jones and Taylor and Perkins and knew their techniques and preferences and habits at least as well as they did.

That intel came down like it used to in the old days right after 9/11, as a classified rumor. It could be an urban legend, like Candy Man or Bloody Mary. It is, at least, the worst kind of ghost story one EOD tech could tell another.

We heard other classified rumors. That the Irish Republican Army and Colombian FARC were training the highest bidder in Iraq and Afghanistan. That the Iraqi kids were tracking us, and that the Arabic graffiti in the worst neighborhoods said "I'm going to kill you bomb man." That the same groups were trying to abduct us or capture one of our robots. That the Engineer had gotten his degree at MIT as a sleeper agent, and that's why the devices were so sophisticated and changed so fast in reaction to our countermeasures. We had inadvertently trained him.

The most frequent rumor said that there was a $25,000 bounty on the head of every EOD technician. I have never found anyone who could provide conclusive evidence, one way or the other, that there really was such a reward. I have asked hundreds of fellow EOD techs, and while no one can confirm it, they nearly all believed it, and why not? While the US Army was instituting "stop loss," forcing infantry grunts to stay in past their enlistments, they were simultaneously writing $100,000 checks to entice EOD guys to do the same. A similar check sealed the deal for Matt Schwartz to reenlist. If even a bureaucrat in the faraway Pentagon saw our value, then surely the other side did too. Not much of a stretch to bounties and videotapes.

So I don't know when the other side learned the nuances of targeting, discriminating both among American military options and in their internal battles. In Iraq, it might have been during the Sunni Awakening in the mid-2000s, when the revenge attacks started.

They killed tribal leaders in Ramadi and Fallujah with sophisticated improvised limpet mines that attached to the underside of cars and detonated when the driver reached a certain speed. In Afghanistan, it started much earlier. When the Taliban ordered a string of assassinations in the summer of 2011, killing specific politicians and police chiefs in Kandahar and outlying villages, they were merely resurrecting an Al Qaeda-trained tactic. The first shot of the post-9/11 wars was actually fired two days before the World Trade Center attacks, on September 9, when Ahmad Shah Massoud was killed by Al Qaeda. Massoud was a hero of the resistance against the Soviets in the 1980s and the leader of the Northern Alliance, the last credible indigenous threat to the Taliban. He was known as the Lion of Panjshir, the Shir-e-Panjshir, the Lion of Five Lions, and he was assassinated by two Arab suicide bombers who posed as journalists. The IED was hidden in their video camera; we still don't know the name of the Engineer who built it.

We also don't know what they call their oil-spot model. I don't know if it has three rings. I've never looked at the maps on the bunker wall of this war's Bamboo Pentagon, and neither has anyone else; we used JDAMs dropped from fighter jets to flatten the apartment building of Abu Musab al-Zarqawi, the one-time head of Al Qaeda in Iraq. We hit the front entrance of Hindu Kush caves to trap the Taliban inside. Osama Bin Laden was no General Giap, and the material discovered in his house in Abbottabad was philosophical, not operational.

But whatever they call their method, and whenever they first discovered it, and whomever can be credited with it, one thing is certain: it worked. They knew the US military was an oil spot too, and they adjusted tactics to combat it.

The point of the Surge was to get past the wall of IEDs, to reach into the oily membrane of the insurgent cell and grab the human will that lies behind. The IED is a machine, the oil-spot third ring human emplacer an automaton. It was in killing the second and first rings, the inner rings of the oil spot, where real damage could be done.

But the enemy has always gotten a vote, as the old saying goes, and the enemy voted to do the same thing back to us. The outer layer of our oil spot is tougher, a technological film of electronics and machinery and plate metal. Armored trucks that take a licking. Robots and drones. They could damage our trucks every day, and we'd just keep repairing them. A Predator could be shot down, and an EOD robot could be destroyed, but there would always be more. Talon robots cost only $100,000, chump change for JIEDDO.

So in Iraq the Engineer developed ever-larger IEDs, and in Afghanistan they appeared in the dirt where soldiers walked. They pierced the veil, and once inside, they knew the relative value of each ring. In the outer layer, a pink farm boy from rural Ohio or an ambitious Latino Marine from inner-city Los Angeles. But even better, the next level in, an EOD technician who disarms their bombs. A special ops soldier who comes to snatch them in the middle of the night. An officer who was successful spreading a counterinsurgency oil spot. They knew where the utility lay.

In *The Outpost*, Jake Tapper tells the tragic story of Captain Rob Yllescas, targeted for assassination because he proved so successful at befriending Afghan elders and leading *shuras*. Yllescas was killed via a radio-controlled IED, the only appearance of such a device in the entire book. Casualties during the Iraq Surge leapt 20 percent for Green Berets and doubled for EOD techs. SEAL teams didn't lose a single man in Iraq until 2006, and then they lost twelve in the Surge.

The bomb maker and the bomb safer. We each sent our technological avatars into battle. We each sought to reach through that curtain and grasp the other. We each persisted, day after month after year, implementing strategies strikingly similar. Why? Because it's a job? Because someone told us to? Or because his brother is dead, and so is mine?

No, this isn't a book about why. Only what and how. Why never makes sense. My own tours in Iraq had taught me that. Asking why only produces an answer too arbitrary or inhuman to apply to any man you love.

Veterans of Vietnam know that when you hit the LZ, you never wanted to jump out of the helicopter next to the guy with the M60, because the VC hiding in the tree line tried to shoot the man with the big belt-fed Pig first. For hundreds of years, as long as snipers and sharpshooters have existed, the powerful and unusual have drawn the attention of the opposing army. How is this different?

Because violence has evolved from the personal to the individual. Because each for the other is not merely a target of opportunity. This is the war plan. We need to move Left of Boom, and the bomb man needs to die.

MATT SCHWARTZ DIED on a route clearance mission. I did those missions when I was in Iraq as well, and even back then the Engineer knew how to target.

When I was in Kirkuk in 2006, we fought in the city, and we fought to the south toward Baghdad, and we fought to the southwest to Tikrit, and we fought to the west to the Tigris, but to the east lay mountains and Iran, and to the north the tablelands rose and rose in a vast emptiness. The land was flat scrub all the way to the Little Zab River Valley, and beyond lay Erbil, where they said the Kurds lived in peace and bombs never went off, and tidy American-style Cape Cods sprouted like green shoots from the cracked earth. We rarely drove north because the war wasn't there and we didn't want to take it there.

But, occasionally, the contractors had to work on the Dibis Dam on the Little Zab or on the power station there and the massive steel transmission towers from which were strung the high-voltage power cables, and so we would join with the combat engineers and drive up the highway from Kirkuk to Dibis, on roads that rarely saw American patrols.

The line of armored vehicles that swept and cleared highways, the biggest vehicles with the toughest armor we had, varied little from mission to mission and year to year. An RG-31 on point, tough as your grandfather's old hickory ax handle. Every mission the RG would hit an IED, the hood would be blown back into the armored windshield, a front tire would shred, and the team leader in the front seat would call back on the radio, "Yeah, we're fine. Just had our bell rung."

Following the RG was the Husky, a Dr. Seuss–inspired one-man bubble perched on a frame with a ground-penetrating radar array hung beneath. Then the Buffalo, another brute with a massive robotic arm emerging from the front bumper. Soldiers called it the "Claw," and they used it to dig and sift through rock and soil. Next the JERRV with the EOD team inside, then a command-and-control Humvee, perhaps another RG-31 or two for extra firepower. This line of horned beetles crept slowly down the road an hour before the Dibis contractors, trying to get shot at, trying to find the IEDs that lay hidden, trying to disrupt them when found, trying to survive them when tripped.

On a perfectly ordinary mission, the RG-31 would drive unaware past a camouflaged IED on the side of the road. The Husky would drive over it as well, but their radar would ping from the magnetic signature, hot and loud in the operator's ear, and WARNING would flash across his video screen, and he would slow and stop and wait, hanging above his death in his egg-like perch, calling in the exact spot for the Buffalo to search. Then the Claw would extend, rake the ground, plow the gravelly crust, and reveal, what? A wire? A 155mm round? A heavy lump in a garbage bag wrapped in black electrical tape. So the EOD team would drop the Talon robot from the JERRV, confirm the IED, place the explosives, make it go boom, scatter the pieces and parts, and pick up the key evidence by hand.

Except on one particular day, a length of copper audio-speaker wire ran off from the side of the road into the distance. This was not unusual; this type of command-wire device was common throughout our area. But in such a desolate land, no towns or settlements for miles, the Little Zab River and Dibis still far in the distance, we felt the need to investigate more. The wire ran off into nothingness.

So off we dismounted to find the wire's end. Tracing a command wire is dangerous; directly walking along its length, such an obvious place to hide a booby trap. So my team zigged and zagged, outflanked it, found it and returned, followed its route from afar across the blank arid uplands. After a full kilometer, it descended into an obscured dried wadi, meandered along the bottom into a concrete culvert. This single mark of man upon the landscape was so far out of place it aroused immediate suspicion, but a quick check found nothing hidden, and so we dropped down into the depression.

The wire ended several feet inside the shoulder-high culvert. A large battery pack lay there, plenty of juice to overcome the resistance of so much copper between here and the bomb. No other sign of human occupation—no cigarette butts or discarded food scraps or sandal impressions in the dust—nothing to see, except this, which made my stomach flip twice:

Scrawled across the inside of the smooth concrete wall was a perfect depiction of our Route Clearance Patrol. Drawn in dark chalk as a profile view, like an ancient cave painting, each vehicle in the childish sketch was blocky but unmistakable: the smaller RG, the high-wire Husky, the fat Buffalo with a three-fingered stick-figure Claw, the JERRV, a tiny Humvee, more RGs behind.

We drove this road so rarely, and they still knew we were coming.

We looked out from the edge of the culvert and back toward the highway. Even a kilometer away, the convoy was easy to see across the empty plain.

We looked down at the sketch. The JERRV was circled in black, and crossed out with an X.

"SO YOU'VE GIVEN this a lot of thought, I'm sure," I asked Frost, sitting on his couch, "After looking through all this evidence yourself, what do we know about the Engineer, the guy who actually knows how this all works?"

"Oh, you mean the Smart Guy," Frost said.

"Yeah, sure, the Smart Guy. What do we know about the Smart Guy?"

"Not much."

We laughed. No, it's not funny.

"You know, you collect hundreds of pieces of evidence," Frost said, as he settled in his computer chair and propped up his stick legs, "which is probably only one third of the total amount of evidence available, and still all we really know about the Smart Guy, or the Engineer, is that there is a gap in our knowledge. There's money coming down, there's logistics coming in, there's IEDs trickling out the bottom, there has to be somebody there, but we have almost no direct evidence. We don't have anybody who's talked about that guy. We don't have any distinct DNA biometrics profile on that guy. We just know that there is an operational signature or an equipment signature, and you only know that if you pay attention to the details. It's like reading the classics, you have to read them all before you figure out they all reference each other. And too many of them that we thought were Smart Guys turned out to be unreliable narrators."

IT WAS LATE in the American Surge in Iraq, in a martyrdom safe house in Tikrit, north of Samarra, in a cement room hidden away from the prying *kuffar* eyes, that the Engineer met the local emir for Ad Dawla al Islamiyya fin al-Iraq wa al-Sham, the Islamic State of Iraq and the Levant. They may have been shouting so loud that the women and children upstairs huddled in fear on their sleeping mats.

You are distracted and have lost your way, the Engineer may have said. Killing the Shia, and killing our fellow Muslim brothers and sisters.

The Shia are apostates, and the others are all *shaheed*, may Allah accept their martyrdom, the emir may have said.

It is unnecessary and against the teaching of our Prophet, peace be upon him, al-Muhandis said. You do not care for the widows and orphans of our slain brothers, as our Sheikh has directed. You do not discriminate. You seek nothing but chaos. You put my *albuyah nasiffah* everywhere.

The collaborators are legitimate targets, the emir said. Everyone knows this.

You have lost your focus on the Great Satan brought near. He must be targeted, and his men and machines who find the *albuyah nasiffah*. Your revenge distracts from the Jews and Crusaders.

The Engineer pointed to a corner of stacked rocket-propelled grenades, the warheads all wrapped in aluminum foil.

And you are ruled by superstition, he accused.

We have heard the *kuffar* jammers protect the tanks with a field of electricity. The covering defeats the jammers, the emir replied.

These are mere rumors. You are superstitious and sloppy. You do not place the explosives around the remote detonator to hide the evidence. You do not use the gloves when making the devices.

We wrap our fingers in tape, said the emir. They will not see our fingerprints.

You leave the tape everywhere, like trash! They will find the fingerprints on the tape and find you.

The Engineer snatched the emir's cell phone from his hand, smashed it with a nearby hammer, and removed the SIM card.

This must all be burned, immediately, said the Engineer. Have you learned nothing from the last ten years? Of course not. When our great Sheikh led the attack on the two towers at the Battle of Manhattan you were still on your mother's dusty tit.

We have killed thousands of *kuffar* while the Sheikh hides, the emir replied. We are not as lucky as our other mujahideen brothers. We have not received the remote detonators and missiles to shoot down Hind helicopters, as you did in jihad years ago. We do not have the *takfir* Persians giving us weapons. We Sunni must do it ourselves. We conduct our own martyrdom operations.

Yes, from throughout the caliphate, the Engineer said, you bring those wishing to be *shaheed* through Syria and then lock them in your safe houses here, and then feed them drugs and girls, like a playboy from the Great Satan. Or you rape them and fuck their asses, like some kohl-eyed Pashtun goat herder. These are not the directives of the Sheikh. We do not need to shame our brothers into obedience. We do not need to tempt our brothers with worldly pleasures. They will submit as good Muslims.

You are the *takfir*, the Engineer continued. I am returning to my Afghan mujahideen brothers and the black banners of Khurasan.

IN MY MIND, the wars loomed over us like the heads of two slaughtered whales hanging from opposing sides of the *Pequod*'s mast. The Sperm and the Right. The favored and the lesser cousin. Kant and Locke, spiritual intuition and technical empiricism, Melville says. But now they are also Afghanistan and Iraq, the good, long war and the wrong, unwanted one. We were all whale hunters now, looking for answers from dripping containers of sperm and blood.

Iraq and Afghanistan. In each Surge we did counterinsurgency and counterterror, we spread stability and we killed specific targets, we oozed our oil spot of peace and destroyed their network. But if the Engineer and his surrogates did the same in reverse, if some IEDs are general mayhem and some have an individual name on them, then the question hangs: what about Frost, and Fye, and Matt?

On May 18, 2008, Frost hopped onboard with a Navy EOD team responding to a call for help from an Army combat engineer's route clearance package. The Husky had been hit, and the driver was hurt. The engineers stopped and created a security cordon and then another armored truck was hit. Two vehicles crippled and five soldiers wounded, and when Frost's patrol arrived to rescue them the dirt road erupted and crumpled his Caiman, and now there were four more wounded, but Branden was quiet from the very beginning and he didn't make it.

Frost knew that dirt track was famous for Christmas Tree Light devices, tiny little pressure strips made with thin motor-winding wire and a string of contacts held apart by clear rubber spacers. Drive over a contact, crush the rubber spacer, complete the circuit, boom.

In fact, Frost had made that track famous; he wrote the reports and drew the cell on his map.

It was nearly impossible to see the strips except in full sunlight and crawling at ten miles per hour. But there had just been a three-day dust storm, the kind of storm that makes the sky glow orange and scours every surface as if the moon dust was sprayed with a pressure-washer. There was no way for the combat engineers to see the Christmas Tree Lights under that layer of dirt.

A few old craters in the road had been packed with explosives and covered with dust. No one had checked the old craters to make sure they had not been reused by the bomb emplacers. No one had checked ASP 3 to make sure the old ordnance wasn't being stolen.

When Frost got hit, his patrol had not yet made it to the route clearance package. They were still two football fields away. It had to be a command wire, waiting for him or the Navy EOD team. The combat engineers had already driven that way; if it was a simple Christmas Tree Light strip, they would have triggered it themselves.

The explosives might have come from ASP 3. Or they might have been home-cooked. Either way, Frost doesn't know for sure because no one ever did a full investigation. Official policy at the time said they should have. To move Left of Boom, a patrol that is hit should stop and secure the site and medevac the wounded and wait for a WIT or EOD team to investigate. If that response team is then hit, they should wait for yet another EOD team from another FOB in another part of the AO.

But no second team was coming. In that complex attack, three IEDs crippled three trucks and produced one killed and eight wounded, and no full investigation was done. It was an eight-to-one ratio, wounded to killed, worse than the Iraq average.

No, not eight-to-one. Remember, the interpreter doesn't count. He's just the terp. He's not a US soldier. But the terp has a name. His name is Max, and he lost both of his legs and now he lives in Jordan, even if he doesn't count for the statistics.

Even in 2008, sometimes no investigation was done. After years of looping repeated failures, the overall strategy had changed to focus on just that sort of attack, but still incidents got missed, reports went unwritten. Whatever happened to the mountain of data anyway? *CSI: Baghdad* is a generous comparison. It implies that someone solves the case at the end of the episode. Only rarely does that happen. Iraq was more like the first ten minutes of the show over and over and over again: collect the evidence, send it to the lab, and then just move on to the next one. Cases open but rarely shut, repeated until the war ended.

Frost learned later that someone took a picture of the crater and measured it, but no one picked up evidence, no one traced the command wire, no one found the firing point, no one pursued the triggerman. Once the helo arrived and carried off the wounded, everyone had had their fill for the day and went home.

Frost didn't feel bad that no one did an investigation. How could you take it personally? So many bombings, you had to focus on taking victories where you could. There was such a small chance the system would produce a worthwhile result anyway.

The truth was, the person who cared most about doing an investigation had just gotten hit. Frost was on his way to the hospital and out of Iraq for good, and in his absence, nothing was done. The Engineer's targeting worked.

Three years later, in 2011, a full post-blast investigation was done for Fye. A follow-on EOD team did just as the Surge policy said they should. By then, the process had become institutionalized, and didn't rely on the drive of one man like Frost.

The final report would determine that Fye was simply unlucky. The IED was not meant for him; it was random chance that he stepped on it. Fye knew it was dangerous to walk across the footbridge or on the main donkey path directly to the known devices in the Taliban Bazaar. It was also dangerous to take the steepest slope of the canal, hop over a wall. Left with a mix of less-obvious and random routes, he picked one. What else is there to do? The question was not what Fye did wrong, but why the emplacer would choose to put an IED there at all.

The investigation also revealed that Fye did, in fact, step on a PMN landmine with an extra charge beneath. In that area of the Horn of Panjwe, the Taliban used PMNs as high-power initiators, connecting them with detonating cord to jugs of homemade explosives buried still deeper. All told, approximately three quarters of a pound of TNT and five pounds of ammonium nitrate and aluminum (helpfully, and without mirth, shortened to ANAL in military jargon) detonated under Fye's left foot.

But the five-liter plastic jugs found throughout that district can hold forty pounds of ANAL, not just five. Why did so little function correctly? Why did the top of the slurry simply blow itself apart in flaming chunks? Why did the lion's share remain in the hole? Why was the mix off, in the wrong proportion, the recipe not followed?

Fye has an answer.

"I was really blessed and God was really looking out for me," he said during my visit. "I can't think of any other reason. You step on something of that size, and to have only the damage I have, I should have lost a lot more."

Fye lived because the *muj* didn't stir enough. They made a bad batch.

"It sucks because I fought an inanimate object and lost!" Fye continued, with a deep belly laugh, humor as defense mechanism.

"Actually, I won because I'm still here," he corrected himself. "But you know what I mean, it's an object."

"You're fighting the deviousness of the Engineer, that's what you're fighting, and you lived through it, so I wouldn't say you lost," I said.

"It's like a scene from *Scott Pilgrim*," he said, referencing the movie about a high school kid who battles a string of impossibly cartoonish ex-boyfriends in hopes of landing a girl, "but instead of actually fighting someone, it's a weird in-your-mind fight." Only now I'm not sure he's only talking about the IED.

But Fye is right. All of us EOD guys—Fye, Frost, Matt, myself, the few thousand of us who served in both wars—had been originally trained to fight a thing. To fight the inanimate object. Success was simply disarming the device, until we learned to go Left of Boom, and fight the mind behind the bomb.

Frost was targeted. Fye seemed to be random. What was Matt?

"Do you know if they ever found the guy who built it?" I asked.

"No. I don't know if they ever got the guy," Fye said, and then he unintentionally echoed a refrain heard daily over the last decade of war:

"All that evidence just goes into that intel black hole, and you never hear about it again."

I never got intel out of the black hole either, but now I'd have to, if I wanted to continue my investigation. The war had changed so much in the four years since I left Iraq, I barely recognized the players and rules of this new game. What is in that black hole, and what are the analysts and interrogators and hunters doing to find the man who killed my friend?

PART IV
HUNT AND KILL

"Let us therefore animate and encourage each other, and show the whole world that a Freeman, contending for liberty on his own ground, is superior to any slavish mercenary on earth."

—General George Washington, 1776

11 • THE BLACK HOLE

IN A REMOTE PORTION OF Afghanistan north of Kabul, where the mountains ease to hills and the hills to lush irrigated fields covering a broad valley, in a tiny village set among the silty channels of the Kunduz River, a pair of Blackhawk helicopters landed near a walled compound and, against odds, a tall thin young woman from West Virginia named Sarah Soliman got out.

A helmet and body armor hung loosely about her, but beneath she wore a stylish button-down and smart business slacks. She claimed no uniform, carried no gun, lacked all the tactical accoutrements the modern soldier found fashionable, and her distinctive long red hair, so bright and authentic one startled upon first glimpse, was sensibly tied back against the rotor wash. With the confidence of a frequent flier she hopped from the side of the bird, one chunky heel on the ground at a time, and with long steps crossed the LZ of dried mud to where a man from the local ODA team was waiting for her.

He was all contrast: unwashed, M4, baggy camo pants, boots, beard. In a spotter's scope they would make quite a matched pair. They greeted each other with comfortable familiarity and hand gestures, few words being possible under the buffet of the blades. At his feet sat six small clear bags filled with blackened junk. He pointed at the bags, hefted one, indicated a white paper report inside each, helped her carry the parcels back to the helicopter, and loaded them on the center jump seat where they would not be lost. The woman reboarded. The man turned his back and returned to his rack in the compound.

The helos never turned off their engines. In a minute they were off, six bags of IED evidence, six bags of hard-core forensics, six bags of pressure plates and fingerprints and distinctive wire snips and hairs, permanently sequestered from the conventional reporting channels and hand-delivered to the central depths of one of the fiercest black holes in Afghanistan.

WHEN SOLIMAN ARRIVED back at Bagram, she delivered the six bags to Zac Crush at SOCOM's IED exploitation fusion cell. Though they worked for the main SOCOM (Special Operations Command) task force in Afghanistan—in the J2, the intelligence hub for activities as varied as hunter-killer takedowns and local police training— Soliman and Crush were not EOD technicians or spooks or Special Forces. They weren't even in the military. They were contractors. Soliman is a biometrics engineer. Crush is an intel analyst in Identity Operations, SOCOM's term for figuring out who people are.

Biometrics is the science of measuring and cataloguing unique human signatures, and it is not a new idea. In the late nineteenth century, French police began tabulating the lengths of forearms and feet and jawlines. At the same time, the US Army, in an effort to catch scam artists who enlisted in multiple recruiting stations to receive multiple bonus checks, began recording the distance from the top of the shoulder to the tip of the finger of each new soldier. Scotland Yard adopted fingerprinting in 1901, the New York City police department five years later.

As a system and theory, biometrics is unchanged. To be "enrolled," a citizen simply has their unique characteristics measured. Then, when they want something (a job, to cross a border, access to a military base or classified information) or when the state wants something of them (evidence connected to a crime), those unique characteristics are measured again and checked against a database. Maybe the criminal had applied for a job; maybe the person applying for a job is an ex-con. In the twenty-first century we turn iris patterns into bar codes, use face recognition software, and flip through fingerprints digitally, but the process is fundamentally the same. Only the scope is different; millions of electronic records can be scoured in minutes versus thousands of paper records in days or weeks.

As a biometrics engineer, it was Sarah Soliman's job to implement that scope. She helped develop the technology, tested it, taught it, and, in a pinch, used it herself. In 2011 and 2012, she traveled across Afghanistan in order to teach Special Forces units to gather the biometrics data—fingerprints, three photos, iris scans—of every Afghan they met. On the side, she was a courier, carrying forensic IED evidence back to the main SOCOM intel cell, but her prime job was that of the evangelist, selling and teaching a new way to fight the war.

Conducting a census of the population is a classic counterinsurgency strategy. It is also classic counterterrorism, a way to positively identify who needs killing.

Iraq was always a conventional war: large traditional Army divisions and brigades, firm AOs and lines of demarcation. In contrast, the war in Afghanistan was, from the beginning, a task force war. The Rangers went here, SOF went there, SEALs on this mission, 10th Mountain Division in a thrust to Tora Bora. That culture persisted as the years went on, and task forces were set up for everything: Paladin did the IEDs, ODIN did the aerial surveillance. Each NATO partner had their own designation. The task forces known only by a number often did the killing. SOCOM set up a tongue twister known as CJSOTF-A: Combined Joint Special Operations Task Force Afghanistan. CJSOTF (pronounced "See-Jah-SO-Tiff") broke the country up into districts that did not match the larger Army regional command system and allowed each ODA team within this proprietary framework to act as a mini–task force itself.

No wonder, then, that biometrics, a system that functions properly only if built on a monolithic foundation, would find a foothold in Iraq long before Afghanistan. In 2007, two systems were fielded: the Biometric Automated Toolset and the Handheld Interagency Identity Detection Equipment, known to soldiers in Iraq as BATs and HIIDEs. The BATs used a laptop and heavy scanner and sat at the front gate of every FOB to check any local who wanted access. The HIIDE looked like an old-fashioned bulky digital camera, and could be taken on patrol. This allowed two important developments. First, the entire country could be enrolled if soldiers would serve as door-to-door census takers. Second, when a unit detained someone suspicious, instead of just dousing them in Expray (which would make their hands turn black if they had touched explosives or fertilizer or both), one could immediately scan their eyeballs to find out if they were wanted men.

Afghanistan did not fully adopt biometrics until the next generation of mobile device was fielded. It was called the SEEK, proof that nerds have a sense of humor. It took iris scans and photos and, unlike the HIIDE, FBI standard nail-to-nail rolled fingerprints. "Ten rolled is gold," Soliman would say in her classes. SEEKs were fielded to both Special Forces teams and average Army patrols during the Afghanistan Surge; the surge in manpower was also a surge in data, to move Left of Boom.

The biometrics database was one of the few that was truly DoD-wide, and if searched correctly, it could reveal a map of the IED supply chain. The same fingerprints were always found on blasting caps or on the tape inside pressure plates; repeat offenders were the norm. Who applies for a job after emplacing IEDs? Soliman met them all the time. The unemployed, the desperate, the poor, the cuckolded, the cajoled, the ignorant. *Computers are magic here*, she thought. *How can the average Afghan even conceive of a searchable database system of fingerprints and iris scans?*

But biometrics could only take you so far. Zac Crush tried to fuse various streams of forensic data and saw the limits every day. He was an analyst in an IED deconstruction office, an intel cell somewhat analogous to Chris Frost's Weapons Intelligence Team. Frost didn't trust his headquarters in Baghdad and so did his own analysis in Samarra. CJSOTF found the national system set up by Task Force Paladin, the main counter-IED organization in Afghanistan, too slow and cumbersome, and so it hired contractors like Crush to do IED exploitation locally. Special Forces needed forensic answers faster than the conventional military could give them, and so it created its own feedback loop in its own black hole, fed by IEDs recovered by their teams. Compared to the experts working in the big evidence labs in Bagram, analysts like Crush sometimes had less specific training and had to do multiple jobs, but he produced reports quickly that could be used immediately. This is what he found:

So you have a fingerprint. So what? A fingerprint by itself is useless unless you have records to check it against, and the biometrics database for Afghanistan was always incomplete. And even if you found a match and discovered that a print on a battery in Kandahar in 2012 matched one collected from an individual who applied for a job in Mazer-e-Sharif in 2009, there is very little that can be done at that moment. You know that guy's name, but you don't know where he is now. So you flag his profile in case he randomly pops again. And anyway, all you really know is that he touched a battery. You don't know exactly how he fits into the process. The complete IED network map does not instantly spring into focus once a match is made; it was always fragmented, a concentration of data here, large holes there.

Tracking individual data points is not enough. Soliman's databases sorted through millions of head/tail penny combinations and set priority lists for the analysts. Crush tied that biometrics info to actual devices. But to move beyond grabbing trigger pullers and tape touchers, to break into an IED network Gallieni oil spot's second and third rings, an additional level of analysis and ingenuity is required.

In the J2 black hole, such profile-building was the job of contractors like Hayes.

Hayes goes by his first name. He is physically forgettable, and his Southern accent is often well concealed. Part psychologist, part anthropologist, part straight-from-a-police-procedural detective, Hayes was trained in multiple types of intelligence collection. He did biometrics and sensors and detainees as well as traditional targeting and analysis, and like an MBA who speaks multiple languages fluently, international business opportunities opened to him.

When he deployed to Afghanistan, Hayes found himself reading as many histories as current reports, and it was the academic texts concerning Genghis Khan and the empire building of the Ghilzais that made the most sense to him. The Ghilzais were the predecessors of the modern Pashtuns that form the bulk of the Taliban, and they had not changed greatly in centuries. Insular, tribal, stubborn. They outlast empires and don't tolerate foreigners in their valleys. Eventually Hayes realized his whole intelligence process was built on so many false assumptions, he thought it was amazing they found anyone at all.

Take, for example, the simple idea of names.

In America and the West, everyone has a unique name. It is generally permanent, and we organize and search for people based on their names. The Western tradition assumes that strangers will interact, and so it privileges the easy building of a large social network, using fixed names as reference. The biometrics intelligence databases are built on this system. The fingerprints and iris scans and photos must be attached to a record, and that record is identified by the individual's name. Iraq's naming system was generally stable, secular, and Western. Iraqis occasionally used a *kunya,* deriving a nickname from one's child, but it was saved for the notable or infamous. Biometrics fit fairly well.

Afghanistan's naming convention, on the other hand, privileges tribal integrity, isolationism, and long-term relationships with a few close family members in one's clan. Why do you need a system to meet a stranger? Strangers stay in their valley, and you stay in yours. Given that, Hayes found that names were fluid and repeated often. The same individual might have multiple public names, depending on his relationship to the person asking. The name might change throughout a life as the person changes. These weren't criminal or *hadith*-directed aliases, but rather natural shades on a theme. The same name could be spelled many ways, often by the same individual. Afghans know the personal history of those in their village— sometimes also assigning traditional Arabic and Islamic titles of *hafiz, qari,* and *mullah* if the person memorized the Koran as a child, speaks it well, or works at the local mosque—and everyone's current name is easily and intuitively understood. Even if the infantry grunt entering the name in the SEEK spelled it right, it was a temporary name alone.

Hayes saw that he was checking fingerprints against a database as impermanent as last winter's snow. But there were so few other means to collect intelligence. No individual American military unit stayed in place long enough to truly earn the kind of trust required to get people to talk willingly. No one watched state-run television, and most villagers got their news at their local marketplace and mosque. It was very difficult for Americans to listen in on that conversation, to even know what the average Afghan was hearing about current events. Analysts used to be able to rely on signals intelligence, inter- cepted radio communications. They called it SIGINT crack, because it was so addicting and easy to use and exploit, but it was a crutch, covering up for a lot of bad methodology and lesser analysis. The enemy in Iraq and Afghanistan had learned to guard their communi- cations, and the good old crack days were now long gone.

Often, Hayes knew, the biometrics was the best they had, the only objective link between individual and bomb.

ON ONE TOUR, while Hayes was an analyst in the J2, Kunduz prov- ince in northern Afghanistan exploded like a pressure cooker heated on the stove too long. Every measurable toll spiked: deaths, injuries, gunfights, IEDs. The lethality of each IED suddenly leapt as well, and new designs were seen throughout the district.

There's a new guy here, Hayes thought. *There's a new trainer in town.*

Hayes didn't call him the Engineer. He wasn't the Smart Guy either. In the J2, the analysts called him the So-Called Expert. But despite the name, an expert he was, and respected. Hayes knew that bad bomb makers didn't live long enough to have the kind of impact he was seeing.

In his databases, Hayes's profile for the Engineer was thin. He didn't have fingerprints or an iris scan or a photo or even a name. Of course, the Engineer's Afghan name might be evolving as well.

Hayes only had one firm hit. A series of fingerprints in the hot glue used to attach carbon rods to wooden pressure plate boards. Mohammed from Kunduz. Not Mohamed or Muhammad. Three M's and an E. *Good luck finding just one Mohammed in Kunduz*, Hayes thought, *here's the phone book*. But this one had previously applied for a job down south, so they had a name and a face to match to the glue on fifteen IEDs. Thank God for the photos. Without those it was almost impossible to pick up the right guy.

Hayes took the reports to his commander. This was a place to start, Hayes said. We start with Mohammed, and we work our way up. They should do a targeted data collection, Hayes said. Verify or enroll everyone living within a few klicks of every IED bearing Mohammed's hot glue.

In a case like this, it would be Soliman's job to get on a helicopter and link up with the local ODA team. She would deliver new SEEKs and software and repair equipment and train them to cast the wide net, enroll every villager and dirt farmer throughout the valley.

That's the funny thing about using biometrics. The only way to find one person is to find everyone.

WE'VE ALREADY ESTABLISHED that all these stories seem to begin on September 11, and Sarah Soliman's trip to that helicopter is no exception.

It was the United Way Day of Caring in the eastern panhandle of West Virginia, and Soliman was with her high school senior class in a local park, picking up trash when the towers fell. She had already planned to attend her local West Virginia University on scholarship, but after 9/11 she decided to apply her interest in math and science to WVU's biometrics engineering program, the only one of its kind in the nation. In her major, she fell in love with data. On a semester abroad in Morocco, she fell in love with travel and exotic cultures. During internships at the White House and the DoD's Biometrics Management Office in DC, she secured her future in government. She spent a year getting her master's degree in the UK, and then she traded idyllic green Cambridge for the Green Zone in Baghdad. It was 2008, and her first job out of college was working as a biometrics contractor.

That was her first tour, and she would come to think of them as tours. It wasn't exactly the same as being in the military, she knew. She didn't take the same risks certainly. But she went back and forth, deployed and home, for the next several years.

In the Green Zone, she worked in a glorified DMV, checking locals who wanted to work on base. She read *Imperial Life in the Emerald City* as preparation, and it was everything she expected: a college campus in the middle of a war she barely saw. She learned all of the cultural norms, kept her arms covered and her hair long. She learned to say, "Welcome," and "Happy to meet you," and "Please open your eyes," in halting Arabic. She wore blouses and skirts and heels and earrings to "glam it up a bit" but avoided black because it showed the dust, swearing to herself that if she ever felt tempted to convert to the standard contractor uniform of polo shirts and 5.11 khakis, then it was time to get a new job. She met a handsome man in her office one day and fell in love with him during Tuesday night country line-dancing lessons under the crystal chandeliers and engraved ceilings of Saddam's marble palace. She married that man when they returned to the United States, and then she did what we all did; she left him at home to go on another deployment.

She spent half of the next year on the flight line at Kandahar, helping to launch sorties for Task Force ODIN. Most military acronyms don't make much sense when their component terms are written out, but the Norse god–inspired ODIN gets pretty close: Observe, Detect, Identify, Neutralize. ODIN was ostensibly an Army unit but really consisted of a mishmash of contractors. The only members in uniform were quality assurance representatives serving as "systems integrators," making sure all of the companies worked together. It was a Go-Co program: the government owned the planes, the pilots and technicians were contractors. They flew a variety of platforms, from the Army's version of the Predator to modified King Airs measled with antennas. The first commander of ODIN was Army Colonel A. T. Ball, and he said their mission was "sensor-to-shooter" fusion, "persistent stare capability," and "dynamic re-tasking." The policy wonks call this Network-Centric Warfare, using our network to take out theirs. More oil spots.

Soliman's role in this process was minuscule. She ensured one small device on one aircraft was functioning. Meanwhile, the other airframes bubbled with sensor pods that listened to radio communications and smelled fertilizer-based homemade explosives and did a million other things she knew nothing about. Most of her tour she was isolated, on one far side of the flight line, killing time in her little parts shed. General McChrystal had recently determined that everyone was having too much fun in the war, and so had made life more Spartan, closing restaurants and coffee shops on base. She was lonely, but she was introduced to a world she barely knew existed. In Baghdad, she had only seen the tiniest sliver of these secret missions. Who flies these planes? She knew that, when she came back, she wanted the best of both worlds, the social and the surveillance, and to transition from building Gallieni oil spots to dismembering them.

And now here she was, assigned to CJSOTF and the J2, working with operators and analysts, on a helicopter flying to train a special operations team to use a technology that continued to fascinate her.

So much had changed since her first tour. Then, she had only one week at Fort Benning as preparation: marching and guns and shots and scary sucking-chest-wound PowerPoints and two green seabags for her gas mask and vest and helmet. The first time she flew on a helicopter out of Baghdad, she was so nervous. Her future husband calmed her fears then, but she didn't know what to wear, what to do. She wore a ridiculous winter coat on that first flight and was somehow still cold. But the flight was a liberation from the Green Zone, and a beautiful ballet in the air, she thought.

Helo and Osprey flights were no big now. She flew constantly, all over the country, training special ops teams. She knew she would never really blend in so she didn't even try. *They don't care anyway, these SOCOM guys*, she thought. They don't care if you are a man or woman, military or contractor, black or white. They only judge you on one thing. Do you contribute to the mission? Do you pull your own weight? She was determined to, and so while she still wasn't tactical, she now had very tactical teammates.

She thought that working for SOCOM as a contractor with no military background was a little like studying abroad in Morocco. Do your research, be a good student, read books, learn the terminology. She read Dick Couch and Linda Robinson and discovered using jargon like "headshed" helped her fit in. She made it clear she wasn't taking anyone's job. There was no biometrics equivalent to her in the active-duty Army, and she wasn't trying to beat anyone, lift more, outshoot anyone on the rifle range. CJSOTF eventually did offer her a gun, and though in predeployment prep she had shot expert on both M4 and M9, she declined.

Soliman also read *War Torn*, a series of first-person narratives of female reporters in Vietnam. Some things had changed—one woman had a baby in Vietnam and got a pass for her family to visit—but plenty about being a woman in a war had not. Not in the military but affected by it, shaped by it, in a tenuous relationship with it, she took inspiration from the reporter who carried a stick of Maybelline coral-colored lipstick everywhere she went, a silent safety blanket. Soliman could order an infinite variety of lipsticks at the Bagram PX now.

She had picked the right field at the right time, she could see. The technology was blossoming just as the war drove need. Senator Byrd—West Virginian of the Century, God rest his soul—had moved the FBI's biometrics lab to Clarksburg and set up the program in Morgantown just as she came out of high school. The 9/11 Commission Report had recommended a national biometric-based entry and exit system based on the government's experience with Mohammed al-Kahtani. He was a candidate to be the twentieth hijacker but was fingerprinted and denied entry by suspicious border agents in 2001. Later, he was captured at Tora Bora and re-identified when his fingerprints were run again at Guantanamo Bay. The DoD would adopt biometrics after a dining hall in Mosul was hit by a suicide bomber in December of 2004; he had snuck on base using a falsified ID card. While an intern in DC in 2005, she had seen the daily hit count, all of the times two biometrics records in Iraq connected for some reason. It was all rudimentary then, no IED forensics added yet, but it was still fascinating, and she had seen the development of the entire program. There were even opportunities with the UN now, in refugee camps around the world, helping people prove who they are so they qualify for benefits. She was on the front edge of a technological wave, she thought. The Iraq War had ended just as the system was finally getting established, but now she was part of an opportunity to demonstrate the full potential in Afghanistan.

This whole country is like a laboratory, like a giant beta-test, she realized. Can we prove the technology really works? And it's a chance we might not get again; if we don't occupy another country in our next war, we won't be able to enroll the population the same way. We'll have to rely on signatures like IP addresses and keystroke patterns. Everyone is obsessed with cyber-this and drones-that. Khyber Scones! Biometrics was advancing in ways those talking heads didn't even realize.

On her first day in Baghdad, her first day in a war zone, her first day in her new job, her boss, a full colonel in the US Army, welcomed her to Baghdad with these words: "You'll be working with the Army's sexiest and most successful weapon." But she had never seen it as a weapon. It made sense on some level, she thought, but I'm an engineer, solving problems. I don't judge if anyone is a bad guy, I just provide the 1s and 0s and let someone else figure that out.

And it's not all about bad guys. She helped people get jobs, let them move around freely, let trustworthy people prove they were so. Most of these people are just caught in unfortunate circumstances, she thought. Sometimes they make bad choices. But she wasn't chasing people anyway. She was chasing data. Chasing the opportunity to have someone else put the pieces of the puzzle together. You would think looking at eyes and fingers all day it would be personal, but it's not. There is so much data it can't be.

It might be difficult to collect all the data now, but it'll pay off in the long run. If not this tour, the next one. It's an act of faith, paying it forward, she knew. You had to have faith in the trickle-down effect. You have to trust the system, to know it's all going to work. Not always, but enough. The system wasn't perfect, and she knew most never saw the fruits of their labor. They either put data into the black hole, or they took it out on the other side in some Einstein alternate universe, but they never saw both sides.

But now that she worked in the J2 and sat in the weekly SOCOM command briefs, she had seen both sides. She had seen the system work, and she was more sure of this big picture than ever. Biometrics was just one part of it, certainly, of what they called Identity Operations or, sometimes, Identity Dominance. Knowing for sure who someone is. But you could see it pay off when an old record would pop, full of biographical info that was really hard to re-create later, and she would always tell her colleagues, "That unit from 2006 just got you a great SITREP today." In Iraq it was about fingerprints, but in Afghanistan now they had the funding and technology to focus on identity generally: iris scans and photos, sure, but also DNA and documents and media and all of the other little trails we leave. And it would only get better. SOCOM was collecting the biometrics data of every indigenous force they trained worldwide.

Sure, it can feel like spinning your wheels when you are collecting and collecting and not catching anyone. But when she was out in the field, working with an ODA team in a village, at least at the end of the day she could report she had enrolled twenty-three people that were unknown before. This wasn't like Vietnam and body counts. This was an achievable goal, a census of Afghanistan.

The two Chinooks crossed high over the ODA compound, circled back over the river, and began to flare as they descended in tandem. They were landing at the compound, good. Once, they had dropped her alone in the middle of a village, and it was summer and she was wearing short sleeves. It still bothered her, that she could have been so culturally insensitive, bare arms and a woman alone.

She began to gather her go-bag and equipment. They had not been shot at on the flight. She had never been shot at while flying, not a single time she knew of, on any milk run or courier mission. After that first flight out of Baghdad, she had never feared flying again. She only feared being slow, being late with a profile or report, screwing up her data, her one little biometrics piece, and then hearing the next day something happened. A green-on-blue attack, an Afghan police recruit that she said was vetted turning out to be Taliban. She only feared that one of her SOCOM teams would get hurt because her system failed.

This was the biggest contribution she could make, be ready to go embed with any ODA or Marine unit or special operations team that needed her. Her little part to prevent more ramp ceremonies. She saw them, all the time, on the flight line at Bagram. The flag-covered coffins, every day it seemed. When she saw them, her gut twisted like a limb caught in a toothed coal shearer from back home. She would see them and then cry and turn away, but somehow there always seemed to be more the next day.

After so many years—9/11 was over a decade ago!—it had taken so long, but she was finally really doing her part. She wasn't just reading about it anymore. It was a privilege and an opportunity and an honor. The tears from that day, out in the park with the United Way, they still came back readily enough too. And always more ramp ceremonies.

She looked out the back of the Chinook, and the ground drew close, and she saw two guys on four-wheelers waiting for her. They looked so thin. They get so little food out here, the air drops are so sparse, and she had so much at her big base.

She slung on her pack and jogged down and out of the back of the bird and into the dust cloud kicked up by the rotors.

No more ramp ceremonies.

THE POLICE CAPTAIN turned off his cell phone and discretely approached al-Muhandis.

Two *helicoptera, malem,* the captain may have said. Two of the big fat ones. My brother's son, out on the ridge with his goats, he saw them and called right away. They will be here very soon.

The Engineer may have sat at the end of a long workbench, a string of students on each side, the tabletop covered in boards and wires and drying glue and black electrical tape.

We must move you, *malem.* Now, to my cousin's house in Baghlan. We can take the police *laarey.*

Too late, the Engineer said. He gestured at the Tea Boy huddled in a corner of the long room. The boy was wary, two black eyes and a limp from the police captain's . . . play with him the night before. But the boy had nothing to fear from him; that was an Afghan indulgence, not his.

Habibi, I need you to send a message, the Engineer called.

Yes, *Haji,* the boy replied. He had studied his Koranic Arabic well, unlike these other uncouth manglers of the tongue. How could they even understand the imam's teaching on Friday at the mosque?

Take a motorbike and go to the *talib* camp just outside of town and tell them to radio the other *katibat* about attacking the *kuffar* when they arrive here, the Engineer said.

But *malem*, the police captain protested. The *kuffar* can hear the radio now.

I know, the Engineer may have replied, they must hear the radio. There is no time to clean the material, but we must all leave this room immediately. Get to your homes and your fields. None of the pieces must be with you. Take off your gloves and throw them in the fire.

No matter his instructions, they were not so disciplined when he was not around.

What do we do if they arrest us? one of his students asked. They will torture us. How can we resist?

Yes, they will torture you, the Engineer said. We have seen this. Everyone knows it. Remember the Throne verse of the Koran. Say the *Ayatul Kursi* to yourself, over and over again, and invoke the greatness of Allah who knows and sees and has supremacy over all.

They all got up and left the room quickly. When the Engineer stepped outside into the sunlight, he saw that the two helicopters had landed on the edge of the village and the Crusaders were already invading the sanctity of each home, gathering everyone outside. Twelve men, and a few women in their inappropriate men's uniforms, and one more that he did not recognize. She was covered, but not in an abaya, and he could see her red hair falling from beneath her scarf. She is Nuristani, maybe, or one of Alexander's Greeks?

She was holding a small black box that looked like his old-fashioned Polaroid camera from university. She was placing the box against the face of each Afghan, showing the uniformed *kuffar* which buttons to push, how to align a white dot on the side with each villager's eyes.

She's a traveling teacher, he may have thought. Just like me.

The men in front of him queued politely to have their fingers rubbed. Some rolled their own fingers on the device. They had done this before, he could tell. Some were confused by it. He had the soft hands of a dentist after years of wearing powdered latex gloves. He stayed in the back of the line, always drifting away if he could. The chance they already had his fingerprints was small, but why risk it?

The Crusaders had scanned over half the village when he heard yelling on their radios. They gathered, and talked, and held their rifles with renewed interest, and rushed back to their helicopters. The woman with red hair followed.

Habibi, always dependable. The Engineer got in a white Hilux pickup truck with the police captain and headed south.

MOHAMMED FROM KUNDUZ squatted against a mud wall.

Five more Mohamads and Mohameds and Muhammads waited in the wings, but this one was different. Hayes could see it on his report. The SEEK scan and check said this was the Mohammed who had been sticking his fingers inside pressure plates for the last month.

None of the others had popped on the scan, but they'd question them anyway, just to be sure. Never know what you might learn. They checked the dead too, the squirters the team guys had to shoot. They always squirt, it's like they can't help it. A few of them kicked out records. You can still run the fingerprints and the iris scan, if you prop open the eyelids.

Hayes and his linguist and a few detainee interrogators were there. None of them wore uniforms, unless you count the standard contractor polo shirt. Hayes knew them all by name and not organization. At the end of the tour he would eventually ask where they were all from. Only half were government agencies.

The commander of the local Afghan commando unit also stood near and watched. He was a major or lieutenant colonel, probably. Hayes swore he was high on hashish and mentally retarded. No, seriously, this wasn't some offhanded insult. Like really, medically mentally retarded. His family would have bought him the job anyway. Get him out of the house.

So this was the game: Somebody had approached Mohammed from Kunduz and said, "You make ten Afghanis a day cutting poppy.

How about fifty a night to wrap tape around wood?" Now, who was that? And who *taught* him to wrap tape around wood? That's who they really wanted.

But getting these peons to talk their way up the food chain was tough. Not under the constraints they had now. You can't hurt them, you can't make them uncomfortable, you can't threaten them, you can't offend the local populace, you can't offend NATO, you can't offend our local partners. Yes, don't offend the mentally handicapped commandoes or child rapists. Not that the locals had such constraints with each other; Dostum put the foot soldiers of his enemies in shipping containers and forgot about them. But *he* could only ask politely, and only for a short time.

So you try to understand them, figure out the right questions to ask, the one's they will answer. First, do you even have the right Mohammed from Kunduz? So you ask his father's name, his brother's name, his tribe, who he works with. Ask about their valley, what is happening there. They only care what is happening in their valley anyway. Of course, if we weren't in their valley, they wouldn't care about us either.

But that usually breaks down too. *Everyone knows they don't value education, but everyone forgets they don't have proper nutrition either,* Hayes thought. They have poor eyesight, their bodies and minds don't grow correctly. Some places, they think they're still fighting the Russians, a bunch of big white guys in standard uniforms speaking a language they don't understand.

So they got the man talking. This wasn't like breaking some high-ranking Al Qaeda guy trained in counterintelligence. This is just another Mohammed from Kunduz we're talking about. Hayes squatted with him, and the main interrogator and linguist too, and they made progress, until they finally asked him, There is a new trainer here, right? A new man that teaches you to make IEDs?

The linguist translated. The only word Hayes picked out was *"mines."* Pashto had grabbed the English word.

Silence. Mohammed from Kunduz, who was happy to tell you about his father and brothers and cousins, got evasive. He shifted his feet, rocked back and forth in his squat, and looked away.

Tell him we found the room, Hayes whispered to the interrogator. That we found the piles of wires and circuit boards and timers and those screens you use for sifting the explosives you cook up. The hot glue guns were even still warm.

The interrogator tried this new tack, so then Mohammed from Kunduz gave up another guy, Mullah Abdullah maybe, and said he was the man for *mines* in this district.

But it was never that easy. You had to pay attention, make sure it was your man.

But Mullah Abdullah doesn't teach you to make the mines, does he? Hayes asked.

No, then a long story, about where Abdullah kept the *mines*, in an old dry *kariz* maybe, near his *qalat*.

See, this isn't right, Hayes thought. We don't want the local man, we want the new one.

So they pressed him, and asked about the new man who had just arrived, and Mohammed from Kunduz got even more uncomfortable, and so Hayes and his linguist and the interrogator pressed harder, shouted maybe, their detainee sweated and rocked and looked far away, and Hayes asked again, What is the name of the new emir who comes to Kunduz and teaches you to make the *mines*, and then Mohammed just put his head in his hands and went completely silent, and no more sound came from him except a quiet and quick mumbling over and over to himself. Arabic now. The Koran.

And that's it, Hayes thought. *There's nothing more we can do, not anymore.*

The Engineer is the one name they never give up. Never, in all his years working interrogations, had he scored it a single time. Hayes was convinced: they're scared to death of this guy.

THE BLACK HOLE doesn't have a name, photo, fingerprint, iris scan, or DNA sample of the Engineer. But his profile is not completely empty, because, as JIEDDO promised, we can learn a lot about him by the IEDs he creates.

Our composite image of the Engineer is the amalgamation of very few men. Explosive device circuit designs are remarkably consistent—one main power supply, a trigger that actuates a transistor, a current dump to the blasting caps, a safety light, an arming timer—and so we can be sure that a relatively small number of minds have been producing many bombs over many years.

One could argue that, like an invasive species, IEDs were introduced into the Levant and Mesopotamia by none other than T. E. Lawrence. His targets were the Turkish railroads that supplied Ottoman garrisons; no way for a train to find a new route to outflank such a mine. Al Qaeda itself began as a movement of intellectuals, an outgrowth of the Afghan Arab movement founded by Abdullah Azzam, a Palestinian who received his PhD at Al-Azhar University in Cairo, and the college-educated Osama Bin Laden. The CIA trained the Afghan Arabs in the 1980s in the use of remote firing devices—they weren't called IEDs then, at least not generally—and they spread from there. In the 1990s, veterans of Afghanistan taught the skills to mujahideen fighting in Chechnya. Fewer IEDs were utilized in jihad in Bosnia and Kosovo, but that was purely practical. Yugoslavia was awash in conventional weapons, especially, and infamously, landmines.

By 2000, Al Qaeda remained an organization of the educated. The core leadership consisted of many former members of the Muslim Brotherhood, including the Egyptian intellectual and physician Ayman al-Zawahiri. The principal planner of the 9/11 attacks, Khalid Sheikh Mohammed, received a degree in mechanical engineering from North Carolina A&T State University in 1986. At least thirteen of the nineteen 9/11 hijackers attended college, four in engineering and law programs. The wars in Iraq and Afghanistan and Syria now consist of poor farmers planting IEDs and half-literate ISIS videographers filming beheadings, but they didn't start that way.

It is no stretch, then, to say that the Engineer is exactly that, college educated with a real engineering degree. Many IEDs that initially appear simple are not. They require a relatively advanced knowledge of the inner workings of electronic components—signal filtering and rectifying, microprocessor programming, the breakdown voltage of specific transistors, how to maximize the gain of an op-amp—that is beyond the scope of a household electrician or hobbyist.

Such complexities do more than imply education. They also reveal how the Engineer thinks, as we can decipher how he solved each engineering challenge. The choice to build a redundant system, multiple blasting caps and firing systems, ensures a device will function. Multiple countdown timers prevent an emplacer from accidentally detonating a device too early. Hand-drawn schematic diagrams of IED circuits have been discovered in weapons caches in Iraq and Afghanistan, and by analyzing them we can even infer where he got his degree: Western universities teach that the symbol for electrical ground should be placed on the bottom of a sketch, while many Asian universities reverse that convention.

In the early 2000s, just as the war was beginning, the cost of consumer electronics plummeted. Basic cell phones became so cheap as to be disposable. Many of these gadgets were perfect for IEDs, giving the Engineer a convenient foundation from which to work. His ability to modify the devices told us even more about him: when one foreign brand of cordless telephone changed the layout on its base station's hugely complex internal circuit board, his wiring adaptation changed with it to a new physical location that was *electrically* the same point in the circuit he had used before. It was as if he had solved the Sunday crossword puzzle, and when someone else translated it to a new language and scrambled the verticals and horizontals, he re-solved it to discover that 5 Down was now 27 Across but, yes, "primer" still fits.

The engineers in CEXC and the J2 fusion labs would reverse-engineer these creative design decisions, but even at an aesthetic level, a lot can be learned by the way a device is constructed. If the splattery frenzy of Pollack or the layered continuous strokes of Van Gogh reveal something of their minds, so too sloppy IEDs versus perfect rows of wires. In every part of the process there is a piece of data left behind, and the circuit design and wiring combinations became a subset of forensic evidence all to themselves.

By virtue of his education, the Engineer's job could not be easily transferred to someone else. Therefore, he would be protected, of the group but separate, an emir apart, traveling between theaters—Iraq, Syria, Afghanistan, Southeast Asia, Georgia, Chechnya, and back—lending his experience as jihad ebbed and flowed via the vastly different insurgencies fighting in each country. The original jihad that arose against the Soviets is now thirty-five years old, and as bad bombers don't survive to influence the war, the Engineer's teeth must grow long.

None of this is to say that the Engineer does not need a robust implementation network in each country. He taught others important and destructive skills, how to build a new trigger or mix home-made explosives, but he would be most effective by leaving the hands-on dangerous work to others. This allows him to, literally and figuratively, keep his hands from getting dirty. When he uploads a new circuit design to a Chinese specialty manufacturing company (not in the business of asking questions) and purchases thousands of mass-produced circuit boards online, he touches nothing. The fingerprints on the metallic green wafers are not the Engineer's or even those of his students, but rather those of the man or woman or child who assembled the board in Shenzhen or Guangzhou.

The vast majority of IEDs recovered in Iraq and Afghanistan adhere to this al-Muhandis profile, and there are only a few examples of freelancers, upstarts like Frost's crooked police captain, who think they can design and field their own bombs. These contraptions became the equivalent of Internet memes within the military's classified computer system: the guy who tried to build a remote control go-kart IED, another who used spinning electric motors to strike matches. In every interview with media, an EOD tech at some point is going to say, using the shortcut, "The variety of potential IEDs is limited only by the imagination of the Bomber." But this isn't really true, and not just because, as we've seen, the term "Bomber" is overly simplistic. In practice, imagination is not enough. Designs are tested and consistent, the main product lines constantly refined and improved but not revolutionized, and the unique one-offs are simply that.

One final note on the Engineer's profile. Al-Muhandis has a practical and analytical mind, but it would be a Western and secular mistake to presume this leads to decreased religious fervor. As an American soldier might value courage or loyalty above technical proficiency, so among jihadists piety trumps any skill in rifles or explosives. It is a litmus test, to differentiate between pretenders and the committed, those on an angst-filled jihad holiday and the hardcore ideologues. There is simply no known precedent for an individual central to the mujahideen effort being unreligious. In fact, the opposite is true.

In the mid-1990s, Grozny, the capital of Chechnya, was a boiling bath of blood and pain. A few thousand mujahideen held off the last vestige of the Red Army, block-by-block, utterly inhuman urban combat that would make the city the stuff of apocalyptic nightmares. To finally dislodge the *muj*, the Russians resorted to World War II carpet bombing and the killing of tens of thousands of civilians. Still, the Chechens recaptured the city twice, through the efforts of leaders whose names would be sung by Syrian insurgents two decades later. We know very few details of the horrors of Grozny, even less about the war stories jihadists tell each other, but we know this one:

On one day, in the midst of the worst Russian artillery bombardment, fighting trench to trench, among the shattered concrete apartment blocks and even as rockets scattered Dragons Tooth bomblets on their heads, when the muezzin sang the call to prayer from the minarets behind them, the mujahideen put down their rifles and faced Mecca and bowed in submission and then lay prostrate and prayed as they did five times every day, as if the war was the least trifle upon the earth.

Not a man was killed by enemy fire during their *salat*. A mighty fortress was their God.

AFTER MATT SCHWARTZ died, I had made it a habit of searching for the Engineer in my own black hole database: Google.

I tried many combinations of "bomb maker" and "traveling" and "Al Qaeda" and "Afghanistan" and "engineer." I found what you would expect: *Inspire* magazine and the *Anarchist's Cookbook*. I had no fear of the NSA or FBI; I was a military-trained bomb tech, and through teaching as a consultant I had access to the classified versions of everything I could find online. And I wasn't looking for ammonium nitrate recipes anyway. I wanted a name and a photo.

Despite my failures, I kept at it periodically, often long after my wife and children were asleep. So I don't remember what exact combination of search items finally worked, but one groggy night Hermes reached out and through kismet or providence or luck, showed me a pattern in the chaos: I stumbled upon an academic paper by Anne Stenersen, a researcher at the Norwegian think tank Forsvarets Forskningsinstitutt. Her 2011 article, "Al Qaeda Foot Soldiers: A Study of the Biographies of Foreign Fighters Killed in Afghanistan and Pakistan Between 2002 and 2006," contained one fascinating name. Ibrahim al-Muhajir al-Masri. Abraham the Foreign Egyptian. Killed in Pakistan in 2006, he was described as a "university-trained engineer and veteran of the Soviet-Afghan jihad. After 2001, he was based in the tribal areas, where he was 'an engineer for suicide operations and made equipment for suicide bombers.'"

This was it. He fit the profile exactly. This was as close as I had come yet to naming the Engineer. I Googled "Ibrahim al-Muhajir al-Masri" and got six total hits, none of them helpful. I Googled his name without the quotes and got the wrong man, Abu Hamza al-Masri, the captured mujahideen London cleric who lost an eye and both hands trying to disarm a Soviet landmine in Afghanistan in the 1980s. I Googled shorter combinations of Ibrahim al-Muhajir, found him, but was immediately disappointed. After all that searching, Ibrahim al-Muhajir was just another name for Abu Abdul Raham al-Muhajir, the builder of the truck bombs that hit the US embassies in Kenya and Tanzania in 1998. He had avoided Gitmo, survived the initial cull of central Al Qaeda members in 2001 and 2002. Was he a smart and savvy operator, to have lived so long, or not a priority for the US? Either way, I had seen his name and face before. In his Wikipedia profile, he looks like the caricature of a Western engineer, a middle-aged wage slave dork in a bad short-sleeve dress shirt who has just taken off his tie for the day.

But maybe Anne Stenersen knew more about these men? I began reading her other papers, published in English in relatively obscure journals. I eventually found Midhat Mursi, also known as Abu Khabab al-Masri, another Egyptian-trained engineer and chemist, a bomb expert, writer of an explosives manual, and a "freelance trainer."

The only references I found to Abu Khabab outside of Stenersen's work were death notices posted by the world's major news organizations, some misreported, some correct. We tried to kill him with a drone strike in 2006 and missed. We succeeded in a similar attempt in 2008. NBC said the FBI had used the wrong photo and the wrong name for Abu Khabab al-Masri for years in their databases; ironically enough, they put the one-eyed London cleric on the official wanted poster.

The black hole really didn't have a photo of the Engineer.

But now I did. All of the correct international obituaries used the same one, endlessly repeated, grainy and two-tone. A square-headed man with a massive beard and intense eyes.

And yet, this still wasn't the Engineer who killed Matt Schwartz. Abu Khabab al-Masri died in 2008, and significant IED development, some of the most lethal IED developments, occurred after he died. But it was the right profile.

THE CJSOTF J2 at Bagram didn't look like much from the outside. Bland and monotonous sheet metal and block, it blended into the rest of the air base, a semipermanent squattersville of plywood huts and temporary trailers and dry-rotted tents that felt overly lived-in, like a hotel room that has changed occupants but never had a visit from the maid. Still, Soliman felt at home in the J2 because it was named in honor of Sergeant Gene Vance, a fellow West Virginian and Special Forces soldier out of 19th Group, who was killed in an ambush in May of 2002. *Montani Semper Liberi.* Mountaineers everywhere.

On the inside, the J2 was likewise deceptively plain. Row upon row of tables and flip-up laptops for the various representatives. There was the Predator guy, the MC-12 guy, the JTAC, the analysts of the different disciplines. And projected on the wall, always, a Predator feed. "Predator porn," everyone called it, a staple of operations centers since generals discovered how to get mobile access over a decade ago.

She had a seat in the J2, as the biometrics girl. When she watched the Pred feed, she dreamed that someday there would be a fusion of their two disciplines, a gait recognition algorithm so people could be identified from the air just by their unique walk. In the meantime, she was content knowing her data was being used at that moment, on a mission watched by that Predator. If a report came in that a match had been made or a team needed more info, she would call the FBI or DoD biometrics centers back home in West Virginia for help. Often, she was talking to an old classmate, a friend. There were only eight biometrics engineering graduates her year at WVU. It was exciting knowing they were all working the same cases together.

She sat with the intel analysts and watched as they put together the big picture, also using data she collected, photos and prints that she took with a SEEK. They were both military and contractors, and she could feel like an outlier. She wasn't a triple tabber, she didn't have the Triple Canopy—referring to Airborne, Ranger, and Special Forces scrolls worn on the left sleeve, as well as the security company of the same name that provided contractors for the DoD—but it was more than that. They obsessed over individuals. They worked the same names every day. It was insular, and exhausting, and she was glad it wasn't her job.

All day the analysts pumped as much data as they could into each profile. Intercepted communications. Biometrics. Geospatial trends; a fancy term for Frost's penny-flipping. Handwriting samples from night letters, the messages of intimidation left on the doorsteps of those thought loyal to the Afghan government. Link analytics that diagrammed the inner connections of each terrorist oil spot. The information from the various exploitation cells: explosives, bullet ballistics, ripped cell phones, computers. It all goes in the portal, because when the commander comes by, the analyst transforms into a salesman.

Sometimes the commanders needed to turn the red metrics green on the weekly PowerPoint slides. Sometimes they just got bored and wanted someone to smack, to feel like they had the initiative. No matter the reason, the commander needed a trigger, an excuse to spend energy on one target over another.

If an analyst wanted to get the object of their infatuation on the Joint Priority Effects List—the JPEL, the hit list of high-value targets—they needed two things: a profile jam-packed with data, and a photo. It was easier to sell the story with photos. It made it personal, more than a list of aliases. It wasn't always the SEEK photo that put the pitch over the top, but Soliman saw it happen often enough to know she was making a difference.

She didn't realize how isolated she really was in Baghdad and Kandahar until she got here. In the J2, she could feel the battle rhythm of the war, especially when the TIC lights came on. Troops in Contact, new military speak for a gun battle, firefight, engagement. The first time the lights came on, she didn't know what they meant, but she sensed the air change in the room. Everyone's body language tightened. Eventually, over watercooler chat, she learned more.

When the TIC lights came on, it meant somewhere, out across the country, maybe with the team she had just trained, maybe in that village where so many had popped in their biometrics screening, someone at that very moment was being shot at. Someone's truck was tumbling. Someone was hoping the jug of homemade bang was unstirred. Someone was burning from QuikClot. Someone was getting some. Someone was letting the machine gun touch hearts and minds. Someone was calling, "Good sparkle." Someone was all business, and someone was quiet. Someone would be carried in a ramp ceremony the next day.

IT WAS THE TIC lights that did it. As Sarah Soliman spoke, I looked at my notes and checked her deployment dates again. Yes, they did line up.

"So, Matt Schwartz and Seidler and Bell died on January 5, 2012, when you were there. Do you have any memory of that at all?"

She gave me a small frown. "Unfortunately not," she hedged. "Not that particular event. You hate to say it, but . . . the TIC lights happen so often."

"No, right, I'm sure," I started. She gave me another look, more pained if that was possible.

"I didn't want to assume that you would," I said. "I thought I would ask, just in case, if . . ."

Yeah, I know there is a lot of data, I get it, but these are my brothers we're talking about now. I pushed on. Maybe I could jog her memory.

"You know, it was actually the single biggest loss of life for EOD guys in Afghanistan ever," I said.

That wasn't true, but I didn't remember that at the time. I've looked it up since. In 2002, three Army EOD techs—Craig, Galewski, Maugans—and a Special Forces soldier—Romero—died when a Taliban weapons cache they were investigating exploded. Their remains were so intermingled they now share a plot at Arlington. But I had forgotten that somehow.

Soliman was still giving me the look, but I kept going anyway.

"You know, so it might have come up?" I said. "Or maybe if any of the evidence had passed your way? Serendipity, if you crossed paths?"

She paused. "Sorry." And that was that.

I had no right to be disappointed, but I was.

"Right, right," I said. "No, that's okay."

FOR A DECADE, Hayes had worked with SOCOM all over the world, and it taught him, perhaps counterintuitively, powerlessness and humility. He put out sensors, electronic and metaphoric, and pulled in data, and still could not predict when, where, or how any terrorist cell would attack. It was at their whim, and all he and SOCOM could do was react.

The J2 was flooded with data—MC-12 and Predator feeds and forensic reports and the biometrics database, of course—but Hayes felt like he knew nothing. Or, at least, none of the things that really mattered.

All of the best evidence, the truly dangerous and important stuff, gets blown up, he thought. The EOD guys detonate the bomb because it's so deadly. Or the IED is so well constructed and reliable, it functions every time. There could be an entire class of IEDs out there no one knows about. The best way for the Engineer to hide his signature is to make sure the device detonates. Then no fingerprints, no DNA, a guess at the forensics only.

American leaders are obsessed with metrics: body counts, biometric records collected, IEDs found, men detained and questioned. Biometrics was its own worst enemy. The same guy could be enrolled in the system five times with five names and we think we did a good job because the stats look good. Worse, biometrics gave the illusion of success, helped us to find the easy guys, the pipe swingers, those that place and initiate the IEDs. But those guys are targetable anyway. You could find them all day long, and we do. But the hardest guys?

All those metrics are irrelevant, Hayes thought. In this war, only one stat mattered, the number of dead Americans. All that capture and kill stuff would make a good story someday, but is the security in Afghanistan any better? Are we winning?

It is so hard to separate an insurgent from the local population, to get them to give up the Engineer's name. Meanwhile, we never break down our big units into small enough bands to infiltrate every town. Could you even do it? We're not going to move the US Army into each village and have them stay there for years. We don't even stay for hours. We go home every night, even to a regional fire base, and the Taliban runs every cluster of mud huts once the sun goes down. They have the initiative. Just another way the Engineer goes first in that chess match.

Units that thought outside the box, that spent days in villages, invested in their security, shared hardships with the locals, they did better. That's the only time they open up enough to talk. But it is hard for commanders do that. Tours are just not long enough. Everyone rotates, the analysts, the collectors, the commanders. When the ODA teams paired up and started to flip-flop tours, so they always went back to the same district, that made sense. It is so draining on each team. But are we trying to win or not? Our enemy is there all the time. They never leave. We leave. We've prioritized each individual soldier's comfort and family over winning the war. The Taliban haven't. They want it more. They have all the advantages.

So what to do?

Sometimes SOCOM caught people by blind luck. Their greatest successes, in fact. They hit a target and just happened to get someone else. Caught them on the one day they were sloppy and made a mistake. The SEALs say that it's not that they're so good, it's that everyone else sucks.

But don't great sports teams make their own luck? You can't just sit around and wait for the key piece of intel to magically arrive. Maybe you can't wait for luck. Sometimes you've just got to try something.

Hayes and his team had compiled the interviews of the Mohammeds from Kunduz and integrated the forensic reports and were building their recommendations for the JPEL when the TIC lights strobed again and the casualty SITREPs poured in and the commander was done with peons.

"I want this motherfucker found tomorrow!"

Data, data everywhere, and not a drop of what he needed. The detainees only talked in generalities and rumor, a whisper that the Engineer was in town. Killing him would be the easy part, it was finding him that was hard.

Hayes thought through the problem. We have a guy working with the Taliban. The Taliban are Pashtun, which makes this guy either Pashtun himself, or an Arab ally from the days of the Soviets. He is in the land of Uzbeks and Tajiks, the historic enemies of the Pashtuns, so there are only a few villages where he would find a warm reception. He probably travels alone, or with one or two very close associates, probably family members. He needs the cover of a Pashtun village in otherwise hostile territory. The IEDs were getting deadlier because he had to choose the most vulnerable targets; so far away from his traditional base of support, he would have fewer resources, he couldn't be wasteful like us. Every shot had to have strategic or symbolic value, every shot had to count. A mayor, a police chief, a commander, an SF guy, a bomb tech.

Anybody can compile data, make a list of everything we know about a person. A really good analyst puts themselves in the shoes of another. Everyone thinks the J2 or their intel headquarters is a black hole, but the real black hole is the analyst's mind. No computer system or organizational overhaul is going to put it together. The analyst does the fusion. You can't rely on anyone else to do it for you. Of course, the lack of knowledge about the Engineer is its own black hole that can suck you in. It's up to the analyst, a black hole searching for the black hole within itself? Maybe the Engineer is the center of that nesting doll after all.

Too metaphysical. Hayes snapped out of his wandering introspection and got back to the problem at hand.

They had identified about 80 percent of the IED process, he figured. They knew the facilitation routes, the rat lines over the mountains, and now they had just discovered where the devices were being made. Since politically they never seemed to be able to stop the supply, maybe they could finally grab the trainer. Maybe he would be with other targets on the JPEL.

We are too reliant on technology, Hayes thought. We don't know enough about these villages. And every time we go very high tech to compensate, he goes even lower tech. But if the villagers wouldn't say where the Engineer was, what else could they do?

Hayes took his idea to that afternoon's brief. He showed his commander overlays of IED trends and types, the local tribal organization, loyalty maps and links, likely accomplices on the hit list. At the end of his sales pitch, he had a recommendation of where the commander should send his few resources, one long-range surveillance team and a Predator above them. Put the Pred here, Hayes said, that's where we need to search.

SOCOM's kill chain was euphemistic but simple: Detect, Identify, Locate, Monitor, Track, Exploit, Interdict.

Frost, Fye, Soliman, they all Detected. Hayes had moved the process forward to Identify. But to Locate and Monitor and Track? Where was the Engineer, so they could watch him and follow him, and, ultimately, Interdict him? Where to look? Where would he be? That's the million-dollar question. Hayes had an idea, to make his own luck.

12 · HELMET FIRE

THE FIRST MAN INTO AFGHANISTAN following the 9/11 attack on the United States was a career spook who started at the CIA when shredding typewriter ribbon was still a standard security measure. Gary Shroen had been professionally attached to Afghanistan since he landed the backwater assignment of junior case officer in Islamabad, Pakistan, in 1978. By the eighties he was funneling cash to the mujahideen to support their fight against the Soviets and was station chief in Kabul in '89 when the last Red Army soldier retreated across the Friendship Bridge back into the motherland. Shroen was fifty-nine years old and well into planning his retirement when the towers fell. He was asked to stay on for one more mission. He accepted, and so, on September 26, 2001, he boarded a Russian-manufactured Mi-8 Hip helicopter in Uzbekistan for infil south, the Cold Warrior on a Cold War–era workhorse. He landed in Afghanistan's Panjshir Valley to the cheers of Northern Alliance fighters, to meet face-to-face with the resistance leaders, to sleep in their tents, to share meals and cigarettes, to be a living and breathing representative of the people of the United States riding into battle on horseback with our sudden allies.

Shroen was the first man, and he's long gone. The last of us, the last man in Afghanistan, will be a robot. He will fly in the air. He won't consider retirement. He need never leave.

Between Shroen and the last robot, waves and waves have deployed, and whenever I sent a team to Afghanistan as the commander at Nellis Air Force Base in Nevada, that wave tracked similar tides each time.

The plane always seemed to fly early, and so some spent their last night with family, and some spent their last night celebrating. Maybe the casinos and then a house party afterward. Maybe the carousing went into overtime, and I had to take the bottle from their lips because, don't you know, you're already twenty minutes late and the chief is going to kill you and it's a good thing you packed last night. Maybe they didn't answer my phone calls, and I had to go searching, knocked on the bedroom door at four o'clock and said that she needed to go home and you needed to put your pants on, it was time to get to the airport. But wait, on second thought, better get in the shower because you reek of vodka and sex and I'm not going to send you off like this.

Others, like Dan Fye, avoided the party scene. Said good-bye to their families at home, while their wives were still in bed, the kids tucked and asleep. A kiss on the lips, a murmur of love, and then to the car.

Everyone met at the unit parking lot on the edge of the desert, only red taillights to see by in the predawn dark. The pickup trucks bound for the airport filled with green bags of clothes, black cases of rifles and pistols, trunks of body armor and helmets and probably an Xbox carefully stowed, backpacks bursting with iPods and cartons of cigarettes and laptops full of porn.

The McCarran airport just south of the Las Vegas Strip is busy at all hours. Three unmarked white long bed trucks would pull up to the crowded departure drop-off point and men and bags would spill in all directions. A small war could be started with the guns and gear unloaded chain-style, $500 in extra baggage fees per for sure.

Next up, at least forty-eight hours of vibrating gloom, wretched in its unavoidability. Usually a commercial flight to Kyrgyzstan. Then a C-130 into country, stuffed with grunts and pilots and mechanics and snake eaters and everyone in between, a great equalizer in misery. Then a last hop helo trip to the FOB or COP or piece of shit outpost, the center cargo rack full of fresh-smelling wooden crates. New robots, direct from the factory. The old ones got blown up.

But all of that was still to come. There at McCarran, we all just tried to avoid a long good-bye. Only a bear hug, with no restraint or self-consciousness in the busy public space, a squeeze, a back slap, a rub of sandpaper cheeks. The next time I see them, it may be with a nubbin. Or two. Or they may have died midsentence.

However it went, I always felt the same, whenever I dropped a team at the airport. It always felt unnatural. Like I should be going too, that I should be flying with them to war.

Across the street from the EOD unit at Nellis, across the unlit road and beyond the dark headquarters of the para-rescuemen and their silent helicopters, past the tarmac still and quiet at that early hour, past the rows of F-16 aircraft all in a line, at the end of the parking apron and across the street and in an unmarked building, brown block, ordinary in every way, a Predator pilot finished a cup of coffee and did just that.

Finding anyone in Afghanistan, including the Engineer, usually takes a Predator.

GENE RICH LEFT the desert heat and dropped his phone in a corral on his way through the air-conditioned control center. He skipped his admin desk, ignored his email and the pile of blue folders with routing slips, dropped off his coffee cup in the ops cell. His boss yelled after him, something about performance reports.

"No queep, man—I'm flying today," he said.

Gene left the main building, stepped outside briefly into the open air, and crossed a tarmac filled with rows of forty-foot shipping containers. He entered one via a side door, got a hand-over brief from the previous crew, and then folded his lanky frame into the tan fake-leather armchair and let down the armrest. Nothing but a glorified airline seat creased with millions of vicarious miles, ratty and stained.

He checked his engine readings and fuel, tracker display and the current inky picture from the ball, glanced up briefly as his sensor operator eased into the seat next to him, put on a set of one-sided headphones, adjusted the microphone, stretched once more in the seat, and then settled in for another twelve-hour day.

"Pilot's up in the seat," he said through the intercom system, and his support team acknowledged. He checked his heading and airspeed again. Two hours north into the mountains until he linked up with the team on the ground. An afternoon rendezvous for him, a still-dark early morn for them; Kabul was eleven and a half hours ahead, the digital clocks on the wall reminded him. Gene sat in silence, seven thousand miles removed from the chopping prop, and flew.

Gene called the Predator an RPA, a Remotely Piloted Aircraft. *Drone* was a term used by those who don't like them, he had long ago realized, and the Air Force was even dropping the term UAV, Unmanned Aerial Vehicle, because that sounded autonomous, as if no one was in control. Unfortunately, Gene thought, the Pred was no such thing. It was just an airplane with a displaced cockpit. No cyborg intelligence here; there was still a human very much in the loop.

That cockpit, a Ground Control Station (GCS) in the precise jargon, consisted of a surprising mix of next-gen and shabby DIY, a big metal box full of computers baking in the sun. Four flat screens dominated Gene's forward view: sensor video, map, gauges of temperatures and voltages and various switches. His sensor operator, who sat next to him, had a similar setup, and in the center column between them were two more flat screens, for email and intel updates and mIRC, a secure Internet chat protocol originally written to support Microsoft Windows 95. Gene had two keyboards, one to run the Predator and one to mIRC chat with various operations centers and other aircraft, and to keep the two separate he built an apparatus out of plywood scrounged from a storage closest. Around the four main screens hung a variety of communications gear, radios, and datalinks to talk to aircraft and Joint Terminal Air Controllers (JTACs) on the ground. Some of the radios looked like they had been simply unscrewed from manned fighter jets and bolted to the wall. To his left was a dry-erase board. He used it for long division, to calculate when he would run out of fuel.

Gene had joined the Predator world even before September 11. He was a cross-trainee, an ex–fighter pilot who made the correct educated guess that the cutting-edge technology was moving away from manned aircraft and into the remote world. If Gene had joined the Air Force in 1947, he reasoned, he would have passed over the sexy P-51 Mustang for the unproven F-80. The P-51 is badass, but jets were the future then, not props. So too now, the robot over the jet. Gene had studied engineering in college, and he knew that was the right way to think about it, an evolution in technology. That an airplane was unmanned was simply a feature, not a thing unto itself. It was the natural extension of thousands of years of military development: knife to sword to pike to arrow to musket to machine gun to artillery to bomber to Tomahawk missile to Predator.

Not that he shot anything very often. Usually they observed, communicated, searched, found, coordinated, and targeted with an infrared laser attached to the sensor ball. That afternoon, he was meeting a Special Forces team on the ground and then serving as their top cover while they watched several villages near Kunduz for a target on their JPEL. Gene didn't know much more than a coordinate and call sign and a time; the fragmented and fractured way these missions came in never allowed for much preparation. A unit requested a Pred, the Air Force's main air operations center prioritized, the central planners kicked out his mission, he got it when he arrived for work. That day his tasking was to fly two hours, orbit at a specific lat/long, and meet up with the team.

Gene arrived on time and called down to the ODA team with his air-to-ground radio. An encrypted signal containing the sampled and encoded sounds of his voice was routed to a computer, copied to servers outside of Las Vegas, flowed via fiber optics to a trunk system, beamed to a satellite, bounced back to the main dish at Bagram, resampled and chopped into individual packets of data, broadcast via attached carrier wave from the main air-ground tower, and then hopped from repeater hub to repeater hub before it should have come out, several seconds later, in an earpiece of a radio strapped to the back of the ODA team's JTAC.

Should have. Silence from the JTAC.

Gene tried again. Nothing. No way to know if the call was making it for sure.

"Hey, guys, can we double-check the freq?" Gene called back to his ops cell. They did, and the freq was right, so they mIRC'd CJSOTF, who confirmed where the team should be, and then, after an hour of radio calls and chat rooms and reconfirmations, a mission to search for the Engineer became a mission to find a lost ODA team.

There was no panic or distress; this was not the first team that was out of comms for a prolonged period, and Special Forces teams are trained to be self-sufficient and operate independently. They could be delayed by weather or terrain or have radio trouble or be stuck in a valley with bad reception. But as the hours dragged by, Gene's no-big-deal explanations grew more hollow. Eventually, he had to turn the search over to another Predator. He had been passed his Pred with far less than a full tank, and so had to call bingo fuel, the point at which he had just enough gas to get home.

If Gene was physically in the air, turning for home would have meant a break from the search process. But not so flying in a Pred squadron. The pilot who took over for him was seated in the next GCS over, and his ops cell only a few feet away in the office behind him continued to coordinate the mission. Gene was stuck drearily piloting his Pred back to base, but the hubbub of the search permeated the room. Then a new ad-hoc tasking was announced in his headphones.

"Hey, Gene, I know you're bingo, but we just got a report on an MH-53 crash. Think you have time to work the rescue?"

In a fighter jet, *bingo* means returning on fumes. But a Pred allowed more flexibility. In reality, Gene had hours of reserves, in case of a strong headwind, weather delay on landing, or a lost signal, which would force the aircraft to take up an orbit and wait for a new command. Gene did the math on his dry-erase board. The MH-53 was about a hundred miles away. If he was smart about it, slowed down once he arrived, he would be able to squeeze out five hours on-scene before truly needing to return.

The MH-53 helicopter is a massive, bulbous insect, pods and fuel tanks and mini-gun spines, designed for long flights to retrieve shot-down pilots caught behind the borders of antagonist states. Gene easily saw the burning helicopter from miles away, a pillar of smoke stark against the white mountainside; in the IR camera it glowed. As he approached, he tried a couple of radio calls, to reach other aircraft that should have already arrived, but got only got static in return. He must be the first aircraft on the scene. He lowered the altitude setting and came in closer to the ground. Next to the wreckage, one of the survivors was carving the letters SOS in the snow. Gene came in even lower and the man paused, looked up, and then waved. Gene rocked his wings and tried to radio again, tried several air-to-ground channels, but no one answered. But at least the helicopter crew knew they had been found.

Gene spent the next several hours coordinating the rescue. He had his sensor operator search the ground for Taliban while he maintained enough altitude to keep a good line-of-sight signal to relay information to inbound aircraft. The Predator was perfect for this job, he thought. Bombers and fighter jets arrived to provide top cover, but because of the threat of surface-to-air missiles, they couldn't descend low enough to be of any use. He and his crew were in no danger in Nevada, and the B-52s and F-15Es and F-16s were left to carve infinity-shaped contrails in the blue sky above. By letting the airframe act as a glider and easing back his throttle—the Pred's Rotax engine sips only a few pounds of gas an hour when managed properly—he was able to stay on site for the length of the extraction, even as jets came and went as they called bingo themselves. They simply couldn't loiter like he, and when the math told him his margin for error was now truly spent, he turned the Pred and limped home.

That was real flying, he thought with satisfaction. He had time, as a young officer, to really develop his airmanship, his "air sense," to work his way up before pulling combat air patrols. He had twenty-four months of flying under his belt before dodging Saddam's pitiful anti-aircraft fire in Iraq's southern no-fly zone for real. Now the whole system was on its head. The new Predator pilots are pipeline grads and don't have any previous flight time. They get twenty hours in a Diamond DA20, and then it's straight to the simulator and the war in Vegas. So few assets for training, they only learn to run the mission once the Predator is airborne, just pass off control without even knowing how to take off or land! They learn it later, and then forward deploy to the launch and recovery elements in Bagram, where all they do all day is lob Preds in the air and catch them on the way back.

His hardest landing ever was in a Pred. That might sound funny, but it's true. One night, he got called out to the box to land in a hellacious crosswind on a single runway. He was the senior instructor pilot on duty, and so it was his job. Every measurement was out of limits, but the Pred was out of gas, orbiting for hours waiting for the winds to change; land the plane now, or ditch it in the desert. He crabbed it into the wind like he would a little Cessna, the sensor ball slewed so it was as if he was looking at his left shoulder. It was all mental gymnastics, flying the airplane down on final, and then, at the last minute, he kicked out the rudder, swung the bird square to the runway, told his sensor operator to lock the ball forward—remember, he can't even move his own eyes, he has to get his partner to run the video—and he lined up the crosshairs on the center line, kept it banked right, saw the runway leap in and out of view in the wind, and Gene is leaning back the whole time now, canted in his seat like he's actually in the plane, flaring, flaring, flaring, not stalling, not stalling, I'm going to be long, one wheel down, keep up the nose, aerobrake, aerobrake, no no I got it, drop the nose. Taxi.

The new guys don't move around in the seat. Sometimes they look at him like he's crazy. But that's what they lose when they skip twenty-four months of pilot training. The air sense.

Gene checked his gauges again. Another hour before he passed off this Pred to land.

"Hey, guys, have we found that ODA team yet?" he asked his ops cell.

"No. Turbo is on searching now."

"Can I swap for him?"

"No, bro. Your shift is up. You're out of here."

Gene looked at his watch. Twelve hours gone. Another pilot approached the back of his chair, and he handed over control to the incoming crew. He left his briefing materials in the ops cell, grabbed his bag, walked out of the control center, and picked up his phone. Four messages, from buddies from his fighter pilot days, in town for the RED FLAG exercises. RED FLAG is the Air Force's crowning achievement, an ideal two-week war consisting of the world's most realistic air-to-air and air-to-ground combat flight training. Several times a year, flying squadrons of all types descend on Nellis Air Force Base, Eagles and Strike Eagles and Raptors and Vipers and Bones and Buffs filling the air over the desert like an ever-shifting flock of blackbirds.

The message from Gene's bros said they got in a day early. No crew rest for three days. Come out to meet them.

It was late. Or early, depending on how you were counting. If he went home to get changed, he would never leave. So he stepped out into the heat and found a pair of jeans and a shirt in his car and got changed in his squadron admin office and then drove down to the Strip. Traffic was thick on Las Vegas Boulevard no matter the time of day, but he fought his way into a secret corner of the Caesars Palace parking garage and found his bros at the craps table just like they had said. He wasn't gambling, but they were, and he hung with them, so he got his Coors Original for free anyway. They were on a tear and tossing back rum and Cokes like it was their J-O-B and Gene never heard if it was mechanical or hostile fire on the MH-53. He never spotted Taliban, but that didn't mean anything. There were survivors, two ambulatory, five badly injured, they said. It was a long flight back to the hospital. If only he could have done more, but you always bet on black, motherfucker, you always bet on black. I hope they find the ODA team tonight, I'm sure they will, Turbo is good, you guys remember Turbo, he was with us in UPT, had the scar on his forehead. Head? Did you say head? I'll take some of that! No, I can't have another beer, I gotta fly tomorrow. Call me, we'll meet again. And he bumped a waitress on the way out but found his car and got on I-15 at Flamingo to 95 and drifted into the endless red-roofed subdivision suburban. He pulled his car up to the consolidated steel mailbox and unlocked his bin. It was stuffed full, three days' worth at least. He flipped through the first several envelopes, bills and credit card applications and rental property flyers, tossed the bundle on the front seat and drove up the rest of the way to his house. A familiar notice was trapped in the front screen door: a warning from the home-owners association that his grass was too long. He opened the door, flicked on the lights, and dropped the notice and mail on top of a tumbling pile of their predecessors on the kitchen counter. He checked his watch. If he hit the rack now, he'd get just enough crew rest. He got undressed as he made his way to his room, set his alarm, collapsed on his bed, fell asleep, woke up, and peered out the window. The sky was brightening, but the sun was still behind the eastern mountains. Better run before it's blazing hot. An easy five miles of familiar sidewalk and sidestreet. He panted up the driveway, took a quick shower, and found every one of his flight suits in a dirty pile on the floor. He threw them all in the washer, express wash cold, made coffee, and ate a bowl of cereal, and when the wash was done, he put on the still-wet flight suit and made his way to his car. There was another crumpled uniform on the passenger seat that he had forgotten. Oh, well.

When Gene arrived at the command center, there was a buzz in the air. Twice as many analysts and staffers were crowded into the ops cell. The base commander was hanging in the back, watching over the floor with his squadron commander, the operations group commander, and several other colonels. Gene checked in, and his boss flagged him down.

"You have thirty minutes to get up to speed and then the seat is yours."

The seat was the GCS seat, the hot seat, the seat his buddy Turbo had been strapped to since Gene left fourteen hours ago. Turbo's video was up on the big board, and every face in the command center was fixed on it, watching rooftops in a remote town. A pilot's work/rest cycle is severely regulated, but the general had already waived the rules, and so Turbo was well into overtime, coordinating a sophisticated strike on a target off the JPEL hit list. But Turbo had troubles with his aircraft, had lost signal in weather, lost sight of the target over a low ceiling, and his strike assets—Vipers, Strike Eagles, and some Hornets off the boat—had kept running out of gas. While they ran to the tanker, Turbo briefed in new assets, and then delays forced them to call bingo as well.

Gene watched over Turbo's shoulder, listened to the radio, got the bare minimum background brief, and then swapped in so Turbo could go home and collapse. Checking in and assuming control of the mission was like wandering onto the Indy 500 track in the middle of the race, and Gene was instantly buried. New weather was coming in, and chop at his altitude was bouncing the sensor image. The VOIP phone rang: F-16 rep needed an update on the replacement two-ship that should have just arrived. Targeteers in the ops cell were arguing about whether they had followed the correct vehicle. Gene needed to confirm. Three mIRC chat windows open, update update update, to CJSOTF J2 and J3 and the CAOC battle captain. Gene's headphones never stopped broadcasting: AWACS, Vipers, Strike Eagles, CAOC, ops cell, the base commander: "Gene, we need to hurry up."

They call it a helmet fire. Task saturation, when it becomes humanly impossible to do everything that needs to be done. Good pilots practice identifying what will kill them first, dealing with that, and then moving down the list. But sometimes, you can't move down the list fast enough. A helmet fire is when a route clearance package is hit and then the response team is hit and the wounded pile up and Max is bleeding out and the helo medevac needs to be called but the Navy EOD team is checking for more secondary IEDs and doing a post-blast investigation and forgets that Chris Frost is still wounded in the back of the truck. You can get a helmet fire in the jet, Gene knew, feel like you are just hanging on to the tails while the engine roars and that's when you get behind.

Now the same thing was happening. The strength of the Pred is that you are on the ground, out of personal danger, and able to make calm, rational decisions. But now the connectivity was too much.

We need to change the strike order again, Gene. Weather is moving up low ceiling forecast. Tell the Bones to get out of the cons, we don't want to telegraph this. Gene, can you confirm white hot and not black hot on the IR feed? Oh, Vipers may have that reversed. Targeteers still working sedan confirmation. Confirm what? Reconfirm the 9-line. Chat windows in flat screens SATCOM VOIP mIRC to TOC helmetfire UHF DUDE 21 confirm helmetfire CAOC slew the ball helmetfire helmetfire helmetfirehelmetfirehelmetfire

Then, his phone rang.

Gene's squadron commander on the headset: "Don't answer that, Gene. That's the boss. I told him to leave you alone."

Gene knew who he meant: the boss, two-star in theater, commander of all Air Forces in the Middle East and Southwest Asia. Calling him on the phone, ignoring the sanctity of the cockpit. This had all gone too far.

He had to settle down. It would have been easier if he could just take the shot himself, but he had no munitions onboard his Pred. And no mIRC in a fighter jet, only a radio and the paper card from their preflight mission brief, so he had to talk them through every nuance of the shot. He coordinated with every strike asset, forced the targeteers to confirm the target, rematched all the intel himself, rebriefed the gunship on each shot, and then officially requested permission to strike.

The sedan trickled down the road.

An autonomous robot? A human in the loop? Try two or three or a hundred humans in the loop. Gene was the eye of the needle, and the whole war and a thousand rich generals must pass through him.

"Hey, Gene, good to go, cleared to engage, but they want to change the order of the strikes again."

These Fighter Mafia guys, who grew up complaining that the F-4s over Vietnam were flown from the White House, would never dare interfere in an air-to-air fight like this, Gene thought. What was unacceptable in their own fighter culture they had made commonplace with the Pred. Gene reconfigured and requested permission and received more mission changes, and he reconfigured and requested permission and received another round of parameters, and he reconfigured and . . .

Gene was done. He threw off his headphones and in so doing, kicked everyone out of his cockpit.

I know this mission better than anyone else at this point, he thought. *This is the right target. I've already switched it three times. I'm just going to execute the last thing we planned.*

The pickle button was Gene's alone. If he fucked up, he had the wings on his chest and he'd fry at the trial, not them. If they wanted to fly the fucking plane, they could come out and do it themselves.

After seven hours in the objective world, fifteen minutes in helmet fire time, the first flash of light in his video monitor. Finally. The gunships would shoot squirters for another hour. Did they get the right guys? To find out, he'd be on station long after the strike aircraft landed, watching, picking up as much evidence as he could from the air.

Gene established an orbit and thanked his sensor operator. Again. Saved his ass every time he fucked up. But what about the ODA team from yesterday? Did Turbo ever find them? No, the ops cell said, he didn't. Search was ongoing, three control stations down.

Gene spent the rest of his shift returning his Pred to base and then flying a replacement out to assist in the search. By now it was clear the team had run into trouble, though no one yet knew what kind, and search and rescue crews were on call to pick up the team once they were located. Gene had just about gotten his Pred on station when the factory whistle sounded. Shift up, clock to punch, time to go. They should stay, Gene thought, work straight through, twenty-minute naps. Until they found this team. This is why it was better to be deployed, launch and recover the airframes. You saw nothing but the GCS and your bed, did nothing but fly and sleep. But you can't do that here. Searching for the team was now another guy's job. You trust them, these pilots were family, but, well, better to stay.

He walked out of the control center and picked up his phone. Six messages from his fighter bros. He put the phone in his pocket and walked out into the dark heat of the parking lot. The ODA team was probably freezing, even this time of year, caught in the mountains. Or worse, overrun by the enemy. Two days, no contact. Gene drove down the highway and took his exit, and, as he passed Safeway, he realized he was out of milk. He pulled into the parking lot, found the milk at the front of the store, and the ODA team probably had enough food for another day or two, if they took MREs instead of extra ammo or bang. A man behind him in line tapped him on the shoulder and said thank you for your service because Gene was still wearing the flight suit, but what about the helmet fire? And he hadn't found the ODA team in two days. Gene left Safeway and drove past his mailbox and stuffed in his front door was a bill for cutting his grass and a seventy-five-dollar fine from the home-owners association. He opened the refrigerator and discovered two gallons of milk. He put the new gallon inside and smelled the open one and then tossed it in the trash. The trash stunk too. He took off his flight suit and paced and paced and turned on the TV and then turned off the TV and then he lay down in bed and fell asleep and woke up and was momentarily disoriented. What time was it? The sun was shining. Heat radiated from his bedroom window. But what does that mean in the bright, seasonless desert? What day was it? Shit, what month was it? They were blurring, bad now. It was day four in his shift week, but the shift weeks were ever shifting. How did guys with wives and kids do this? He checked his phone and found three new messages. He rolled out of bed and threw on shorts and a T-shirt and ran his five easy miles. The heat drained him and renewed him. He took a shower, shaved, went looking for a flight suit. It took him a while to remember they were all still in the washing machine from the day before, spin-stuck but only half-damp. He put one on, put the rest in the dryer, and got in the car and drove to work. Had they found that team last night?

Across the street from the main entrance to the base was a group of protestors. He had seen Code Pink around Las Vegas, and honestly, didn't mind them. He had been at a lot of events where they show up, and they do their protest, they have a point, they yell and show their signs, but they leave when asked. They aren't out of control, are respectful even. Not for the first time he was tempted to stop and talk to them, but he didn't think it would go well. He imagined it.

Gene: Why do you hate drones?
Them: Because they kill people.
Gene: Would you rather we carpet bomb people with a B-52?
Them: No, we don't think we should be dropping any bombs.
Gene: Well, that's a different point, isn't it?

When people say they hate drones, what they mean is they hate war. Well, I'd like world peace too. But if we do go to war, shouldn't we use minimum force and the best information? Why demonize the thing keeping soldiers out of harm's way? The answer, which nobody wants to admit, is that they think without dead Americans, or at least Americans at risk, there would be far more dead Iraqis and Afghans. They can't say it, but that's what they think. That American bodies are a flotsam driftwood dam, holding back a raging river. For years we've been using cruise missiles, one-way drones that get launched from a Navy ship and fly for hours and go to a single preprogrammed spot, and that's okay? Cruise missiles really are the autonomous robotic version of Slim Pickens in a B-52, but who protests? Now that we actually have more control, can stop a mistake before it's too late, we've discovered a moral problem? In the control station in Vegas, he had no self-preservation instinct to distract him from making the best possible decision. How does putting bad guys outside his door make him more effective?

But Gene didn't stop and have that conversation. He drove through the guard post and along the road paralleling the runway, the Eagles and Vipers and Raptors and Bones launching to play RED FLAG war games. *I wonder if my bros are flying today*, he thought, before parking and entering the control center and grabbing a quick cup of coffee before work.

Hard to believe that on 9/11 they all still thought they had to deploy the pilots and GCSs to the war zone to do this job. Saddam actually shot down a Predator the morning of 9/11, not that anyone remembers that now. But on that particular day, Gene had a deployment drill. He had gotten up at 0330 to go sit in a hanger, pretending to fly on a C-130 to set up a new Predator mission in a foreign country. During the exercise, while they were killing time on their fake flight, a colonel rolled in a TV on a cart and turned it on, and the towers burned and he said everyone should go home but keep their bags packed. Gene deployed again right after. They were flying from Kuwait then, over southern Iraq, and suddenly they had to work in two theaters, the new war in Afghanistan and the same old no-fly zone drag. They made that work, with satellites and fiber optics, and that's when they realized: if we can fly over Afghanistan from Kuwait, we can do it from anywhere. The mission started small at Nellis, then doubled at the backwater Indian

Springs Airfield north of Las Vegas. The Springs grew so big so fast they renamed it Creech Air Force Base. Now they could fly up to sixty-five simultaneous missions, all over the world. They had come a long way in a decade.

Fields and fields of ground control stations, human connected to machine, and they still hadn't found the ODA team.

You can see so little through the soda straw, Gene thought. In a jet, he could use his eyes and ears, vestibular sense of balance, the haptic feedback of vibration and pull. He could tell how fast he was going just by listening to the wind break over the canopy. But in a Pred, you lose everything but vision, and even that is constricted. The human eyeball sees in a 140-degree arc and swivels instantly. The Pred looks down a 20-degree view, fixed to the nose, and a separate sensor operator is required to slowly pan this way and that.

The Predator solves a problem and creates a problem, Gene knew. It identifies objects but not events. It sees but does not interpret. It measures existence but not intent. It tells Dan Fye where some IEDs are, but not necessarily all of them. Gene had a video ball and a laser but no sensor for "suspicious." No sensor for "lost." They were developing an algorithm, he knew, to cull the terabytes of video data recorded every day, weed out the large chunks of innocuous nothing, and let the human brain spend time analyzing the right snippets.

Gene punched in and checked in with the ops cell. No, they hadn't located them, but he wasn't searching today. He had to watch a safe house and track who came in and out.

No, he needed to respond to a team caught in a TIC. Provide top cover. *It's "combat" for us, but combat for them*, Gene thought. He did the math and flew two hours, and then they called him off before he even arrived. TIC was over.

No, he needed to check in with another task force humping to an objective, watch it before they hit the target. Gene found the team at the lat/long, called them on the radio. Silence. "Check the freq," Gene said to his sensor operator. "What freq are they supposed to be on?" "Ask their TOC on mIRC." "No answer." "Which window are you in?" "What window should I be in?" "Ops, can you call their TOC on the VOIP?" "They say they hear you and the team is trying to call you back." "Do we have the audio up on the datalink?" I'm messing up I'm messing up I'm messing up I can't even get the radio right. "I can't hear the datalink over the UHF speaker." "mIRC them to see if they have a Rover, we can do this without audio." "Which mIRC room are they in?"

No, now he needed to link up with a NATO element, watch the highway ahead of their convoy. Gene arrived and called the commander on the radio. "What are you?" the commander asked. "I'm a Predator," responded Gene. "What can you do for us?" the commander said. "I can watch," said Gene.

No, now he needed to search for the ODA team that had been lost three days. Forgotten was that team's original target; al-Muhandis would have to wait.

If he was there, Gene thought, at least he would see the ground forces every day, in the flesh, eat with them at the chow hall, share a little of the risk. He'd know who he was searching for. He'd know when there was a rocket attack on the FOB before a mission. He'd know what time it was, by looking at the sun and not a clock.

What time was it? His stomach rumbled. He had skipped breakfast. And lunch. Maybe dinner. Not enough coffee either.

Gene orbited the search area until the factory whistle blew. He asked around at the end of the day. No, no one else had found that team yet either.

Sometimes, it not about what you did, it's what you failed to do.

Gene stepped out of the secured room, picked up his phone, and walked out into the dark parking lot. He checked his messages. Marathon run at the blackjack table at TI's, and if he skipped two nights in a row he was a fucking pussy.

ON HIS WAY to Pakistan, the Engineer may have changed drivers and vehicles four times.

In Baghlan he changed police trucks, and in a small village north of Kabul a young *mujahid* picked him up in a sedan. They traveled when the skies were gray and slept for two days at a safe house when the skies were too clear. It became more dangerous as you approached Kabul, the Engineer knew. Patience and perseverance. Then one morning he woke early and saw that the winter winds and rain had returned, and he whispered in the ear of his young, slumbering driver, "Prayer is better than sleep," and the two men got back in the car and drove on.

They drove around the edge of Kabul and continued south. The Engineer did not teach in Kabul, the *takfir* central government made it too dangerous, but he may have connected his laptop to the Internet briefly to conduct business.

He avoided email, and the camera above his screen was covered in black tape. But he ordered supplies, including a hundred units of a new device he had just designed. The ability to outsource construction, send the computer file to Alibaba.com for official manufacture, like one of those companies in the Great Satan's California valley, that was one of his most important new developments. Other companies could do it, sure, but Alibaba.com was cheap and always the best quality.

Not that he was an Ali Baba. He was no honorless thief. He relied on no *takfir* Persian state. The work was his.

He finished his order and then checked on an online explosives course he was teaching. He never interacted with the chat rooms directly; he had an intermediary for that. He had placed several self-learning courses there, to assist in jihad around the globe, but interest was languishing. He just could not update it regularly enough, he was too often traveling and out of contact. It was more effective to teach in person anyway. He could teach them anything, and yet his brothers here in Afghanistan, what do they ask for? Only *mines,* simple *albuyah nasiffah* that he could make from the trash on the street.

He left Kabul quickly and proceeded south. At an underpass he traded drivers and white sedans again. Sometimes he could just feel the *kuffar* drone watching above, he thought, or hear the motor buzz, a mosquito whir at the edge of his hearing that would send him searching the sky for a dot that never quite materialized.

He changed cars again at a safe house in Gardez. A courier told him they had received word that his driver of the last car had been killed along the road, a flash from the sky as random as any of his *albuyah nasiffah.*

Bury him immediately, the Engineer may have said. He is *shaheed.*

The gray clouds settled low, and he drove his little white sedan across the plain. At each checkpoint they knew him when he said his name, and he drove out of the mountains and across the Khowst Bowl.

13 · Khowst Bowl

"Abdul? where is abdul?" the Afghan man called down the narrow streets, even at this late hour teeming with fruit stalls and goats and children running barefoot at play.

"Have you seen my friend Abdul? Abdul!" He put his hand to the side of his mouth and called again. He was a middle-aged man, graying beard, long plain *shalwar kameez*. He swung his arms when he walked. He was just another man on another street in the sprawl of Kabul, average in every respect.

So were the two men who followed him, within earshot, thirty feet away.

"You are looking for Abdul?" a taxi driver called out to the man from his open window.

"Yes, my friend Abdul. Where is he?"

"He is at home, two doors past the market," the driver said, and waved south in the general direction.

"Yes, I see now. Many thanks to you," the man said, and wandered through the vendors, past shop windows shut tight. The two other men followed at a discreet distance, lost in a crowd. One raised a long-sleeved arm up to his face, scratched his beard.

"FREEDOM, ALPHA ROMEO, do you have visual on the Objective?" Evil heard the New Zealand accent over the radio.

From twelve thousand feet above, silently circling the market, Evil compared the video off the sensor ball with the SEEK photo on the profile he pulled up. No one matched the face he saw on his screen, and the analysts watching the video back at Bagram had not called him with a positive ID.

"ALPHA ROMEO, FREEDOM, negative, intel has no PID for Objective Castle. His pad is in the 10 series. He must be inside," Evil responded. Lucas, his sensor operator, zoomed out to display the wide view of the market and surrounding low homes.

Evil watched the Afghan man walk up to the doorway of Abdul's home, saw him knock, call inside. Evil took in the scene of the choked alleyways and mud-walled shacks, draped wagons and carts, sheets occasionally stretched as sunshades over the streets. He noted the rifles in the hands of most men in the market. But the Afghan man did not have one, and neither did his two shadows.

A small boy appeared at the door.

"*Habibi*, go get your father," the Afghan man said.

The boy disappeared. Evil watched the Afghan man wait at the door, watched the other two men stand back-to-back a short distance away, watched the busyness of the night-cool city around them, watched the few automobiles crawl through snarled traffic on the main streets just off the market square, watched one white panel van begin to inch toward Abdul's home using a back alley.

"Lucas, watch that mover," Evil called back to his sensor operator. The video on the screen in front of him shifted as the sensor camera panned. Lucas cropped the view, put the panel van under the crosshairs. It was driving in reverse and picking up speed.

Evil turned to his copilot in the seat next to him. "Check out what's about to happen," he said.

Evil flew an MC-12. It had no weapons. It had no side-mounted mini-gun like an AC-130, or Hellfire missiles like a Pred. It had only a sensor with a video camera and an IR laser, to sparkle targets. But their Objective was inside the house, so nothing to do but watch as the van and the two men began to converge on the door.

A larger figure appeared in the door frame.

"*Salaam*, Abdul, I have found you," said the Afghan man.

"*Salaam*. Do I know you?" Abdul replied, and he gripped a rifle in his hand.

The two men moved more quickly now. Evil could see one scratch his beard again.

"FREEDOM, ALPHA ROMEO, here we go, van is with us."

The vehicle burst from the narrow alleyway and screeched to a halt in front of Abdul's door. Pedestrians on the street scattered, the Afghan man stepped aside, the two men moved with sudden purpose. Abdul fell back in surprise as the two figures leapt toward him, closing the gap in an eye blink. A truncheon flashed from its hiding place, caught Abdul on the side of the head with a hollow thud. Abdul dropped but never hit the ground; the two men clamped him about the shoulders and stuffed him in the open back door of the van. The driver threw the stick into first, spun the tires on the slick gravel as it tore back up the alley from which it had come.

A woman and child appeared in the doorway and looked out on the empty street. The Afghan man had disappeared.

Evil turned again to his copilot.

"Kiwis are fucking crazy, dude."

WHEN THE BLACK hole is looking for their target, they'll send a Predator. And if that Predator eventually corners him, if the black hole is sure—they know not just who but also where—they'll plan a raid, and flying top cover will be a pilot like Evil.

Major Ben "Evil" Cook does not say the word "um." Upon careful reflection, I have decided that if you met him for the first time, this is the only discernable clue of what lies inside his otherwise average exterior. Nothing in Evil's gait or posture would alert you to his profession. When not wearing his green Nomex flight suit, harnessed and wrapped chute hanging about his ass, helmet under his arm, you would not guess Evil was a fighter pilot. Formerly dark hair has faded gray with time and sun. The faint residual smell of a hangover, last night's rum leaking from his pores, drifts about him less and less; Evil has a wife and two dogs and a mortgage, and the nights are ending earlier and earlier. Never thin, the stresses of so many flight hours have thickened Evil all over. When he turns the jet at 9G, the helmet by itself weighs over forty pounds; Evil's neck and body are now designed to compensate for such forces.

He doesn't wear aviator sunglasses, the simple Eagle-profile tattoo on his back is well hidden, and he has learned not to talk about the jet all day to civilians who didn't care.

"When you go to the bar, you don't tell people you're a fighter pilot," Evil often said. "No one likes fighter pilots except little kids and other fighter pilots. We tell people we're plumbers. They usually believe us."

Away from the flight line, Evil is just another middle-aged guy in flip-flops with a short haircut and a little too much around the middle.

But if you know what to listen for, his speech does give him away. The faint Tennessee twang is rapid and precise. Evil never says "um," and not a word is out of place. Ever.

First Lieutenant Ben Cook became Evil at a private naming ceremony in the bar at the squadron headquarters, with the alcohol flowing. One fellow conspirator told a particularly nefarious story involving the general's daughter and her unceremonious curbside drop-off at her home at dawn. "Evil" seemed appropriate. Pilots don't choose their own call sign. Evil's peers bestowed the honor, the best fighter pilot name around.

And yet when the fighter pilot with the best fighter pilot name first flew in combat, finally flew in combat, it wasn't in the single-seat, high-performance, enemy-aircraft-killer F-15C Eagle that had dominated his professional life. It wasn't in the airframe he had spent thirteen hundred hours of flight time training in, teaching in, specializing in, aching and puking and sweating in. It wasn't in the great white shark of fighter aircraft, the crowning achievement of one hundred years of military evolution, the peak predator species that defied further improvement.

By the time Evil left for Afghanistan in 2011, the American people had spent nearly twenty million dollars on jet fuel alone to make him one of the best air-to-air killers in the world. But that's not the job he went to war to do. No, when one of America's last true fighter pilots finally went to war, it was for the same reason the rest of us seemed to go to war in the years after 9/11: Evil went to hunt IEDs and the Engineer who made them.

To get the chance to log his first combat hour, Evil took a temporary assignment to fly the MC-12 Liberty, a twin-engine modified Beechcraft King Air, used the world over by freight companies and business executives to hop between stateside corporate headquarters and sales meetings. Its mission was to provide "manned tactical ISR," the highly sought-after buzzword of special operations support. The term "ISR"—Intelligence, Surveillance, and Reconnaissance—could refer to many types of platforms, from satellites to U2s to Preds to drones the size of model airplanes. The MC-12 was "tactical" as opposed to "strategic" because it supported small units in real time during their missions. It loitered for only four or six hours, much shorter than a Pred, but a local commander could ask for an MC-12 and there was a fair chance he could get one. "Strategic" assets, such as the unmanned Global Hawk, worked for bosses in Washington and Qatar and the CIA. And the MC-12 was "manned" because four human beings were in a tin can in the air above the battlefield.

How quaint, to put people in the plane. The MC-12 was a relic flown by a dinosaur.

A sense of amazement surrounded the MC-12, an awe that it existed at all, not because of the breakthrough state-of-the-art electronics that it contained but because it broke every rule of the military's acquisition process. Evil claimed it went from "bar napkin to combat in ten months," a blink of the eye compared to the typical decades of aircraft development. This timeline so impressed the wider aviation community that the MC-12 was the runner-up for the Collier Trophy, the Pulitzer of flying given by the US National Aeronautic Association. Past winners include Howard Hughes and the crew of Apollo 11. In 2010, the MC-12 design team lost only to the Sikorsky X2, the fastest helicopter ever built, clocking in at over two hundred miles per hour.

This plane that should not exist would not look so special to the untrained eye, and that was the point. It used an airframe designed in the early 1960s. It was painted two-tone gray, dull on deep. Antennas and pods were stuck on the fuselage at various unobtrusive places. Every bit of spy hardware was a commercial-off-the-shelf purchase, stolen from other military programs or obscure supply catalogs. The video from its targeting pod could be broadcast to soldiers on the ground using a system called Rover, originally designed to slake the Pred porn appetite of deskbound generals, now distributed to the masses. Once airborne and absorbed in the mission, Evil would place a standard touch screen tablet in a rack over his aircraft instrument displays, pull out a keyboard and track-ball mouse ordered online, and, like Gene, chat via mIRC for the majority of the flight.

The Army bought a fleet of MC-12s and immediately loaned them to the contractors of Task Force ODIN. The Air Force retained a military crew, recruiting a slate of almost over-the-hill fighter pilots who were facing job losses, base closures, and a war passing them by. There was a period of cultural adjustment that, from the outside, might appear shallow. The MC-12 was a prop-job puddle jumper and not a jet, a buzz and not a roar, a minivan that cruised at 145 knots, not 450. Flying it required little "real" skill except in cases of extreme weather. And most jarring, rather than fly solo, pilots like Evil were suddenly the Aircraft Commander for a crew of four: a copilot in the left seat, boss in the right, and two enlisted technicians in the back, one to operate the sensor and the other to work the cryptological programs around which the aircraft was truly designed.

In the Eagle, Evil had no one sitting in the back. Just him and one airplane and two wings dripping with missiles and (with luck) a sky full of similarly hostile aircraft to shoot down. That was how he always thought war would be. Gene had a thousand humans in his loop, but for Evil, three could be too many. He had to smell their farts, listen to their snores, keep them engaged to alleviate boredom, and jar them loose when they locked up in an oversaturated helmet fire.

While chat rooms viscerally held little of the same urgency as air-to-air combat, there was a dearth of enemy aircraft to shoot down over the last fifteen years, and fighter pilots had to find new ways to get in the war. Some, like Evil, waited until the last minute and ended up in the MC-12. Others, like Gene Rich, permanently switched to Predators early on. Either way, they didn't go meekly. Evil and his brothers seized the opportunity before them, bullying their way into the operations development offices that were writing the new book on how each aircraft would optimally be employed. In both cases, manned ISR and unmanned RPAs, the fighter pilots applied to the task their two primary skills: obsessiveness and tactical thinking.

"You get a bunch of fighter pilots in a room," Evil told me, "and if they are real fighter pilots, it doesn't matter what they fly or what country they are from, they all tell the same stories. It's why our wives hate us. We are all competitive, and we all try to make everything perfect."

Perfection in an MC-12 meant applying the philosophical underpinnings of BFM, Basic Fighter Maneuvers, the fundamentals of air-to-air combat, to their new less-than-ideal circumstances. Novelty is at the heart of the aerial duel: highly trained humans are not only trying to out-think each other, but they are attached to a machine subject to ever-changing weather, electronic interference, and malfunctions.

Evil specialized in this tactical thinking, first breaking a problem down into its component variables, and then solving the equation repeatedly as each variable changed second by second. In the Eagle, the variables had become comfortingly familiar: air speed, heading, altitude, missiles, gun, radio, radar, wind speed, direction, cloud ceiling, the Cons, restricted airspace, wingman's location, wingman's heading, target, tactics. Double that number to consider the ene-my's equivalent of each. Computing and computing and computing every second as he pulled the stick and pressed the pickle button and killed another jet.

And all the while, compartmentalizing the fear of killing yourself or someone else. Your rickety old airplane tries to kill you. Your new inexperienced wingman tries to kill you. The thunderstorm tries to kill you. Can you put that aside, shut off the reptilian in favor of the distantly sublime and rational, have the poise to put the sensor on the one person who needs to be shot, and not the three that don't?

Fighter pilots in the low and slow MC-12 discovered this same process—continuous problem solving, fear suppression—applied to hunting IEDs and the Engineer on the ground. It was a problem to be solved, an opposing mind to outwit, a climate to endure, a gizmo to optimize, a team to lead, a plane to fly. The variables changed but the tactical process for beating them looked familiar. Some pilots from other backgrounds, tankers and heavies, were unused to the pace but learned to adapt quickly. Others struggled with the fluid schoolyard pickup game nature of the fight and descended into hel-met fire.

The crews of the MC-12 became very good at hunting bombs and emplacers and tracking their networks to target the inner rings of their oil spot. This was the breakthrough of the aircraft's employ-ment: the realization that the greatest weapon in its arsenal was not its camera or laser or antennas but the finely tuned human brains of its occupants. In an age of long-range air-to-air missiles, fighter pilots still teach BFM to their hatchlings because they have discov-ered no better way to train people to think quickly and confidently.

"If you are going to put a man in the platform, give him that much more situational awareness, how do you want him to think? What will they do with the increased knowledge?" Evil asked in a rhetorical way that made it clear he knew the answer.

Under optimum conditions, and when his crew was engaged to their highest potential, Evil would act as mission commander and coordinate all air support for a given special ops mission. His copilot would fly the plane and act as air warden, providing clearance for a variety of other aircraft to transit their airspace. His enlisted sensor operator would run the camera and sparkling targeting system, "put the thing on the thing" in Evil's words. A good one was worth their weight, Evil said, and could make or break the mission.

The last seat in the airplane was filled by the cryptological tech.

"And what did your cryptological operator do?" I asked Evil.

"They worked all the beeps and squeaks," Evil said. "Dude, you should have seen the shit we had onboard this thing. The stuff it could do was scary. Things I can't tell you a lick about. I just hope we never need to fly them over this country."

Unlike Gene in his Predator, Evil did have a sensor for "suspicious."

A SNAKE EATER in a tight black Task Force 373 T-shirt walked up to Evil in the chow hall. Every detail about every task force was classified—their members, their branch, the countries that supplied them, their targets, their capabilities, their sources, even their code names—so Evil always wondered where they got the T-shirts made. The super secret spy shop?

Evil recognized him. Here at the main base he was a task force liaison to headquarters, but previously, when he did time out at Salerno, they had surely worked missions together, over the radio. Based on the perfect hair and the fact that his waist and shoulders formed an equilateral triangle, he was probably a SEAL. Evil knew if he asked, the guy wouldn't tell him. Might mention he was from Little Creek, a hint that was close to confirmation. Everyone here was from Little Creek or North Carolina, all from inside the fence. In the Khowst Bowl, the US had given up on creating Gallieni oil spots and was only dismantling them.

Evil got one meal a day, between flying and workouts and sleeping, and he preferred the task force chow hall. Hang out a bit with the guys in the ground, the few people on this massive air base who knew what was going on. The Pred crews just stayed in their little shelter, launching and catching, talking to pilots at Nellis rather than operators here. The rest of the base was even worse. One day he tried to stop into the finance office to get his pay fixed, and there was a sign in the window that said they were closed for training. *Closed for training?* Evil thought. *Do they even know a war is breaking out?*

Evil waved, and the unnamed Virginian laughed as he approached, pointed to Evil's jet-black mustache, the ends twisted up into *l'as Adolphe Pégoud* fighter-ace points with wax; Evil was a Dapper Dan man.

"I got a team prepping now. You flying tonight, bro?" the brick wall asked.

"They're calling for weather, 19 to 02," Evil answered, and had visions of his last late winter mission, hail beating on the side of the plane, tossing ice from his prop every couple seconds, the updraft relentlessly trying to push him over the border and into a Pakistani mountain.

"Scared it'll be rainy?" They both knew the ODIN contractors never flew in weather. It was a running joke.

"No. But for me, it'll be lightning-y too," Evil said.

"Touché."

"No, we'll be there. I'll make sure I take their line," Evil confirmed with a nod, and earned a clap on the shoulder as he tucked in to his cold, hard chicken nuggets.

"TYRANT 17, DUDE 21, checking in for ROZ Boggs."

"DUDE 21, FREEDOM 64 is the air warden for ROZ Boggs, target Objective Wade. When able go with laser codes, Rover codes, and products. You are approved Echo-5 for ROZ Boggs, angles 240 block 260."

"FREEDOM 64, DUDE 21, copy all, laser codes to follow: DUDE has products v2.1 for Objective Wade."

"DUDE 21, FREEDOM 64. Those products are current, time-line is as fragged. Stand by for follow on to the 200 series when LZ is cleared by JTAC. Report exit ROZ Boggs."

"FREEDOM 64, DUDE 21, copy all, wilco."

And so ended the chatter in Evil's ear, as his air warden copilot Two Time coaxed the pair of F-15Es into the three-dimension column of space above the small house where Objective Wade slept. The air warden built the stack, the layers of fast-mover B-1s over these new F-15Es over their MC-12 over Predators over Apache gunship helicopters over the CH-47 Chinooks dropping off the task force, the JTAC and snake eaters, to kick in Objective Wade's door.

Evil could see none of these aircraft. Out the MC-12's front window he saw only deep night, a cloudless sky after the weather passed, a faint moonshine outline of mountain peaks that formed the imaginary border between Afghanistan and Pakistan, sporadic cooking fires along the ground. The Khowst Bowl, the valley containing the city of the same name, was a busy place at night. Multiple Restricted Operation Zones (ROZs), their five-mile radius circles overlapping due to the density of the targets, and a pile of airplanes above each. Not for the last time, Evil scanned the ridges and Hindu Kush foothills that nearly completely encircled the bowl. He and his crew always kept skulls out, watching for the bright flash of a surface-to-air missile (SAM) against the uniform dark. There were Soviet SA-7s, and classified rumors of 14s and 18s, all over this country. Plus we sold Stinger missiles to the Afghans when we called them anti-Communist freedom fighters instead of insurgents or *muj* or Taliban or Al Qaeda or bad guys.

The MC-12's only defense against SAMs were flares. SA-14s and 18s don't see flares. With his lights off, Evil hoped the bad guys couldn't see him. He circled his ROZ, two-mile orbit, checked mIRC, checked his watch. The task force with his JTAC—his air controller contact on the ground that served as his conduit, his link to the shooters—would be landing at their LZ soon. Evil couldn't see them either.

THE ENGINEER APPROACHED the outer wall of the compound. Two machine guns were trained on him. DShKs? No, PKMs probably. He said his name, and the large steel doors opened and he drove inside.

His host met him in the courtyard. They exchanged *salaams* and news. But his host could tell he was impatient, and so he took his leave and directed the Engineer to the small guest house against the outer wall.

The Engineer opened the door and looked inside. His newest wife sat on a *toshak* next to her teenage brother. She was young, and her brilliant white eyes sparkled when she saw him. He approached her and knelt and kissed her hands and then the top of her head.

We are going home, the Engineer may have said. We will leave for Pakistan soon.

AS EVIL FLEW over ROZ Boggs, waiting for his team to snatch Wade, the JTAC on another team texted him in the mIRC classified chat room.

```
TYRANT 33: Hey FREEDOM 64, u up there 2night?
FREEDOM 64_MC12_MC_EVIL: Yo bro, it's Evil,
what up?
TYRANT 33: Hey, we're about to go. You're
supposed to have 2 Apaches for Boggs and I
only have one Pred for Mantle. Your JTAC says
I can have your gunships. Cool?
FREEDOM 64_MC12_MC_EVIL: Cool with me.
TYRANT 33: We've got a long walk and your
guys have a short 1.
FREEDOM 64_MC12_MC_EVIL: I got ya. Callsign
for ROZ Mantle Pred?
TYRANT 33: Disco 11 on feed Red 11. + check
the latest products on Wade. New update on
the satellite.
```

```
FREEDOM 64_MC12_MC_EVIL: Already got them
TYRANT 33: Awesome. peace out
```

Evil checked the map, found ROZ Boggs and ROZ Mantle were close but didn't overlap. He and the Pred wouldn't be sharing airspace, so Two Time hadn't put him in the stack, but still, it was good to check in and be sure.

```
FREEDOM 64_MC12_MC_EVIL: Disco 11 what's your
latest?
```

A flood of other chatter in the busy virtual room, but nothing from Disco.

```
FREEDOM 64_MC12_MC_EVIL: Disco 11 latest for
ROZ Mantle?
```

TF_INTEL_DO and CSAR_TOC and RC_EAST_FIRES and DUDE_OPS and TYRANT and PYRAMID, but no DISCO. Evil scrolled up through the mIRC history, found the last DISCO 11 entry, over an hour old.

```
DISCO 11: Copy - I'll watch the house.
```

Not a good sign. Predator crews had a reputation for simply taking their last tasking and mentally checking out. Evil had access to the video feeds of other ISR platforms in the Khowst Bowl, and so he swapped out his own sensor picture and pulled up Red 11 on his touch screen tablet. The grainy gray IR picture appeared, a gentle circling of a walled compound. The target was multilevel, a center courtyard and a variety of stables and maintenance buildings and larger living quarters in the back. Not a soul in sight, ours or theirs. Nothing but the slightly shifting view as the Predator rotated on its orbit and the sensor camera panned to follow.

But however frustrating it was that the Pred had checked out, this wasn't his mission tonight, so Evil turned back to the task at hand.

"Hey, Painter." Evil swiveled to his cryptological operator sitting in the back, using her last name. "Can you pull up the latest on Objective Wade off the satellite?"

Objective Wade was not the Engineer. He was a cell leader and organizer and financier, but not the original brains. But if we're lucky, Evil thought, we might catch more guys while grabbing Wade. Maybe somebody like the Engineer would be with him.

Who has time for kingpins? Frost had asked. Evil only did kingpins.

Evil read through the JPEL dossier that appeared on his screen. It was packed with information from Soliman and Hayes, listed Objective Wade's name and noms de guerre and variations thereof, a photo of his ugly mug from the SEEK for visual confirmation, fingerprints taken from a sweep through his village, a history of him and his family, and a laundry list of every attack US intelligence could tie him to. Dates, locations, IED types, triggers, smuggling routes, cell identifiers, and names of the dead.

Evil read the list of names. Every American solider Wade had killed, every amputee. It would fill a small-town obituary page. Evil flipped from dossier to dossier on the satellite, from Objective to Objective, Wade and more and then finally on to the Engineer.

Evil checked the Engineer's list of dead and maimed Americans. It could have read Schwartz and Fye and Frost. It could have read those names and then thousands more. Each name was one too many, as far as Evil was concerned. One name was every name.

It was this list of names that scrolled endlessly through Evil's mind as his task force of snake eaters hopped off their blacked-out CH-47 helos, snuck the short way to Objective Wade's *qalat*, broke down the door, and latched him in flex cuffs. It was over in less than a minute. There was barely a shot fired. Evil's help was hardly needed at all; he did nothing more complicated than eat a bag of sunflower seeds. His JTAC, TYRANT 17, kept him informed out of courtesy, a line of radio updates until a new sound emerged in Evil's ear.

Explosions. Evil was startled to full awareness. They were distant, muffled, yet unmistakable. They had to be detonations, filling the background of TYRANT 17's radio calls.

"TYRANT 17, FREEDOM 64, are you taking fire?" Evil radioed down.

TYRANT 17 stopped speaking, as if to listen. Another explosion. Two Time reached in the bulkhead-mounted pocket next to him for the opera glasses, the night vision goggles that he would hold up to his eyes to better see out the left side of the aircraft. If there was a battle going on, he would want to watch.

"FREEDOM 64, negative. You hear the intersquad radio speaker. It's the next op over, ROZ Mantle."

The JTAC switched radios to talk to his counterpart on the other team, but kept the aircraft radio keyed, to maintain the connection. Evil overheard the conversation.

"TYRANT 33, this is 17, bro, you okay?"

"Our Pred's not answering the radio. Tell Evil we're pinned down and we need some help." Detonations, gunfire, gunfire.

"Hey, dude, did you hear that?" TYRANT 33 said to Evil.

"Yeah, I got the products right here," Evil said.

Evil swapped his tablet video to Red 11, saw Mickey's compound awash in light. The Predator feed continued silently, unmoving, an inert witness to a task force's ambush.

In the view from the opera glasses, Objective Mickey's multilevel compound was visible several miles away, the bright green flare of muzzle flashes forming a continuous ring around the perimeter. The center courtyard, where the task force took cover, was dark.

Evil keyed the radio for the general aviation freq.

"DISCO 11, FREEDOM 64, you there?" Evil spoke into the mic. Seven seconds later, a speaker in Las Vegas should have come to life.

"DISCO 11, FREEDOM 64, do you copy?"

```
FREEDOM 64_MC12_MC_EVIL: Disco 11 - answer
the radio
FREEDOM 64_MC12_MC_EVIL: Disco 11 - please
respond
```

Evil pulled up the mIRC direct message system—whisper mIRC they called it—and opened a private line with Disco 11. It would automatically pop open a new window on the Predator pilot's screen; no way he could miss that.

```
FREEDOM 64_MC12_MC_EVIL: where are you?
FREEDOM 64_MC12_MC_EVIL: answer the fucking
radio
```

What could he possibly be doing back there?

"Hey, Painter, check the log, how long ago was it that the Pred last checked in?" Evil yelled to his crypto in the back of the aircraft.

Painter kept detailed notes of every interaction. Her answer was to the minute, and far too long.

Fuck. The multi-factor equation in Evil's brain was solved almost instantly.

"I'm swapping over to the other op. You guys run this one. Call the JOC and let them know what's up. I'm going to work ROZ Mantle."

The Joint Operations Center (JOC) on FOB Salerno looked like SOCOM's J2 at Bagram: a miniature version of NASA's famous control center in Houston, and the TIC lights would have been flashing away. It wasn't Pred porn but the MC-12's live video feed that held a place of honor there, projected twenty feet wide by twenty feet tall. So when Evil's crew called the JOC to inform them of a rapidly deteriorating mission at ROZ Mantle, the staff listened.

Evil had not spent time studying the specific products for the snatch of Objective Mickey, the detailed maps identifying the code for each structure, the sources and methods used to track him, the names of the dead Americans notched in his belt. But because of his previous mIRC chat with TYRANT 33, he did have the video feed code for the Predator and the JTAC's radio net. A picture and a voice will have to do for now, he thought.

"TYRANT 33, FREEDOM 64, it's Evil, what's going on?"

In reply, Evil heard a barrage of noise. The pop and thump of small arms and heavy machine-gun fire. The crack of frag grenades. A flood of words. If Evil's human ear were a digital signal demodulator, if it could have parsed out each background voice from the layers of confusion, he would have heard this: "Contact front!" and "Moving!" and "Covering" and "Man down—medic!" and "Fuck, PK in the tower" and "Contact right!" and "Where are the fucking gunships?" and "Grenade!"

Yet somehow, through the din, Evil managed to also hear TYRANT calmly say this: "Hey, what are you seeing up there?"

Buried in the cacophony and ignorance was a request for the one thing Evil could provide. Vision. He studied the Predator feed closely.

"You've got shooters above you. Heavy fire from southeast tower, heavy machine gun. Two additional vehicles in-bound to the compound. No, three vehicles. Movement in the 50 and 60 series. Where are the gunships we sent you guys?"

"Apaches had to RTB. Mechanical. You and the Pred are it."

So with a radio and another aircraft's camera, Evil began to provide the patient reassuring over-watch to talk the task force through their ambush. They had hit the LZ on time, completed their overland patrol to the objective undetected, blown a hole in the flimsy plywood outer wall, and entered the courtyard in a perfect stack of hedgehogging rifles. Then was the trap sprung, as gunmen from other nearby modern fortresses, alerted by the telltale crack of a breaching charge, arrived and began to shoot down and into the courtyard from the adjacent walls. The task force was hit from all three axes. Evil saw the good guys take cover behind donkey carts and engine blocks, return fire sporadically, pinned down and unable to identify and target the greatest threats: the heavy PK machine gun, the line of barricaded insurgents who had high ground and cover and space to reload their AKs.

Evil provided real-time updates to the JTAC as best he could from a video feed that never showed him quite the picture he needed. It drifted, uncontrolled and haphazard, as if on autopilot. How long did Evil have his arms tied behind his back before a new window popped open on his computer? The whisper mIRC had sprung back to life.

```
DISCO 11: Freedom 64, you looking for me?
FREEDOM 64_MC12_MC_EVIL: Yeah, I've sent 10
things. Been trying to get a hold of you.
Can't you see your boys are getting shot at?
DISCO 11: Yeah.
```

Pause.

```
DISCO 11: I can't get them on the radio.
FREEDOM 64_MC12_MC_EVIL: Is your radio
working?
DISCO 11: I think so.
FREEDOM 64_MC12_MC_EVIL: Have you heard the
last 20 min? Your guys yelling for you to move?
DISCO 11: No, I didn't hear any of that.
FREEDOM 64_MC12_MC_EVIL: Ok, do not leave
mIRC and do not shut this window. I need you
to move the sensor when I tell you to.
DISCO 11: ???
FREEDOM 64_MC12_MC_EVIL: I've got the JTAC on
the radio. I'll relay.
DISCO 11: We take our tasking from the CAOC
and JOC. We don't work for
```

FREEDOM 64: STOP FUCKING AROUND. THESE GUYS
ARE GETTING SHOT AT. DO WHAT I FUCKING SAY!

Evil had started typing before reading the rest of Disco's opinion
of the chain of command, and felt only a little better when he hit
Enter and took off the Caps Lock. He took the silence from Disco
as acquiescence.

With aplomb, Evil returned to the general mIRC chat room, for
the benefit of those watching from the Salerno TOC.

FREEDOM 64_MC12_MC_EVIL: Disco 11 - Move the
sensor half a frame to the right and zoom out

The video feed shifted and expanded and a blaze of light erupted
from a high guard tower now in view. The gunmen were spread
about the roofs and eaves and windows of the various buildings in
Mickey's compound and beyond, above the task force on outhouses
and stable shades and the rooftop open-air patios where sleeping
families retreat to escape the summer heat. Now all awash in light
through the Predator's infrared camera.

"FREEDOM 64, where is the worst of it coming from?" the
JTAC asked on the radio in Evil's ear.

FREEDOM 64_MC12_MC_EVIL: Pan down and zoom in
on that main tower next to the gate

"Heaviest fire from the guard tower to your south," Evil radioed back.

"Can you sparkle him?" It was not desperation in TYRANT's
voice, but a first twinge of hope. The sight of an ice-cold glass of
water on a hot day.

FREEDOM 64_MC12_MC_EVIL: sparkle the guy in
the crosshairs
DISCO 11: which one?

`FREEDOM 64_MC12_MC_EVIL: doesn't matter—they`
`are both shooting`

On the road to Damascus, only Saul could see the light. An infrared beam from on high touched the forehead of the Taliban with the PKM.

"Good sparkle!" Two Time called, watching through the opera glasses.

"Now we see 'em, Evil," the JTAC said.

But the gunman never saw, not the sparkle or the 7.62 mm round that entered his eye and exited in a mess from the back of his head.

Everyone heard the sound, though. Plywood and bone and a wet splatter across the mud, laid down over hundreds of years, applied in the wet season and baked in the rest of the year. The top of the *qalat* wall exploded like the back of the head, and ancient mud rained down.

"Sparkle the next target," the JTAC radioed back. Now his voice was nearly drowned out by the close unleashed dam of American FN SCARs and M4s and H&K 416s.

`FREEDOM 64_MC12_MC_EVIL: half a frame to the`
`left, roof top, sparkle`

"Good sparkle," confirmed Two Time.

`FREEDOM 64_MC12_MC_EVIL: quarter frame down,`
`pickup truck, sparkle`

"Good sparkle."

If you were in the task force, crouching in the dust behind a splintered wagon, body armor and pocketed vest and magazines and spare sidearm and flash-bangs about your chest, rifle to your shoulder, through your four-tube night-vision optics you saw a computer-green world of rooflines and mud walls and gunfire flashes, and from a night sky blanketed with enhanced stars, this: an impossibly bright pulsing tunnel of light. A sign from above directing you to your next target, to the stable roof, to the main compound. Beam after beam after beam, until the flash ran out of targets, and you stood among a ruin.

Evil's aircraft-net radio crackled back to life in his ear.

"TYRANT 33, this is DISCO 11."

"Yeah, this is 33," the JTAC called back. "Where have you been?"

"Oh, we were having radio problems," the Predator pilot said, and then, as calmly as if he were calling the control tower of the Jackson, Mississippi, airport on a clear day, he continued, "I just want to confirm that we have three more hours of loiter time, that the timeline remains as fragged. Just a reminder we're using products V3.1 for this Objective, and our primary sensor tasking will continue to be in the 10 series before moving to LZ Hornet. And one other thing, I'm not sure who this other guy was, but he was telling us to move the camera. As a reminder, we take taskings from the JOC so other requests need to be worked through that ATO system."

"Stop talking," the JTAC said. "Never use the radio again. Do whatever Evil tells you." Gunfire continued behind his words.

"Uh, confirm Evil is on FREEDOM 64?"

"Shut the fuck up! I don't want to hear the Predator ever talk again. Do whatever Evil fucking says!"

```
FREEDOM 64_MC12_MC_EVIL: Hey Disco, see the
name. Im Evil, BTW, on the MC-12
DISCO 11: What's he so pissed off about?
FREEDOM 64: Ill tell ya later
```

THE ENGINEER AND his wife and her brother drove up to the checkpoint in his white pickup truck. He handed over three fake passports and was quickly waved through. There was nothing to find in his vehicle; he had left the laptop with his mujahideen brother for safekeeping, and all the designs remained in his head. Tonight he had been a squirter, though he would not know to use that name. They had left through the back door of his host's compound once they heard the detonations two doors away.

Inshallah, the *kuffar* did not seem to be watching tonight.

Pakistan, his adopted home, a long visit with his other wives and children. He missed them so. The Sheikh and his confidants could always keep their families close, but not him. His jihad demanded travel. But now, a break, many days of rest with his sons and daughters. And then, where? The Maghreb? Nubia? Or, perhaps, the Levant and al-Sham?

Yes, Syria. His mujahideen brothers in Syria needed his help.

14 · Long and Messy and Gray

MATT SCHWARTZ'S MILITARY CAREER BEGAN in Clovis, New Mexico, an overgrown railroad stop on the empty high plains border with Texas. Matt got on the train and hit Qatar, Kuwait, two Iraq pumps, and two Afghan. There he died.

I tried to follow. I found the amputees, the evidence, the intel, the interrogators, the analysts, the Pred, Evil. There is one last step to nab the Engineer. I took the train to the last station. This is what I found.

The contractor shooter world is a first-name-only world. His first name was M———.

It's a tale told countless times. Airborne to Ranger School to EOD to Special Forces selection to the Special Mission Unit to private practice. One of ten thousand, then one of a thousand, then one of hundreds, then dozens, until, in the end, only six people in the world did his job. It is an ever-narrowing pipeline. You self-select and are selected. Until, finally, you punch and work for yourself. Army of One.

Ranger school ain't bad, but battalion sucks. If Big Army wanted you to have a wife, they would have issued you one. Honeymoon was an 1,800-mile cross-country drive to North Carolina.

The bullshit eased when he hit EOD. It got even better once he made it through SF selection. Once you're on the team, once you're inside the fence, no more bullshit. Finally. No bullshit.

When he was in the Ranger Bat, he was on a training patrol at Fort Bragg and their dumb-ass lieutenant walked them right into the middle of the live range. Private First Class M—— almost stepped on a set of tail fins and discovered they were in a field of impacted mortars as thick as potatoes on an Irish farm. They had to sit and wait all night, until first light, and then, what do you know, at the butt-crack of dawn, here comes a pickup, driving, where they didn't think they could walk. Two dudes in T-shirts and shorts and sandals got out. "Hey, guys, come with us!" PFC M—— jumped in the back of the truck. It was the first time the Army didn't make him walk somewhere. The guys in no uniforms pulled out explosives, set up a demolition shot on a cluster of live 81s, and then walked back to the truck, kicking over tail booms as they went.

"Who wants to blow something up?" one yelled.

"Hell, yeah, I'll do it," PFC M—— said.

He cranked the shot, and the guy in sandals didn't skip a beat.

"You owe us a case of beer," he said.

Who the fuck are these guys? M—— thought.

"Classic EOD move right there," I said.

"I know, right?" M—— said.

"Did you buy them the beer?"

"Damn right I did. I wanted to join up."

On his first EOD tour in Iraq in 2003 they had one robot for the entire company. They walked up to every IED and placed a charge and made it go away. Their security was the Puerto Rican National Guard. The gunners rarely let their *máquinas* speak.

In those days, when you did get a robot, sometimes the wireless signals would cross, and you'd see the Predator feed on your robot screen. You'd see yourself working, from above, Pred porn for some curious general, rubberneckers looking over your shoulder.

M—— was pinned down and calling for backup. He called on the radio in English, and the quick reaction force called back in Spanish. They waited and waited, their convoy trapped between the IED and the incoming. How long did it take to find a bunch of soldiers and throw them in vehicles and leave the FOB?

Suddenly, three Ford Excursions pulled up to the back of their convoy, put their up-armored civilian trucks between the gunfire and the thin-skinned EOD Humvees. Bearded men in polo shirts and light plate carriers poured from the trucks, firing as they went. M—— knew they must be Blackwater guys, but how did they know to come? They didn't work for the Army, they couldn't hear his radio calls for help. They must have just showed up.

The men set up fields of fire, assaulted a strong point, shot and moved and called for covering fire as they reloaded. A company's worth of bullets poured from the rifles of twelve men.

They shot until no more rounds came in. It was quiet on the street.

"Deuces, bro! We're out!" they called, two fingers in the air in a V, and then they drove away.

Later in the tour an ODA guy in khakis and a baseball cap showed up at their shop and looked over the crisp and conventional uniforms of the men in his company.

"Hey you, Ranger tab and jump wings," the man said, pointing at M——.

"Me?" said M——.

"Yeah, you, Airborne Ranger. We need an EOD guy. You're working with us now."

War is not all destruction. Sometimes war gives birth to a new man.

The ODA team hit the desert fedayeen compound, and when the Apache helicopters opened fire he thought he was dying. The rockets and missiles whooshed from behind like some tidal force, stole the air from his lungs as they passed, detonated in the houses before him, and cracked open his chest. The Apaches beat their way in, fifteen feet off the deck, turned the gun on the hotspots and squirters. One peeled back toward him, tipped the bird on its side, and, as it passed overhead, he could see the pilot through the glass give him the middle finger.

The ODA team hit the desert compound in the middle of the night, and the men and the women and the children were all snug in their beds. They dragged the men to the other room and began an interrogation without questions. The children screamed, and the women screamed, and the men could not scream because the blood caught in their throats, and something inside M—— screamed and he walked outside the compound and paced and paced and paced.

The ODA team hit the compound, and the breacher hit the door, and the stack hit the room, and motherfuckers bit it. The booby traps on the cache were ready to go. The car bomb in the courtyard was ready to go. The birds were inbound, and the team leader called, "Blow through it," and M—— hit it all with a charge where it lay.

The ODA team hit, and M—— blew through them all. He blew through every dead-dog bomb and dump-truck bomb and suicide bomb. He blew them all where they lay until he made it home.

He kissed his wife.

His dad met him at the airport when he got back from the first Iraq tour. His dad was a sniper in Vietnam and had never ever talked about it, but now he said, "Son, the first time sucks, but every one after that gets easier," and he wasn't talking about the tours.

People only know what gets reported. Taliban over here. Hajji's over there. Ten times as many IEDs between 2003 and 2005? That's only because there were ten times as many EOD operators, ten times as many reports getting written. If an operator hits a house and an IED detonates and no one has time to fill out a report, does it make a sound?

One day he got a phone call. "Hey, bro, I hear you're thinking of getting out." "Yeah," said M——. So his buddy sent him a plane ticket and said, "Come out to meet me," and the two went out for dinner, and his buddy passed over a sheet of paper and said, "Here's what I can start you at," and M—— signed before he was even out of the Army.

Some contracts were ninety days. Some sixty. Some a hundred eighty. But who wants a hundred eighty? One contract had no end date. He was allowed to go home and cash his bonus check when they got two specific guys on the hit list. Kill *or* capture, technically.

"I can't talk about that contract," M—— told me even after I turned off the tape recorder.

He eventually worked for the big ones: Blackwater, Triple Canopy. But it was the smaller companies that did the interesting work, small and under the media radar, smart enough to keep their business as quiet as their names.

When M—— was still in the Army and at the Special Mission Unit, his job was to save the world. That's not bravado, it's true. Think of the worst kind of IED you can. Condi Rice's mushroom cloud, right? If that device gets found, somebody has to take it apart, step by careful step. What else do you call that, except saving the world? God created EOD techs so firefighters could have heroes too.

But M—— always wondered. Who finds that device? How do we know where it is? Something major must go down to get the call in the middle of the night and get on a plane. In military training, the answer was always, "Intel." The black hole finds it. Intel says where the device is. Now he knew better.

It turns out contractors find it. It turns out contractors track and seize it. It turns out contractors kill every motherfucker in the room and present the device to the military team like a shiny gift. Merry Christmas, bros! Why not? Better to keep the military out of that part. The job is long and messy and gray, as he learned when he was hired to do it himself.

But that device doesn't get found very often. And he could only board so many cargo ships that came up empty, listen to so many breathless emergency video teleconferences with world ministers that amounted to nothing. So he got other contract jobs, ones with far fewer dry holes.

Contract it all out. FedEx is way more reliable than those yahoos at the military cargo terminal. The KBR pastry chef and seafood cooks at Camp Victory were amazing. And when he was a contractor attached to a Special Forces team, he could do things they couldn't. Blow in walls. Ask questions second. Contractors don't have to pay reparations or fix broken windows. Keep the green-suiters clean. Let him work.

A 2010 study by George Washington University found that contractors accounted for one-quarter of the total American fatalities in Iraq and Afghanistan, that in 2010 the Department of Defense employed over 250,000 contractors in the Middle East and Southwest Asia alone, that in 2010 thirty thousand more contractors served in Afghanistan than military personnel, and that in

2009 and 2010 more contractors died in Iraq and Afghanistan than military personnel. A 2013 study by the RAND Corporation found that 25 percent of contractors who have seen combat duty have post-traumatic stress disorder, a rate roughly equivalent to that of the military population.

Contract it all out. Contract out the shooting, contract out the dying.

"Truth is, military, CIA, contractor, I don't care which one of our guys get their guys, as long as it happens," M—— said. "Even now, when I drink a beer, I think about it and smile."

M—— took being a contractor seriously, and he decided that if he was going to play the part, he needed to look the part. He was never scrawny or out of shape, but he noticed his fellow contractors were big, real big, and it looked good. So he crushed it in the gym twice a day, and took some stuff to help him along and add weight. The community affords respect based upon appearance, and the bigger he got, the more contracts started coming his way.

He put on a new attitude, decided to carry himself differently. He moved his frame in a new way, and it didn't take long to look like the real deal. The beard, the traps that shrunk his neck, the tris that stretched his sleeves. It was about the job. And maybe a little bit vain. Okay, maybe a little bit more than a little bit vain. But it helped him get jobs and do jobs.

He bought a smaller plate carrier, one that covered only his vital organs, so he could move his arms more freely. To protect his femorals, he bought tight leggings with stitched-in armored plates and wore them under his khaki pants. You couldn't even tell he had them on. He bought a titanium face mask with slits for eyes and the Punisher logo painted on the front. He used it only if he went in the house first, when the threat was completely unknown. It was badass, but it cut his peripheral vision.

He bought a Glock pistol because once he had seen a demonstration where one soaked in dirty salt water for a week and then took a mag while still dripping wet and cycled perfectly and put fifteen rounds in a one inch group. He used the M4 the company bought him, but he modified it and preferred the shorty barrel. He bought an EOTech sight because he liked the bright dot and the ring. He could hold his rifle from any angle, and just put the ring on the target, put the thing on the thing, and know that's where the bullets were going.

In *Call of Duty: Black Ops II*, you can get an EOTech sight. The reticle is pretty realistic.

He was happy to do the job in Sadr City. Most of his bros wanted to be there too. If something crazy was fixing to happen, it would happen there first.

When the American military pulled out in 2011, left Iraq for good, or so they thought at the time, he waved at them as the last convoy drove off the FOB.

The base wasn't closing; a full compound of contractors remained. That night it rained mortars, and small arms fire poured from the police station and the old police academy, a fifteen-story building with a direct view inside the wire.

Ironically, the day the military left, that's when all the bullshit started back up again.

"We're worried about the base being overrun," his boss said.

"I'm not," said M——.

"Well, what do we do with the bunkers of ammo and explosives?"

"I'll throw a few thermites in there. There's magnesium in the floors. It'll burn for days."

"But what about everything inside?"

"Fuck all that."

"You can't just leave."

"Watch me," said M———. "This place gets overrun, I'm out."

Every time he had one of those conversations, M——— smiled. *Ch-ching.* He just got paid $100 to listen to his boss bitch about bullshit.

When the military left Sadr City, they took more than air support and laundry. Now the State Department was in charge, and that well-oiled machine couldn't make a fucking decision to save their lives.

Bullets pinged off the armored glass on the far side of his Suburban. The cop car sped away from the checkpoint. M——— had a mother-fucker by the collar. The shitbag's interpreter and bodyguard were still in the backseat, two bros drawing down and another pulling out the flex-cuffs.

He keyed his radio, called the embassy. "What do you want us to do with this guy?" Silence from the State Department, whistles over his head. "He's the head fucking honcho you guys wanted. What the fuck do we do with him?" More silence.

This is why you don't capture anymore.

"Throw these guys in the trunk. You two, get out here and button this bitch up. You're driving their Escalade. Do not let that cop get out of your sight."

Four armored Suburbans and a bad guy Escalade, one hundred miles an hour, chasing an Iraqi Police car.

M——— hit his radio again.

"Tell us what to fucking do or we're about to open fire on a dirty local cop on the busiest road in Baghdad."

"Remember when we used to get Apaches whenever we wanted them?"

"Remember when they used to at least fucking answer the radio?"

Sometimes he called home, in spite of the nagging two-second delay that poisoned real conversation. He just wanted to listen to his girls laugh.

These guys have become such assholes, M—— thought. But that's our fault. We trained the Iraqis that way.

Some of these fucksticks were idiots and dangerous. Better to let them go first into a room. And some guys, during training, you just knew, you'd see them again, on the other side of the rifle after they deserted. But some guys, the assholes, you could trust them.

M—— checked the line of Suburbans and Iraqi armored trucks and called to the army captain.

"Hey, Mohammed, we ready to rock?" M—— said.

"*Salaam*, brother, let's go," Mohammed said.

Iraqi National Guard. I bet half these guys would like to shoot me in the back of the head, he thought.

"Be polite, be professional, have a plan to kill everybody you meet" (Marine General James Mattis).

Up at 0500. EOD guys make good planners, so guess who was doing the convoy plan that morning? M—— studied the maps, picked a primary route, picked three alternate routes, planned every ambush, planned every break in contact.

A late dawn. Convoy rolling down the streets, principal tucked away, M—— in truck one navigating the route on the radio.

A barricade of cars. That doesn't look right.

"Go to Charlie. Go to Charlie. Go to Charlie," he called on the radio.

When the IED detonated under the Suburban, he was tossed sideways, into the middle bench seat, his weapon caught and pinned, eardrums pounding as if on the outside of his head.

This job doesn't pay enough anymore.

"I'm done. Dunski. I don't need this bullshit," said M——.

"Come on, man, stay," said his boss. "We need you here. We want you to stay."

"I bet you do, cuz no one's coming to replace me. Everybody knows this job is fucked. The rules are fucked. I don't need to go to court for shooting somebody. I'm not playing that game. I'm out."

"You could just leave?" I asked M——.

"Hell, yeah, I could do that! My contract said ninety days, I had already done one-twenty. Fuck that place."

Contractors measure pay by the day. You get a base daily pay and then extras for being an EOD guy, extra for each badge and qual, extra for hazardous duty.

M—— got $825 a day for his first gig. He got $1,240 for his second. That doesn't include signing bonus, end of contract bonus, anniversary bonus, Memorial Day bonus, Fourth of July bonus, or any of the other holiday extras.

The guys who sign up for a grand a day are pissed their buddies are making twelve hundred. The guys making twelve are pissed their buddies are making fifteen. The top M—— ever heard was an ex-DEVGRU guy, a trigger-puller who ended lives via immediate lead poisoning, making $1,850 a day.

Asshole.

Those were the good old days. Then the economy went sour and tons of veterans came home to no jobs, and suddenly the market was flooded with grunts who thought they were operators. The free market at work, everyone's pay went down. The really qualified and experienced guys got bumped to the more delicate missions. The young guys, the lance corporals with one tour guarding an ammo dump, got the average protection missions.

That's why you started to hear so many stories of contractors shooting civilians. The young guys still asked, "Can I shoot?"

instead of, "Should I shoot?" They didn't know when not to shoot. They didn't realize that they got paid not to shoot. Well, except for sometimes.

M—— kept going back, because he got the more lucrative delicate missions, and because when his team leaders called on the phone, he couldn't say no. There were some guys, if they needed him, he'd drop everything and follow them anywhere, to hell and back.

He kissed his wife and girls and packed his bags.

It was different, the first time he went after a person. It was cool, true. His first tour in Iraq with the Army in 2003, he was just a tagalong, he didn't really understand. Now he had the seasoning to appreciate it. How it was different than going down on an IED, different than getting ambushed, different than getting shot at. Finally, to be the one doing the ambushing.

Fye worked in the official system, and his evidence went in a black hole. Frost didn't trust the official system, so he worked alone. SF didn't trust the official system, so Sarah Soliman delivered evidence to their J2, who worked alone. The companies and agencies who hired M——? They didn't care about any system.

"Biometrics? Awesome idea. Never saw it work."

When M—— went on a raid, he was given just enough information to plan the hit. A picture, always grainy and black and white. A note that the target supplied arms, explosives, manufactured IEDs. Nothing like what the MC-12 had.

You always knew when the raid intel came from a Pred. How else would they know a certain guy would take so long to get to a certain place? They must track his car, for hours, right?

Every day he thought about the guys who built the bombs. It was impressive, it took real *cojones*. Can you imagine getting some folded-up piece of paper with a half-ass, third-hand schematic on it and actually wiring it up and putting bang on it? Some people, when they do basic demolitions for the first time, have trouble just trusting that the blasting caps won't kill you. But rather than trusting the quality control of American manufacturing, you are trusting your brother in jihad. Biggest balls in the world to build an IED. Even bigger to place it. *Inshallah*. And they got good, survival of the fittest. They ain't all got dead yet. They place them and get alive. It's impressive.

"Do you remember those original Spider Mod 1s? From way back in the day? How they all had yellow, red, and purple wires, just like the ones OGA sold them in the eighties, because they thought the wire color mattered? They learned, by the time they made Mod 2s we couldn't jam anymore."

Every time they caught a builder or emplacer, you had to interrogate them hard, because who knows, they might cough up the Engineer. You had to hope. They always sing like songbirds. It's funny. They're hard-asses until they get caught, then you can't shut them up with the names.

He doesn't know, I thought, *that they never give up the Engineer's name. That they give up every other name and not his.*

These intel weenies that say there's only a few Engineers. How could there be? There have to be hundreds, maybe thousands. How else could there be so many IEDs in Iraq and Afghanistan and Pakistan and Uzbekistan and so many Shitstans all over the world? How else could there be IEDs everywhere—everywhere!— if not for hundreds of Engineers with hatred in their heart? He hates us, he has to, and loves blood and pain and death and the taking of limbs.

Let's call it what it is. The Engineer is utterly evil. And he is everywhere.

"Do you still think that?" I asked M——, after telling him everything I had learned about the Engineer, the evidence Frost collected as weapons intel, Soliman's biometrics search, Hayes's analysis and profile on the JPEL, the one photo of one Engineer I found on Google. Did he still think there were that many?

"I never actually got him, but I know who we used to get, the guys we used to tag. So let me think about that, and I'll get back to you," M—— said.

People don't understand that being a contractor isn't about being fancy. Professionals do the basics well. That's it. Blocking and tackling, shooting and moving and communicating, each footstep deliberate and precise and correct, every time. Soldiering is easy if you don't mind a few mistakes. It's really hard to do it right every single time. That's what he got paid for.

Walking on night patrol, silent. Then, a whisper on the radio, from their overwatch. "Fifteen degrees, nine o'clock." Everyone takes a knee. One PEQ-15 laser from behind them sparkles the ridgeline. Twelve lasers from their line patrol swing up and sparkle and dance. A single sentry on the horizon, the unknown star of an infrared rave. Another hushed radio call from the overwatch. Their sniper laid out in the bed of a truck, three hundred meters away. One pop and one pop only. The target falls but the sparkles remain. A breath: "He's down." Light show over. The patrol continues.

People don't like Guantanamo or Abu Ghraib, but nobody notices if you just shoot them instead.

In Iraq M—— fought hajjis, but in Afghanistan he fought the *muj*. Think there is no difference? That both are Muslim men with dark skin and turbans and a wish for virgins after death? They all are suicidal, right? They all hate us for no reason, right? They all are *crazy*, in the most basic sense of the word, and this is the important part, because their actions are illogical and disconnected from reality. It's easy to kill crazy people, if they want it anyway, right?

They aren't crazy. Hajjis are effeminate urban hipsters, and the *muj* are tough inbred hillbillies, but it's more than that.

The hajjis are Iraqis and their Arab allies from Syria and the Gulf. They take disorganized potshots from hidden spaces. They flee from gunfire. They fight only when backed against the wall. They hide IEDs and fire them from kilometers away. Hajjis kill through deceit. They don't set out rocket launchers when it's too hot or too cold or too wet. They cut off your head on videos. They burn and drag the bodies through the streets. They lie and dissemble when caught. No one respects hajjis.

The *muj* are different. The *muj* are holy warriors. The *muj* stand and fight. The *muj* will assault your position. They'll ambush and aggress. They'll defend to the last man. They'll march over snowy mountains in slippers. They hit what they shoot at. When they set off an IED, it signals the start of an attack, not the end. The *muj* started getting shot at as children, running ammo for older cousins. The *muj* were worth training by the CIA in the 1980s. The *muj* have won before.

Hajji or *muj*? The Engineer was neither and both.

Sometimes, M—— rode a helicopter to work. If a VIP convoy got hit, if a team was in trouble, if one of our guys got snatched, if we had to snatch one of theirs, the Little Bird would land on the X and disgorge its shooters, and they would get the motherfucker or motherfuckers no matter what. The best part of the job was the "no matter what."

It's not that the principal was bait. That's bad business. But you can tell a lot about an ambusher by who they target. If they knew where your VIP would be, in what vehicle, and when, if they used the right IED and the right tactics, then that was a bad guy worth having a long conversation with.

The breeze cooled him on an otherwise hot night, and M—— kicked his feet in the open air. He looked around at the other operators sitting on the side-mounted seat pods. Ex-CAG guy. Pararescue. Two ex-DEVGRU. Another EOD tech like him. No Marines—they all worked for Triple Canopy. Grunts and squids and zoomies. In this business, all you are is what you were.

His earpiece came to life and said it was time to do the job. M—— didn't actually know whose voice it was, or where the intel came from, or if the target was on the JPEL, or what profile Hayes had created, or if it was the Engineer or another crony, or if the call came from the State Department at the embassy or his company or another government agency, one with three letters.

He was a subcontractor for a subcontractor, an independent contractor for a subcontractor for an agency that may or may not be the CIA or the DIA or JSOC or an independent White House office that had acquired a budget line.

None of that really mattered anyway. When the voice on the secure radio said to go, you go. Roger that, two thumbs up, two sandbags full, pop smoke, we're moving, bros in contact, a target worth tagging.

I thought: *Do the TIC lights come on for contractors?*

M—— looked down off the side of the Little Bird and saw a line of Suburbans stopped in a herringbone on the busy urban street. A squad of his mates had dismounted and were firing toward a number of cement-walled homes, using the armored doors as cover. Tracers and sparks and muzzle flashes drew out the contours of the gunfight below him in bright light.

The Little Bird set down between the trucks and the homes, directly in the line of fire. He unclipped his safety lanyard and hopped to the skid and then the packed earth in two steps, firing his M4 before he had taken his third.

"We want the guys in the houses," his earpiece said.

M—— ran into the dust cloud kicked up by the rotor wash.

"The Armed Forces of the United States are here to seek justice for our dead" (Leaflet dropped in Afghanistan, October 2001).

The men from the Little Bird, pop-pop pop-pop pop-pop, doing their do, doubled the firepower in the multi-factor equation. The ambushers became the hunted.

M—— took cover behind the hood of a truck, felt his bros next to him reload, saw three *muj* motherfuckers pop up from behind the wall. Three on one. Oh fuck. He flipped to full-auto, turned up his left elbow, c-grip, pushed down on the upper receiver, stitched half a mag from lower left breadbasket to upper right shoulder, *first time I've had to do that for real,* he thought, three went down, no rounds came in, his bros reloaded, did he even hit anyone?

He shifted position, saw just an AK pop up over the wall, spray and pray. He could see it coming. One round ricocheted off the hood. Oh shit. A sledgehammer smacked him square in the chest.

That hurts like a motherfucker!

The next day his chest would bear a green and purple bruise, the exact outline of his plate. It was a multi-hit plate, really expensive, rated to take six rounds. But for $1,240 a day, why put that to the test? He bought a new one.

"Were you thinking, if I was still in, I'd be getting a Purple Heart for that?" I asked.

"Fuck no," said M——, and then he cocked his head, as if he was examining me in a new light.

"You still think that stuff matters? All those little ribbons and that bullshit? I don't see you wearing no uniform right now."

The man appeared again from behind the wall, shot all over the damn place, his bros pop-popped, no more spray and pray.

"We want the men in the houses," the voice on the radio said again.

M—— and the ex-CAG guy and an ex-DEVGRU guy bounded out of the street and to the closest house. He slid the titanium Punisher mask over his face and whispered, "Moving," and his bro confirmed "moving" with "Covering," and the door opened easily and the first room was empty. He slid the mask back up.

"Moving." "Covering." Whisper, whisper. Second room, clear.

"Moving." "Covering." Third room, squirming and wails. He put the thing on the thing. Mothers and children. They left.

Kids usually mean no booby traps, but they make using grenades tricky.

Fourth room, a man huddled in a corner.

"I live here!" he yelled in accented English.

Like anyone gives a fuck.

They had all the men flex-cuffed and lined up on the street, separated so they couldn't collude their stories. Their contracted terp went to each one in turn, whispered in their ears. They all pointed fingers at each other, but everyone pointed at the man who said he only lived in the house.

I knew it, thought M——. *Now we shake him down and work our way up the chain.*

M—— walked over to the man. He was quivering. M—— called the terp over.

"Tell him where he's going and who is going to be asking the questions."

The man blanched and shook harder and collapsed in a ball.

"Where was he going?" I asked.

"Can't tell you that," M—— said.

"Do you at least know who you captured?"

M—— shrugged.

Everyone benefited when the process was gray. M—— didn't know who made the call on these guys, and it was better that way. They ordered him to go because, as a contractor, he didn't fall under anyone on the organizational chart. And conversely, if he got snatched, by a cell or foreign government, he couldn't say who ordered him in. He wanted neither the credit nor the special treatment that came with being knowledgeable or important.

"I thought about it last night, and I have an answer for you," M—— said to me.

"All right. Do you know who the Engineer is?" I asked.

"I don't, and that's the issue. Nobody does, across the board. If someone had the answer, we would have won by now. We would have . . . the Engineer. Maybe it's a millionaire. Maybe it's guys like us. I started thinking, I could be that Engineer. It could be somebody like me, like you. Maybe it's just guys like us on the other side who travel around and consult and get paid. Maybe they get paid in money or women or religion. Extra wives. Little boys. Whatever."

M—— took a sip of coffee.

"I'd like to get a hand on him rather than a drone strike on him, to find out," he said.

PART V
THE DEAD REVISITED

"I swear by Allah your troops can't go on! Your troops are tired, tired, tired!"

—Sheikh Khalid Husainan, open letter to President Obama, 2011

15 · All the Ways We Live and Die

IT WAS 2012, AND I was a contractor, teaching basic IED circuits to another EOD unit before they left for Afghanistan. Up on the screen at the front of the classroom was the Engineer's electronics manual. It matched our syllabus almost exactly, and why not? Ohm's Law is the same for engineers of all nationalities.

It was getting to be the end of a long week. We had started with voltage and current and resistors and in only a few days made it to silicon-controlled rectifiers and photodiodes. We had made devices—in fact, the Engineer's same device—that had been seen from Africa to South America to New York and Philadelphia. Throughout the classroom, every flat surface was covered with tiny electronic components and half-built circuits, booby traps that beeped when the lights turned on and off, doors opened and closed, radios were keyed or cell phones called.

The weekend was approaching, and the student soldiers were laughing and goofing around, as young people do, thinking more about their last party before deployment than antenna theory. So I took a break from lecturing and asked a question, the question I always ask every class I teach.

"Who's the youngest guy in the company?"

Everyone started pointing and yelling, turning around to stare at the baby-faced private slumping in his seat, covering his eyes in embarrassment. He was tall and lanky, a colt who hadn't grown into his body yet, all elbows and knobby knees and pimply cheeks that rarely, if ever, saw a razor.

"What's your name?" I said to him.

"Andy," he mumbled.

"How old are you, Andy?"

The room started loudly answering for him, but I needn't have asked. The youngest kid in every class was always someone who enlisted right after high school, got selected for an abbreviated version of M——'s high-speed pipeline, made it straight through EOD training, had arrived at his unit only in the last month or two. Maximum age: nineteen. Andy drooped farther in his chair, letting his brothers answer for him.

"And where were you on 9/11?" I asked.

"Aww, come on, don't make me say," Andy pleaded. Jeers and catcalls filled the room, snickers about the expected answer.

"No, tell us. Where were on 9/11?" I said.

"I was playing Xbox before school," Andy answered, to laughter. "My mom made me turn it off, and then we watched the news before I got on the bus."

"And what grade were you in?"

"Second."

Pete Hopkins, Fye's medic, was right. So was Vonnegut. Wars are all fought by babies.

M—— WAS DRIVING. I sat up front. Another contractor sat in back. We were just chatting.

"I heard about a new job," I said. "A buddy shared it on Facebook. Syria. Four months, a hundred and twenty. Advising. By, with, and through. You know how that goes." It was the summer of 2013. ISIS had just declared itself but had not yet attacked Fallujah or Mosul in Iraq. The American bombing campaign would not begin for over a year. All we knew of Syria came down like it did in the old days, as classified rumors.

"Syria is no joke right now," said M——.

"I know. No air cover or backup," I said.

"You can be straight-up stabbing motherfuckers," the other contractor said from the backseat. He was new, fresh out of the military.

"That's right," M—— said, nodding.

"You can be cutting motherfuckers' heads off!" the other guy said. He was thinking of the "unknown Russian soldier" video, I knew. James Foley was already captured, but his murder was still months away. Trust me: don't Google either video.

"Hell, yeah," M—— said. "That's how it is, you're out on your own, no one is coming to get you."

M—— thought a moment and then turned to me.

"How much did you say it was? Hundred and twenty grand? Fuck, I'll do that for one twenty. Then fucking sleep on the beach for six months. What's that dude's name?"

TO LOOSEN HIM up at dinner, I ordered alcohol first, hoping he would follow my lead. Hayes, the black hole intel analyst, wasn't so easily fooled. He was still in his shirt and tie and said no, no drinks, he needed to head back to the office after dinner. Throughout the interview, he was sober and measured and careful, but once I leaned forward and turned off the digital recorder, Hayes, ever the interrogator, immediately asked me the question that had clearly been on his mind all night.

"So, tell me," he said, "do we catch the Engineer by the end of your book?"

He's the only one who ever asked me that. Sarah Soliman had said the best analysts get obsessed.

THERE ARE NO windows on a C-5, so Soliman couldn't see the Afghan countryside flowing past. She couldn't see the beautiful landscape she had fallen in love with, the green summer of tall cedar trees in Jalalabad, the scattered simple brown shacks. Breadhuts, she called them. *Someday*, she thought, *I'll buy a* qalat *in Nangarhar, in those craggy, majestic peaks.*

No view, but she was excited to be on the C-5. She had recognized it as a National Guard bird from home, with a distinctive red stripe on the tail and the name "Martinsburg" with an inset W and V, like the mountain bumps of the state. When she got onboard, she conducted some identity intelligence, pulled out a pen and paper, and showed a note to the armed crew member in the back.

"Are you all out of West Virginia? I'm from Martinsburg!" she wrote.

"The actual crew is. I'm fly-away security," he wrote back.

Home. It was more and more on her mind. As a contractor, she could leave whenever she wanted. Just put in her two-week notice. This shamed her; her SOCOM teammates couldn't just up and leave, not the military ones anyway.

Not that home fit right anymore. Back in DC, a city full of civilian helicopters, her heart would race whenever one would fly over. It was Pavlovian, the check for the go-bag. A moment of panic, she didn't have it, the loadmaster would be pissed she was holding up the mission. Then a look at her oblivious friends. Why weren't they grabbing their bags too? Do they even hear the helo? Then the stress would fade, leaving the moment sad and fond. *War is a little like summer camp*, she thought. A tight community, pledges to stay in touch, and then? She had no unit designation, no annual reunions, no contractor memorial on the National Mall.

If she left, she could go work in the Syrian refugee camps. Or maybe she could find a stateside biometrics job. It would be different, though. Fingerprinting has become normalized, but it still carries a criminal connotation, and iris scans are new and even scarier. Soldiers always give up everything when then enlist—prints, DNA, stool, everything—but there's a different expectation. The military buys the body with an option to sell it back, in the same or similar condition if you are lucky. It's different as a civilian.

But she would do it. She had been in the J2 job for eight months, and it was time to be done. Time to go home. She had things to do.

She was going to donate the money, she decided. Take all that dirty contractor money and atone by starting the scholarship at her alma mater, like she had talked about since college. She wouldn't miss it. It was always about the work and the data anyway, never about the money. Endow it, permanently, so more engineers could study abroad like she did. Morocco had prepared her for Baghdad and Bagram, and there were problems all over the world for engineers to solve. Other students should get the same chance she did. And who knows, maybe a veteran would want it too? See another part of the world, one not full of conflict. One night, when she was in Kandahar, a C-130 landed with a West Virginia tail, and she threw on her muffling headphones and ran out to greet the plane, and a kid from her high school was a crew member. Maybe he would want the scholarship?

And she was going to do it now, she thought, not wait. No time like the present. Do something in her twenties that normally philanthropists do at the end of their lives. She never felt in danger in Afghanistan, not really, but she read *Stars and Stripes*, she knew to appreciate even being alive. Some guys have plans to go back to school, and they never get a chance to use their GI Bill. And some go back because their friends can't. And some children go because their parents can't. The widow and the orphan and the lost brother. She had seen all the ramp ceremonies. If this C-5 crashed, there would be nothing left behind, but if she donated the money, something would always be there. This scholarship would be her good-bye letter.

A year later, Sarah Soliman and I were sitting in a DC coffee shop. She had come from the office, was wearing a fashionable skirt and suit jacket, still no contractor uniform, but her striking red hair had been reduced to a bob. She had cut it all off when she had gotten back to the States, donated to make wigs for kids with cancer. And now she was telling me about the scholarship. Maybe it wasn't all about the data, I thought.

"So, there's some carpe diem there?" I asked.

"You realize at a much younger age than perhaps most people do," she said. "Life doesn't always go on."

I had to ask and I didn't know how, so I just did.

"Do you have any ghosts?"

Sarah's eyes filled with tears, and she gave me the quick tiny nod of a little girl.

"Me too," I said, and my eyes matched hers.

GENE RICH POURED himself a cup of coffee in a to-go mug, kissed his wife and kids, straightened his tie, and got in his car for the long commute to his new civilian job.

It was a big day, a briefing day, not that his company used that word, of course. Maybe they would call it a sales pitch? If so, he was selling an idea, a vision, a way forward.

These growing pains were difficult, the transition from one pilot flying one Pred to total situational awareness. Convincing the military pilot community might be toughest of all. It was counterintuitive, removing the pilot to make the whole system more human. But it made sense. He had been in ops centers when the Pred feed suddenly pops up. Whoosh, everyone drops what they are doing and looks, like an open window letting in fresh air on a stifling hot day. Gene had seen a theoretical mission directed from an antiseptic headquarters become real when the generals in the ops center could see real people on the ground, real helicopters, real compounds, bad guys getting shot. Some people think drones create warfare without consequences, because it's a robot driving around shooting things, but they have it all wrong. It's the opposite. For the generals, drones make the war more human.

So how to give them an even better picture?

Many of the developers of the Pred program were traditional aircraft pilots, so the ground control station made sense as an evolution. But what about for the new guys? They've never felt the sinking feeling on approach as the buoyant ground effect gives way. They don't know that in a tiny-winged T-38 you can get yourself in a

square corner on final, wing rock and stall and pancake with no fixing it. These ex-pilot engineers want to put all the human cues back
in, to give the new guys the experience by simulating wind noises in
the GCS. Make it feel more like you are in the aircraft.

But that's moving in the wrong direction. The goal shouldn't be
to recreate the flying experience, it should be to automate the whole
thing. Consider takeoffs and landings, where most accidents happen. The commercial 757 and 767 can take off and land automatically, but it hardly ever happens. Not unless the weather is 0–0, zero
visibility, zero ceiling. Why? Because the human pilot is the backup
for the automated system and needs currency, needs practice to keep
his or her rating. The computer doesn't need practice, so the safer
system is put aside for humans to hand fly. It makes no sense. The
Army's Gray Eagle, their Predator variant, uses an auto system. No
one takes off and lands, and it works just fine. Yes, there are a few
cases where the computer is out of rating and crashes, but over time,
you lose fewer aircraft by using the autopilot. Different aircraft, but
still fewer.

This idea should be applied to the whole system. You'll never
make the GCS as real as flying, so don't even try. Instead, let humans
supervise the system and make decisions. Save the person for the
higher functions, the problem solving. Let the plane turn right, left,
slew the ball.

Gene imagined a map on a light table, ground teams tracked
by sensors, multiple Preds displayed three-dimensionally. Want to
know what a certain Predator sees? Flip to it on your flat screen.
Want to see what's on the other side of the building? Flip to a different angle. Need a vehicle tracked? Task a Pred with a point and
click, it follows the truck on its own. No more air warden; let the
computer deconflict flight paths. The operator, the human, isn't in
one point in space. The human is at every point in space.

This makes Evil's situational awareness in the MC-12 look pid-
dly and weak. Evil wouldn't like hearing that, Gene knew. The two
had flown together so long ago, when they were new lieutenants.

But technology was passing those guys by, even if they refused to see it.

There was more. Automate the search too. So many petabytes of video to look at, how to find the right bit? Write a better algorithm to sort through the data feeds, predict where IEDs are, provide a better product to operators on the ground, narrow in on bad-guy behavior only, so we have maximum situational awareness and know whom to target.

We'll get there by 2020, Gene thought. *It's just growing pains until then.*

EVIL RENTED THE hangar space at Ferguson Field, a strip of hot asphalt and a row of sheet metal stalls on the west side of Pensacola near Perdido Bay. He had decorated it so it felt like home: a small bar adorned with stolen street and traffic signs, a half-size college beer fridge. On one wall hung a neon light-up emblem of the 2nd Fighter Squadron with their American Beagle badge. The 2nd flew P-39s, P-40s, and P-41 Mustangs over Europe in World II, trained new interceptor pilots during the Cold War, moved to Florida to train the nation's F-15 pilots for twenty-six years. The unit was shut down in 2010. America is nearly done training F-15 pilots.

Most of Evil's decorations were small, almost comically under-sized in the large space. But the hangar was the perfect size for its two main occupants: an airplane and a something else.

The airplane was Evil's. He owned it fair and square, without even a loan to pay down, paid for out of his own pocket with saved-up deployment cash. It was an experimental Glasair IFT. In the world of general aviation—those aircraft that are neither commercial nor military—the "experimental" designation indicates that the plane had been built from a kit at home rather than by a manufacturer in a factory. Evil didn't build his own plane, though; he bought it complete and certified.

The Glasair IFT is airshow small, a modern tummy-rumbling throwback for those with only Boeing 737 eyes. A single prop on the nose turns under the direction of 160 horses, a small automobile engine. The wings are attached to the underside of the narrow fuse-lage, and to climb into the cockpit one must walk up specific rein-forced sections that are labeled Step Here. Step other places, and you are liable to put a foot through the skin and into a fuel bladder. Evil's Glasair was painted in American stripes: blue about the cockpit, a layer of white the length of the body, red wings and undercarriage. A fiberglass flag.

The other occupant of the hangar, that something else, was the very idea of the plane, and it took up nearly as much space as the aircraft itself. A breezy and easy confidence filled the space, a casual defiance of human physics, a perpetual attitude drawn from the ear-liest days of aviation, when experimental aircraft were just that.

When I walked into the hangar on that warm morning, it seemed to me more likely that a fabric-skinned De Havilland Tiger Moth should emerge, or that we should load up bags of airmail, or prepare to map some unexplored Arabian desert. I thought Evil might toss me a scarf and a leather helmet and goggles to wear for our flight, totems from a more trusting time when all would have intuitively understood this truism: the only people who fly airplanes are those that love it and are passionate for an elevated freedom above all else.

I opened the wide hangar doors via a clattering chain as Evil removed the wooden chocks from the plane's wheels and tossed them in the rear of the open cockpit. We were nearly ready to fly together for the first time.

We pushed the plane out onto the well-trimmed infield grass, and Evil started to prep the engine. Calling the Glasair IFT a two-seater strains the definition. Evil sat on the left, to be closer to the modern electronics mounted on the dash. I sat on the right. Shoulder to shoulder, wall to wall, the stick rose from between our knees, and Evil shifted the right side of his torso in front of mine for an easier grip.

"Comfy, huh?" Evil said with a smile. Ten pounds of potatoes, five-pound bag.

We put on our headphones, and Evil flipped on the motor using an ignition switch and a push/pull throttle with a novelty-size black knob. As cool as starting your car, the engine buzzed to life. In a plane so small, I felt the engine as much as I heard it through the thick earmuffs, a vibration in my seat that made me burp. We kept the dual-gullwing hatches of the cockpit open as we taxied over the grass, my right arm and elbow hanging outside over the lip like I was on a Sunday drive out in the country. Maybe Evil was; he flew this plane nearly every day.

At the end of the runway, we latched the doors shut and Evil asked over his microphone whether I was ready to go. His voice was clipped and static. I gave him a thumbs-up. Evil flipped through the dials on the avionics and radioed the closest air traffic control, and I looked around the cockpit and noticed that at my right shoulder, written in bold black stenciled capitals, was the word EXPERIMENTAL. Beneath was an FAA label warning all potential passengers that the plane they were sitting in was built by an amateur. The moment before takeoff in any sort of plane—widebody commercial jet or regional puddle-jumper—is all about trust. Whom should I trust now?

Evil pushed the oversize knob, and the quivering plane suddenly jumped down the runway. The sea-level air was fat with moisture, and the little plane was airborne before half the asphalt was gone. A flick of his wrist and Evil raised the nose, the airplane elevating as if lifted by a magician's hidden string. A crosswind grabbed the tail and immediately yanked hard on our backside, but Evil kept the nose true, and with a buzz we bounced over treetops and turned east in a free pattern of the pilot's own design.

We flew to Tyndall Air Force Base, following the white sand coast, and I managed to not throw up before we landed. Once on the ground we parked, chocked, and wandered over to the F-15C flight simulator, where Evil offered to dogfight me, pilot versus EOD robot driver. Time compressed, and though he whooped my ass continuously for an hour, it felt like only minutes. By then the light was fading, so we got back his tiny Glassair and took off for home.

In less than a year, Evil would upgrade his plane to a six-seat Bonanza, called the Bro-nanza by his buds, because of the ski trips and bike excursions and tropical island booze-fests he could now swing. But he had room for other cargo as well. He volunteered to transport rescued dogs to new owners, and flew veterans to specialist medical appointments up and down the Eastern Seaboard, especially amputees like Fye and Frost.

"I only really get along with fighter pilots," Evil had said, by way of explanation. "But as I say, there are a lot of guys who fly fighters that aren't fighter pilots. And there are a lot of fighter pilots who don't fly jets. There were a lot of fighter pilots among the sensor operators and the SF guys in those task forces, they just didn't know it."

I'm not sure it's possible for Evil to give a higher compliment.

The flight back to Pensacola was smooth and clear, westward into a sunset over the Gulf. As we flew across a nectarine sky bracketed by thunderheads, I thought of the vicious storms that raked Evil's MC-12 over Afghanistan, and a conversation we had about the terrible night that followed.

"A couple of weeks after the fucked-up op where the Predator never responded back, I saw that JTAC, the one whose team was pinned down. He traveled all the way from Salerno, and he came to the MC-12 compound looking for me," Evil had told me.

"What did he say?" I asked. "Did he have an explanation for what happened? Why they were left high and dry?"

"No, he didn't," Evil said. "All he did was shake my hand and say thanks for helping him out. He said, 'We'd still be getting shot at if you hadn't come. I fucking hate the Pred. It's never there when you need it.' So, believe it or not, I try to be diplomatic, and I say, 'Yeah, but it's got a nice camera?' And he says, 'Fuck that camera. I need guys I can trust. Me and all my guys would be dead if you weren't up there.'"

Among fighter pilots, praising yourself with another's words is not a cause for embarrassment; it is a simple statement of fact. Evil went on.

"It was probably the proudest and most humbling moment of my life. But it's a funny thing. If there hadn't been a Pred out there, I couldn't have helped him. But if there was another MC-12, they wouldn't have needed the help to begin with."

The government wants safety and efficiency and distance and thus drones, but the warriors just want brotherhood.

JENNY SCHWARTZ LEFT her anatomy class and walked across the small bit of green lawn that serves as the grounds of Laramie County Community College in Cheyenne, Wyoming. The campus consists of a single main building surrounded by open parking lots, asphalt plains that quickly give way to equally empty high grasslands stretching to the south and east. The unremitting wind blew her hair into her mouth and eyes as she made her way to an obscure corner of the campus. Her destination was not her Jeep or a counselor's office or a class but, most unlikely in this prairie setting, a tree.

They planted the tree for Matt. *Well, not really*, she thought. *They planted it for every soldier who died in the war that was somehow affiliated with the college. But Matt never actually went to school here, so I guess they really planted it for me. I'm the one left in Cheyenne, trying to go back to school to fill the days.*

The tree is on the back side of the main building, jammed in a corner up against two walls. No walkway or path leads to it. There is nothing to do once you get there, no bench or picnic table beneath, no one seeks out its shade. She wondered if anyone else ever visited this abandoned tree. It was a stunted thing with no leaves when they planted it. There was a little ceremony, about fifteen people, including the school president. *That was nice, I guess*, she thought.

Jenny doesn't go to the back of campus to look at the tree very often. What's the point? Why bother? It's nothing but a terrible cliché. What am I supposed to say? What are my kids supposed to say? What does a tree fix?

She started to get angry again and thought, *See, this is why I don't make it a point to see this tree more often. Every time I do, its nothing but rehashing all of the futility and half-measures and misunderstandings and the foolishness of Matt enlisting and following him to Florida in the first place.*

In the end, the argument in her head always ended the same way: *I never thought my kids would be able to say that their dad died in the war.*

Who says that? It's such an old-fashioned statement. Dads didn't die in wars, or, at least they didn't anymore. No one she knew had a father who died in Vietnam. Nor a grandfather in World War II. Who are all of these people who died in the Argonne and Iwo Jima and the Mekong Delta? Real people, they really fought, and then they died, and some of them got trees too, but they were as distant to her as the dead of Iraq and Afghanistan were to all of the students she sat next to in class every day.

But there could be a purpose in planting a tree, Jenny thought. A tiny, tiny purpose. The war is so far away, the people who planted this tree have no idea what it really means, what it represents.

This little tree is not about remembering, like they said. It's about the washing of hands, putting the war and its obligations behind them. They planted this tree to forget.

IN THE CENTER of the northwest Florida military coast that stretches from Pensacola to Fort Walton Beach to Panama City, along the inward side of Okaloosa Island, off the main tourist drag but against a dock on the water, on the narrows that connect the larger bay to the Santa Rosa Sound, there is a run-down bar named Helen Back. It is not an especially large or nice place, and the view is limited. The rock and reggae bands that play on a small wooden stage are only all right. The beer selection is basic, and to a New Yorker, the pizza is just okay.

This dive is a dingy local watering hole in all aspects but one: the stickers that cover the glass doors and bar back, insignia that form a wallpaper of fighter squadrons, mobile units, SEAL teams, SF outfits, and EOD companies. Helen Back welcomes us all home.

Every year, over the first weekend in May, the EOD community of all four services gathers at the EOD Memorial at Eglin Air Force Base to remember our dead. The official service is held at the memorial wall on Saturday morning, rain or shine. The unofficial ceremony, at least since the wars in Iraq and Afghanistan began, is Friday and Saturday night at Helen Back.

Thursday night too, Wednesday and Sunday sometimes as well. My wife, Jessie, and I usually fly in Friday morning and find the party already started. One year, when we arrived and dragged our bag upstairs to our shared rented condo in a huge beachfront tower, our old friend Matty from Las Vegas met us at the door. He had a glazed look in his eyes.

"Matty, are you drunk already?" I asked.

"I got drunk on Tuesday," he said. "What day is it?"

We all hit Helen Back before the sun was even down that night. The bar was full, and loud, and the bartenders were already moving at double speed filling drink orders. Matty bought two pitchers for the three of us, and we clinked plastic cups and so the memorial begins.

Jew, our other roommate, meets us on the deck by the water. Some people take that name the wrong way. Jew is what he calls himself. I've heard his mother call him that. He's got a tattoo with the EOD badge except the stars are replaced with six-pointed Stars of David. Anyway, Jew is crashing with Matty and us, but he's been drinking down by the beach all day with Reese, so this is the first we see of him.

First thing Reese always does is shake your hand. I've decided he loves doing that because his right hand is a mangled mess; in Afghanistan an IED blew in his face while he was lying on the ground disarming it. He lost an eye, part of a leg, most of his hand.

Don't like shaking his claw because it gives you the creeps? Fuck you! He's the one that only has three fingers.

Matty wants to drink Yuengling because it's cheap here, but I can't drink that fast enough to get drunk, so I order a couple of rum and Cokes. Straight well drinks—don't ask for anything more complicated than one liquor and one soda.

The sun finally sets, and the bar is packed like grandma's church on Easter morning. A congregation of EOD techs is mostly young men, though some are middle-aged and a fair number are women, not just wives and girlfriends but operators too. More muscular, not especially short hair, beards if guys are going over or just back or contractors. Lots of tattoos, on just about everyone, men and women, sleeves and legs especially. More cigarettes and dip spit cups than is currently fashionable. Only a few guys pay close attention to their clothing—who cares about such frivolities?

Since Iraq and Afghanistan, we have a few new rituals. When we arrive at Helen Back, we usually go to the center section, between the main bar and the outdoor patio, and without asking we stack all the plastic lawn chairs and move them to one side. This creates a space free of obstacles for the wheelchairs. Many of the wounded guys are drawn to each other to catch up, relax, talk surgeries and rehab and new prosthetics. After a long day, some of the double and triple guys have taken off their legs and are resting in the chair. One is excited he is getting new lips soon. Another has a T-shirt that reads "$10 for the leg story." A third is fending off a guy trying to ride him like the Tilt-a-Whirl at an amusement park; just because you lost a leg doesn't mean you are given quarter from the relentless shit-talking and pranks that every other EOD guy must endure. On a bet, someone licks Reese's fake eye. Ty is showing off his new arm, and how it can grip a beer. The old one would spontaneously squeeze and spill; the new one is as steady as the cup holder in your minivan.

A robot finds the IED, and then you try to use a robot to disarm the IED, but the robot blows up and then you blow up and when you get home you get a new robot leg and a new robot arm and become the robot yourself. If you're as lucky as Frost. Wars are all fought by babies, sometimes babies without arms and legs.

Wheelchairs everywhere, but also dogs. A few retired military working dogs since adopted, most specifically trained therapeutic dogs. Reese got a dog because he lost that eye and he was sick of bumping into shit. If you lost your leg, you get a big dog, so you can lean on him for support when you tire. And if the crowds still bother you, you get a smaller companion dog, so you can just find a corner and rub his ears and stare into his eyes when needed. And if you have nightmares, you still take your dog everywhere, because that dog saves your life every night, licking your face in the worst of the thrashing until you snap out of it and wake up, and how can you leave a companion like that in the hotel room alone?

The talk is of work and guns and motorcycles, and the sequence goes like this: take a job overseas, sell your bike before you go, come home, buy a new gun and new bike to celebrate. Everyone wants to know if you're going back. No, I'm not. Not as a contractor, not as a writer. Not yet. I'd go back now if there was a way to ride with Matt Schwartz on patrol. All of us would, for a whole list of such names.

And everyone wants to know about Fye, since I've seen him most recently. I pull up pictures on my phone and show off the new brace he has for his leg. It's called the IDEO, and it is a sort of exoskeleton, providing support for the right leg he is trying to save. I talk about how Fye is off the narcotics, his memory is slowly getting better, he's finally walking, and has started powerlifting to stay motivated during the long bouts of therapy that keep him from running or riding a bike. In the end, Fye wouldn't grow back all 12.7 centimeters of tibia and fibula bone that he lost. He was six-foot-two when he started, but infections and complications slowed the regrowth process. After eight months of prolonged traction, doctors noticed his new shin was growing in a curve, so Fye endured another round of surgery to break the fresh bone and straighten it. After a year of fighting, the doctors gave up at eight centimeters of reconstruction.

Fye is six foot now, though he reminds me he's taller when he wears the brace and the right sneakers. Those few inches make a difference; Fye looks slightly out-of-proportion in the photos on my phone, his torso just a bit too large compared to his lower half.

One of the people asking about Fye is Angela Olguin, the EOD tech who originally texted me to say Matt Schwartz had died. She wants to know about Fye, but she also wants to talk about Matt, and we finish our drink and I pour another from the pitcher, and soon Angela is wiping tears from the underside of her eyes so her makeup doesn't run. "Fuck, sir!" she says, mad I'll ruin her mascara. So she changes the subject: "Hey, look at this. Haha. Jew balls!" She shows me the photo on her phone, and yes, there is a picture of Jew's scrotum, shiny and clean.

There is a shout from the bar, and the crowd pushes in and then a rush of orders. What just happened? Matty passes the word. Somebody just reenlisted, and he put a fair chunk of his bonus on the bar. It's a race, how fast can we drink it away? We all get at least a few.

Reese's Alive Day is the same day his best friend Tony died. We don't talk about that much. In the men's bathroom, John rolls himself into a stall while other guys piss in the urinals. John's a triple amp, got one arm left, and more. "Yes, I still have my dick, in case anyone wants to know!" he shouts from behind the door. Better than some, but we don't talk about that much either.

Then Jew arrives with the bottle of Don Julio and a Helen Back waitress who doesn't drift far from his elbow. Someone says tequila makes their clothes fall off and then we do a round and the waitress refills the shot glass and then we do another.

Normal sights at Helen Back: shouted stories, whispered tears, men hugging, women kissing, pass the cherry, chants of "E-O-motherfucking-D" followed by silent drinking.

Jessie has been arm in arm with Jenny Schwartz all night, and the two are deep into their cups when I find them again. Jenny left the girls asleep in their hotel room, an older cousin offering to take the trip and babysit so Jenny could break free and relax for the first time in months. Jenny seems desperate for the opportunity to unwind, exhale, droop, like a dress let off the hanger that puddles on the closet floor. A friend of Jenny's brought a tray full of shots, and we all take one and toast Matt.

Oh, it burns, hot as Satan's hoof. For today, from hell's heart, we weep.

Eventually, it starts raining, and we are driven under the few awnings and thatched tiki roofs. Who cares? By now we can hardly hear anyone speak anyway. The goal is not to reminisce but rather simply find the faces of old friends. We are used to long separations from one another, so there is comfort in physical proximity, as if we are all each other's security blanket. I put my forehead on Jew's back and breathe.

THE NEXT MORNING, despite all that had happened the night before, Matthew Schwartz was somehow still dead, so we put on our suits and uniforms and drove to the memorial ceremony on the other side of the bay.

The EOD community is not often known for demurring. EOD stands for many things besides Explosive Ordnance Disposal: Every One's Divorced, Egos On Demand. But where it counts, at the memorial itself and the ceremony associated with it, we are a model of restraint. We live well, and we mourn well. The memorial weekend inspires a certain quizzical awe of one's personal continued existence, and while there is a lustiness to be found in each unexpected breath, there is also humility.

The monument to EOD technicians who died in service is physically unassuming, on the side of a sand-pitted back road, away from the flight line and main hub of Eglin Air Force Base. It is a sanctuary on the grounds of the main EOD training center, as shrine to monastery. A simple wall, not overly tall or long, curved and tapered, constructed of poured concrete, not marble, and the small open-air plaza it encloses is paved with average bricks. Four brass cenotaphs are struck to the wall, one for each service. Over three hundred raised brass names are attached to the plates. Behind the wall, a single American flag, a line of palm trees, a thicket of piney woods, and then, appropriately, acre upon acre of old bombing range as the final backdrop.

Nothing is gilded. No statue of a general upon his horse or green copper man in a bomb suit. When a mainstream military unit, such as infantry or armor, held a memorial service in Iraq or Afghanistan, the physical monument to gather around was always spare: boots, rifle, helmet in a cross, dog tags hanging like a shroud. The EOD wall doesn't even have those.

A thousand or more men and women attend the service where we add the names to the memorial. The men wear dress uniforms and suits, and the women wear dress uniforms and short spring dresses and cork wedge heels, tattoos on shoulders and babies in strollers. Most sit on bleachers and open-air folding chairs, but special tents are erected to protect the families of those honored; the ceremony and flag presentation can be hard enough without the oppressive sun or a chilly late-spring soaking rain. The memorial is particularly well attended by our wounded brothers, though an outsider would have to be observant to spot all the steel poking out of pant cuffs. Guys who were relaxing in their wheelchairs the night before seem to make it a special point to put on their legs and stand in uniform for the event.

The ceremony opens with a famous general or admiral speaking words of glowing praise, about glory and self-sacrifice, about skill and danger and the fear we instill in our enemies. It is the one day a year we let others brag for us. In the seats, faces are stone and eyes are red.

The second part of the ceremony is the simple reading of every name already on the wall. Each service takes a turn reading their own list, Army, Marine Corps, Navy, then Air Force. It is the only point in the ceremony that the average EOD technician speaks. I timed it once; it takes twenty-seven minutes to read the entire list of our dead. Recently, they had to change out the old plates that bore all the names because they were running out of space. The monument was almost full, so they installed new plates, and the names are printed much smaller. Now there's plenty of room for more.

Everyone who died has a name, and they read them all and you start to get numb. By Korea and Vietnam, they start to blend. But then there is a little shock when they say the first name you recognize, a name you really knew, then another name of a guy younger than you, then a good friend from your first assignment. They haven't said your best friend's name yet, and you think they might not. Maybe it's been a mistake the whole time. But then they do say your best friend's name, they say it like any other, and you want to stand up and yell *STOP!* just so everyone slows down and realizes what just happened. Can't we just stop a while, and think about him for a good long time? Just a moment ago, this person was. No, in all of the most important ways he still is. But they read the name as quickly as any other, and the moment passes, and you squeeze your wife's hand.

When the representative of each service is done with all their names, they say this: "We remember."

Do not be deceived by this simple declaration. It is more injunction that reflection; carries the weight of duty, not hazy peace. It is a task to be done now, and the day after, and the day after that. It is fresh mud to labor through. It is a soaked log to heft and split and stack. It is an already sharp blade to hone. There are no laurels upon which to rest.

When the Marine Corps gunnery sergeant says, "We remember," after reading the seventy-eight names on the Marine tablet, what he is really saying is, "Stop!" just like you wish you could. He's saying, "You volunteered for this. You are the one who wanted to join up. Well, now you're here, and my best friend in the world is on this wall, and the least you can do is remember his goddamn name for the rest of your life. He's dead, and you're alive, and it's a tiny thing to do, remembering, and you're going to do it because the only way his sacrifice begins to make a lick of sense is if it isn't forgotten."

"We Remember" is scrawled across every program and banner and website associated with the event. It is the Facebook update for every EOD technician on the morning of the memorial. It is the mantra of everyone with a personal friend on the wall, and after fifteen years of war, only the newest graduates do not have one.

The official motto of the EOD community for decades has been: "Initial Success or Total Failure." Iraq and Afghanistan have all but replaced it with "We Remember."

We remember that there were 184 names on the wall when we started these wars. We remember that we have added 130 names since. We remember that this has been our bloodiest conflict ever, twice as many EOD dead as in World War II, three times as many as in Vietnam. We remember that in 2012, at the height of the Afghan Surge, we didn't add eighteen names to the wall during the memorial ceremony, but rather Chauncey, Christopher, Mark, Eric, Michael, David, EJ, Daniel, Nicholas, Stephen, Kraig, Nicholas, Chad, Kristopher, Joe, P-Nut, Matthew Seidler, and my friend Matthew Schwartz.

We remember that the oldest name on the wall is that of Navy Ensign John M. Howard, born 1917, graduate of the third-ever mine disposal class at the Washington Navy Yard, killed in Britain in June of 1942 taking apart a booby-trapped German underwater mine. We remember that, as of the editing of this book, the newest name is that of Army Specialist Justin Helton. He was thirteen years old on 9/11, and killed in June of 2014 in the Arghandab district of Afghanistan, in the heart of the valley that had taken so many limbs and lives. Helton was killed along with four Special Forces soldiers, their interpreter, and an Afghan Army soldier, via friendly fire, when the air control and coordination system broke down and a B-1 mistakenly dropped a bomb on their position.

We remember that there will surely be a newer name by the time you read this. We remember that there could be new names before this book is even published.

The final portion of the ceremony is silence. Not a word is spoken or a note of music played, as folded flags are presented to the families of those whose names are newly added to the wall. The length of the silence depends on how many names there are. In recent times, it has made up more than half the ceremony.

Back in the 1980s and 1990s, chunks of years went by when no one was added to the wall. The annual ceremony was almost a formality, a lightly attended reading of the names, somber and respectful but small, with none of the immediacy that the post-9/11 wars would bring.

Did they know then how good they had it? I think so. I think enough Vietnam and Gulf War veterans knew what was coming. Not the specifics, of course, but the potential, the inevitability of war-brought grief that lay just beyond the next ridge.

"Screw up and you go on the wall" was the regular admonishment in EOD school. No one had to ask which; there is only one wall when EOD techs converse. Across the street from the school, every EOD student saw the wall, the stakes, every day as they trained.

But the rebuke itself reveals a prejudice in our prewar thinking. For twenty-five years, since the Vietnam War ended, nearly every name we added to the wall died because of a mishap: accidental explosion, mishandling of ordnance, plane crash in Egypt, a Humvee rollover while clearing a desert bombing range. The lessons we learned in EOD school kept us safe in an accident-prone world. One ended up on the wall because of stupidity or ignorance or bad luck, but not maliciousness. Working with unstable ordnance was dangerous enough, but at least no one was actively trying to kill you.

Those days are long since passed.

In the *Iliad*, the dead fall into two categories. The named characters—Achilles, Nestor, Paris—know that if they die in battle they will be remembered. The second group, the unnamed masses that throw themselves on Troy's walls, are as forgotten in death as they are anonymous in life.

No more. Not only do we now remember every individual soldier, but we kill our enemy by name.

JENNY SCHWARTZ AND the girls sat under the white tent with the rest of the honored families. Matt had died five months ago, but having a general kneel at your feet and hand your daughter a flag for her daddy wasn't getting any easier. They already had a pile of flags back in Wyoming. Eighteen names were just added to the wall, and Matt was second to last. Her girls watched every other family cry and then tried to bite their lips when their time came. It was like a second funeral, but worse.

I should have buried him at Arlington, Jenny thought.

Put your husband in Washington if you want to have a life and move on. Bury your husband at home and consign yourself to purgatory.

She understood that only now, that the question of burial is not about where but with whom. Whom should he lie with? That's what she should have asked. In Arlington, you lie with your brothers and the circle is closed. In Traverse City, though, he lay there alone, in a field of snow-covered gravestones, waiting only for her. No matter what she may do for the rest of her long life, she is abandoning him if she doesn't loyally return.

The Engineer's detonation on that road between Leatherneck and Kandahar, first a flash and then silence and then thunder, was an atonal shriek that cannot be silenced. It threw Matt's truck in the air, threw her whole life into the air, leaving her very existence ringing like an unresolved chord until she go lie down beside him. She must eventually. The natural order demands it.

In Arlington it would be done by now, but in Traverse City it hangs, always on the edge of hearing.

AFTER THE MEMORIAL ceremony, the main crowd trickled away, but the afflicted still gathered. Some approached the wall as they would a relic or shrine, to have their picture taken with a particular name or to simply feel the raised letters under their fingertips. Others wandered the halls of the EOD school, searching for their class photo now twenty years gone. As these unaffiliated mourners milled about, several families—Schwartz, Seidler, and Bell—separated from the group and went into a spare classroom adjacent to the main hall.

That morning, Jenny Schwartz and her girls and Matt's parents and family would receive two briefings: the personal story of the team's last day, and the Air Force's official post-blast investigation.

First up was Senior Master Sergeant Chris Schott—Schottzie to everyone who knew him—the ranking enlisted EOD tech in Matt's unit. He had returned from Afghanistan less than a week prior and chose to be with the families of the dead instead of his own. Jenny thought he looked like he had some things that he clearly needed to say.

Schottzie told them all the whole story of January 5, 2012.

He told them how he started every day the same: getting a cup of coffee and then texting every EOD team that was out on the roads and away from the main base at Camp Leatherneck, to check on their status and spirits and health and to show them he loved them. And the whole team, Schwartz and Seidler and Bell, Team Tripwire they called themselves, were chipper and motivated and eager to roll. He told them how that afternoon, at a boring administrative meeting at the EOD battalion headquarters, a Navy ensign had stepped in to interrupt and ask, "Who owns Tripwire?" How the ensign had said there was an IED strike, all occupants were unresponsive, and Army engineers were breaching the doors. How he had called his friend, the chief of the Air Force pararescue squadron, and had asked for their help, because they had jaws-of-life to breach armor, and he couldn't stand the thought of his men being trapped. How there had been initial confusion, because the ops center was receiving reports that three "soldiers" were down, instead of three airmen. How he went to the hospital on the British side of base, because guys got hit in the JERRV all the time and the truck was so tough, and it had been so long since the EOD community had lost a team this way, he expected to be bullshitting with all three of them by sundown. How the British officer who ran the helipad had approached him at the ambulance port and said he could go inside because they didn't have three "soldiers" coming in, they had three "heroes." How he didn't understand at first, how he had said, "Of course they're heroes, they're Air Force EOD techs!" How he didn't understand until the Air Force rescue bird arrived with three flag-draped stretchers. How he had then broken down in tears, and vomited, and beat the concrete blast walls with his fists until his hands bled.

They needed to know that all three men got the white-glove treatment. He had personally identified each body. They looked like they were asleep. He knew Bell and Schwartz had expressed a preference for a Catholic service on their records, so he skipped the British Protestant chaplain on duty and found the priest, a Marine Corps lieutenant colonel built like a cathedral. He had helped load them on the C-130 during the dignified transfer. He had searched their armored truck for a week to find every personal effect. They needed to know he had done everything he could, which would never be close to enough.

When he was done, he asked if anyone had questions. The room was silent. No one moved, except for young Aliza, Matt's eldest daughter but only eleven years old, who looked around at the adults as she tentatively raised her hand. Jenny nodded at her.

"Yes, honey," Schottize asked.

"Was there a fire in the truck?"

One of her daddy's shirts had burn marks all over it. She didn't know where they had come from. Jenny knew Aliza meant it to be an innocent question. The families don't know all of our nightmares; Matt had shielded them from all the worst ways we die.

But then Jenny saw all of the color drain from Schottzie's face. It looked like he had stopped breathing. Over the last eleven years of combat, Schottzie knew what a fire meant. He had seen more than his share. He understood what happened when a team got trapped in a burning truck. Short ribs in the Alabama smoker.

Schottzie finally inhaled and answered.

"No, sweetie. There was no fire. Your daddy didn't feel a thing."

THE SECOND BRIEFING, the post-blast report, was borne by Major General Timothy Byers.

General Byers had two stars. His title was The Civil Engineer. The Air Force, like the Marine Corps, ultimately organizes their EOD forces under the engineering branch, and so General Byers was responsible not only for every carpenter, backhoe operator, plumber, electrician, draftsman, and firefighter in the Air Force but every EOD technician as well. He had attended the memorial specifically to speak to the families of every Air Force EOD technician placed on the wall that May morning. General Byers carried a binder and briefing, and with the aid of Senior Master Sergeant Tom Allen, who had compiled the official post-blast study, he intended to tell every wife and mother exactly how their husband and son died.

In 2008, there was not even an investigation into Frost's attack. In 2011, Fye's report went into a black hole, and he never heard what happened. In 2012, a two star general sat down with the family of a sergeant to explain every detail.

Matt was on a route clearance mission, between Helmand Province's Camp Leatherneck and Kandahar to the east, this much Jenny knew. She didn't know any of the rest that follows.

General Byers was formal and clear. He told Jenny that Matt had done everything right. The report explained the training Matt had received before he deployed, the equipment he was issued, and the type of truck he was in, that it was the stoutest the military had. The report said Matt's team was on a route clearance mission with Army combat engineers, supporting the Marine Corps grunts of the Second Battalion, Fourth Marine Regiment in Operation Double Check, a push into a remote area north of Sangin to find

IED manufacturers. General Byers didn't say it this way, but we understand: Matt was hunting for the Engineer.

The report said that Matt's route clearance team discovered an IED on the road and they had stopped to disarm it. That they successfully used the robot, disrupted the device, searched for others but found nothing. That just as they had remounted and moved a short way up the road, a second device detonated as Matt's truck drove over it.

General Byers told Jenny that Matt was targeted, they were sure. It wasn't an accident, or the general chaos that struck Fye. Matt wasn't just unlucky. Two Army vehicles had driven over the device, but it wasn't triggered until the JERRV arrived. The explosive charge was massive, meant to kill the indestructible EOD truck. They were looking specifically for Matt's team.

The report said the JERRV's doors were locked and damaged, and initially Matt and his team were trapped. But the soldiers in their convoy attached chains to the back hatch and successfully ripped it from its hinges. The chains didn't snap, they made it to Team Tripwire. The report said their vital signs were checked three times—by the medics in the convoy, by the helo crew, by the surgeon at the hospital—and there was never any hope. The three had died instantly, they had died midsentence, just as the autopsy showed.

Another EOD team from the Marine Corps then responded to the scene and did a complete workup. The blast was so large it had thrown Matt's JERRV into the air and dropped it on a mud wall. They found evidence in the crater in the road. They found a command wire running between the road and the hide the ambushers had used. They found a battery there, other evidence too, and because you couldn't see the road from the battery, they knew multiple attackers had set up the shot. There had to be a spotter and a triggerman at least. General Byers gave Jenny a map that showed everything, where Matt's truck was hit, the security arrangement, the *qalats* and walled compounds, the command wire, the triggerman.

The report said that they had found a water bottle at the firing point, and that it was covered in fingerprints and DNA. That they had used the biometrics database to find the triggerman.

The report said they knew who killed Matt. They were actively monitoring his area, they were searching for him at that very moment, and when they found him, they were going to kill him.

IT WAS ONLY a couple of weeks later that Schottzie got a text.

The text said: *Spec Ops targeting op, 3 High Value Targets KIA, positive biometric match to Tripwire evidence.*

Schottzie smiled, just a little.

I got a similar text at the same time, from an EOD brother on the inside, who still had access to the real-time communiqués of the war.

All my text said was *Call me*. It was like that message in front of the Christmas tree months before. My hands shook. I did.

"I thought you'd want to know," my brother said. "They got the guy who killed Matt."

My head swam. Lowering Matt into the frozen ground. The lucky who lost their legs. JIEDDO said, to win the war we had to move Left of Boom. They said the evidence is how we would come to know him. The battery and the command wire and the water bottle went into the black hole, and some analyst had put it all together. A pop from the biometrics database. Who worked all night while the TIC lights strobed? What grainy photo did they use? A task force, a contractor, a trigger pulled, a sparkle on the forehead. Did they read Matt's name in the MC-12 during the mission? Did they remember why they hunted?

I thought about Jenny and her three little girls and whether this news would bring them comfort. At the memorial wall weeks before, we had spoken every name, and now Matt's killer had a name as well.

For my part, I never cared as much about the actual name as the certainty it conferred. That name, whatever it was, represented specificity, the discrimination of one target over another, the knowledge that the system had worked and that the right man had been identified and hunted and killed. So I had to ask:

"Did we just get the spotter and the triggerman?" I said. "Or did we finally break through and get the Engineer?"

"I don't know," he said. "How can you really know for sure?"

The Engineer's brother is dead, and so is mine, and now, perhaps, he too. I would never know for sure, but we have learned that the point is this:

Some people are worth killing more than others.

Epilogue

THE GHOSTS IN THE WOOD behind my home are not of the wood, they are of me, and I am the one who takes them there.

I cut a path in that wood. It is a young wood, not yet second growth, and the stands of green ash and thickets of sassafras swarm so tightly that the way was nearly impenetrable before I labored days with axe and handsaw and great long-handled loppers to cut a trail through.

Now I walk that path in all seasons, I walk it alone with the ghosts of my dead brothers, and I tell them stories, and point out each item of significance, and note each change from one felled tree to the next.

Be careful when you walk here, I say, this where the sharp stump of young ash pokes through; it could snare a foot or ankle and trip the unaware. And here is the last vestige of a two-thumbs-thick sassafras trunk; oh, you should have smelled it when I cut it down, sweet and oily and fit for old-time tea.

And if you ever get lost, I say, just follow the trail of dismembered wild grapevines, each guillotined shoulder high, their fat woody foundation cut out from under them, leaving the bulk orphaned in the canopy above. The wild grape so terrorizes the wood, attacking only the oldest and tallest trunks, it's as though some nameless malignant gardener planted them at the base of each grand tree. See, here is the maple I saved from that choking viny infestation.

This one lived. And that elm. And another ash farther in. They lived because I lopped off the strangling vine and withered the grape's leafy blanket and gave them a new chance to find the sun.

This is what I tell myself.

I walk my path and show the grapevines to ghosts, because my friends are at war thousands of miles away or dead already because of it or bound in wheelchairs and propped on unsteady metal poles. They cannot walk the path with me, so like a museum tour guide with no patrons, I show it to myself.

And here was where I found piles of ancient sheet metal that crumbled to red dust as I cleared them. And here you can see what remains of a farmer's furrows, diverting rainwater through the clay-heavy soil to the remnants of a shallow retention pond beyond. Each year the depression fills a little more with layers of leaf crop, so that now it is more marsh than watering hole, but you can still find the bermed banks among the honeysuckle bushes and nearby, growing feral, the odd apple tree that has far outgrown its fruit, and see how the pond bed has filled with cottonwoods, the only tree that can survive such persistent wetting.

The sheet metal and furrows and shallow marsh and sparse untended apple trees, now stretching to the sky like their maple cousins, are all the evidence you will find that farms once covered my island where my house and wood now reside. But the orchards proved unprofitable, the land more valuable abandoned, and so the wood came in and slowly undid generations of labor as it retook the soil for itself. Now it is all I can do to keep the worst of the wild grape off the mightiest elms and oaks along my path. Kill this one to save another. Save that one but not another. I can't clear the whole wood, I know; one by one I do what I can.

In winter the snows come and turn the wood into a web of black wet trucks and white-lined branches, and the wind scours the forest clean like an astringent that scalds your red face raw. In spring the mud and mire overtake, but the observant can find the path by following the cookie crumb trail of just-exposed deer droppings. In the summer the sun will bake the path hard, and a fair wind cools, and every weed and twig must grow grow grow to form a knee-high net that tangles every step.

But in the fall the ground cover falls away, and the insects are gone, and the ash yellows and the maples become red and gold, and my wife Jessie says she loves me and she will now come with me since it's her favorite time to the walk in the woods. I hold her hand, and she smiles at me, and she knows the ghosts walk with us, even in the brilliant sun. But we can almost forget it on such a day and anyway, if the ghosts are in my woods, then they are no longer shut tight with us in our home.

When I'm alone, it takes me only a few minutes of brisk walking to get to the back of our property, but once you break through the last thicket, a new country is revealed. I remember the day I cut that final section of path and saw it for the first time. The land opened to brush like a hedge, then tangled scrub, then stunted oaks covered in gout-like puffs and tumorous spiny galls. Behind them lines of tall pines, and farther on cedars rose and blotted out the sun, leaving mold and moss and the decaying limbs of their neighbors below.

The gunshots of hunters rang. A snowmobile track crashed through from one side, then an uneven path broken by muddy pools ready to suction off an unwary boot. I considered, standing at the edge of my yellow wood.

I have heard that, past the wall of undergrowth, a maze of trails leads to coyote dens and deer hides and creeks that have no name. I have heard there is a deep pond guarded by a thick wall of cat-tails and swarms of thirsty mosquitoes claim it for their own. I have heard the swamp is growing, that groves of massive drowned willows bulge into the sky like great mastodon skeletons, their bare bones infested with metastasized wild grapevines so pervasive and hungry you wonder if the leg-thick tendrils are reaching for you.

I have been told all this but never seen.

For then I heard my Jessie calling to me, calling me to come home. So I turned back and retraced my steps and some of my ghosts followed me but some carried on alone.

ACKNOWLEDGMENTS

OVER THREE AND A HALF years of writing and editing, I am indebted and grateful to many.

To everyone who agreed to speak to me for this book, especially Jenny Schwartz, Grandma B, Bill Hailer, Dan and Nicole Fye, Chris and Cathy Frost, Pete Hopkins, Sarah Soliman, Zac Crush, Ben Cook, and Chris Schott, plus Hayes, Gene, and M———, who requested anonymity due to the nature of their work.

To my EOD brothers, whose input and feedback kept me in line: Josh Tyler, Landon Phillips, Dee Downing, John Ismay, Stephen Phillips, and Jason Knapp. To Matt Higgins, for the conceptual breakthrough. To Rick, for technical background. To Mick Cochrane, Janet McNally, and Eric Gansworth, the creative writing faculty at Canisius College, for camaraderie and commiseration. To Jim Holstun, who constantly filled my reading list. To Jessica Shearer, for getting me to finally read *Moby-Dick*, and to Jack Kenney for explaining what it means.

To US Navy Captain Jane Campbell, the Director of Defense Press Operations in the Office of the Assistant Secretary of Defense, who authorized interviews with active duty members of the military during the research phase of this book, and to all the local Public Affairs offices that arranged the interviews.

To my fellow writers who are also my first readers: Aaron Gwyn, Matt Gallagher, Matthew Hefti, Joydeep Roy-Bhattacharya, and Chris Chivers.

To my agent, Bob Mecoy, for perseverance, and to Cal Barksdale, who is the kind of editor every writer wants to have, a dispenser of tough love always in the service of the book's potential.

To my parents, for letting me escape to write in their house. To my children, who waited far longer than they anticipated for our family's traditional post-writing celebration vacation.

And finally, to my first and best reader, my primary investor, the love of my life, Jessie.

GLOSSARY

abaya (Arabic)—a large dress that leaves only the hands, feet, and face exposed

abu (Arabic)—father of, typical start of Al Qaeda nom de guerre

ACOG—advanced combat optical gunsight, popular among soldiers

Agha Sahib (Pashto, from the Arabic)—honorific for a military commander

albuyah nasiffah (Arabic)—literally, explosive container. Common expression for IED.

Allahu Akbar (Arabic)—God is great, the typical war cry of mujahideen

ANAL—ammonium nitrate and aluminum, a type of HME

ANCOP—Afghan National Civil Order of Police, an elite "surge" police unit, compared to regular Afghan National Police

ANFO—ammonium nitrate and fuel oil, a type of HME

ansar (Arabic)—helper, slang for foreign fighters in Kosovo in the late 1990s

AO—area of operations

ASP—ammunition supply point, a bunker or other storage area for ordnance

baba (Pashto)—casual honorific for a grandfatherly old man

BAT—biometric automated toolset, a camera and laptop system to enroll people in a biometrics database

BFM—basic fighter maneuvers

bingo—pilot slang for the minimum fuel necessary to land safely

Bone—slang for B-1 bomber

BUFF—big ugly fat fucker, slang for B-52s

CAG—Combat Applications Group, the official name for the Army's Delta Force

Caiman—a type of MRAP

casevac—casualty evacuation. In common usage, the transportation of patients via vehicles on the ground.

CEXC—Combined Explosives Exploitation Cell, the central crime lab in Baghdad and Bagram, where all IED evidence went

CIDNE—Combined Information Data Network Exchange, pronounced "Sydney." The main database for IED post blast reports.

CJSOTF—Combined Joint Special Operation Task Force, pronounced "See-Ja-So-Tiff." Multinational, and included members of all branches of the US military.

COIN—counterinsurgency

COP—combat outpost

CT—counterterrorism

DEVGRU—Naval Special Warfare Development Group, the official name for SEAL Team 6

dhabihah (Arabic)—in Islamic law, the approved process for slaughtering animals

DShK—large 12.7mm Soviet machine gun, the counterpart to the American .50 cal machine gun

Eagle—slang for F-15C fighter jets

emir (Arabic)—commander

EOD—explosive ordnance disposal

FN-SCAR—a new advanced rifle

FOB—forward operating base

fobbit—slang and derisive term for a soldier that never leaves the base, the subject of David Abrams's novel of the same name

golden hour—in the field of emergency medicine, the idea that a patient's chance of survival drastically increases if they enter surgery in less than sixty minutes

H&K 416—a rifle popular with special ops

habibi (Arabic)—someone you like, used between sweethearts or adults to children

helicoptera (Pashto)—helicopter

HESCO—large expandable containers made of fabric and wire mesh. When filled with dirt, they form effective barriers against bullets and detonations. HESCO is the name of the British company that produces the barriers.

HIIDES—handheld interagency identity detection equipment, a device that collects and matches iris scans, fingerprints, and photos. The precursor to the SEEK.

HME—home-made explosives

Hornet—slang for Navy F-18 fighter jets

ICOM—a type of radio often used by insurgents

Identity Operations—the US military's process for determining and confirming who people are

IED—improvised explosive device

ifranjiah (Arabic)—a board game, also known as tables, and similar to backgammon

imam (Arabic)—a worship leader in a mosque

Inshallah (Arabic)—literally, if Allah wills it. A very common phrase.

ISR—intelligence, surveillance, reconnaissance, often (but certainly not always) from a UAV

J2—the intelligence section of a joint military unit, comprising members of multiple branches of the military

JDAM—joint direct attack munition, a smart bomb

JERRV—joint EOD rapid response vehicle, pronounced "jerve"

JIEDDO—Joint IED Defeat Organization, pronounced "Jie-dough" or "Ji-E-dough"

JOC—joint operations center

JPEL—joint priority effects list, the consolidated list of targets

JSOC—Joint Special Operations Command

JTAC—joint terminal air controller, the airman or soldier on the ground responsible for calling in air strikes

KAF—Kandahar Air Field

kariz (Pashto)—underground canal and irrigation system, and a great place to hide IEDs

katibat (Arabic)—brigade, mujahideen term for an independent company of soldiers under a single commander

kuffar (Arabic)—infidels

laarey (Pashto)—truck, from the British

lala (Pashto)—older brother

LZ—landing zone

M4—the standard US combat rifle

M9—the standard 9mm pistol

malem (Arabic)—teacher

MC-12—a type of spy aircraft based upon the civilian Beechcraft King Air

medevac—medical evacuation. In common usage, the transportation of patients via aircraft, usually helicopters.

MICLIC—mine-clearing line charge

MIMID—a type of mine detector

mines (Pashto)—landmine, but used for any kind of IED

mIRC—Mardam-Bey Internet Relay Chat, a civilian Internet chat capability developed in 1995 but currently used by the US military to establish real-time secure chat rooms

MRAP—mine-resistant ambush protected vehicle, distinguished by the V-hull that deflects blast from below

muezzin (Arabic)—a man who sings the Call to Prayer from a mosque's minaret

mujahideen (Arabic)—those engaged in jihad. Singular is *mujahid.*

NAI—named area of interest

ODA—Operational Detachment Alpha, a Special Forces A-team trained to partner with indigenous forces

ODIN—Observe, Detect, Identify and Neutralize, a task force in Iraq and Afghanistan

OGA—other government agencies, sometimes a euphemism for the CIA, sometimes used when the speaker really doesn't know the specific intelligence agency (NSA, DIA, etc.) in question

Paladin—the counter-IED task force for Afghanistan

patu (Pashto)—a wool blanket, often worn as a coat or slept in

PID—positive ID

PKM—a common 7.62mm machine gun developed by the Soviets in the 1960s and used around the world

PX—post exchange, the military's department store

qalat (Pashto)—the standard multifamily housing unit in Afghanistan. Often made of mud. Originally from the Arabic, for castle.

queep—fighter pilot slang for paperwork and other bureaucratic trivialities

Raptor—slang for F-22 fighter jet

RG-31—a type of MRAP

ROZ—restricted operating zone. The airspace around the target of an operation, where all aircraft must check in for clearance by a JTAC or the air warden.

RPA—remotely piloted aircraft, the military's preferred term for Predators and other similar airframes

RTB—return to base

salaam (Arabic)—peace, a typical greeting, shortened from the more traditional *as-salaam-alaikum,* meaning "peace unto you"

salat (Arabic)—the obligation to pray five times a day, and one of the five pillars of the Islamic faith

SAM—surface-to-air missile

SEEK—secure electronic enrollment kit, a device that acquires a variety of biometric data. The replacement for the HIIDES.

shaheed (Arabic)—a martyr

shalwar kameez (Pashto)—the traditional dress of south Asia, baggy shirt and pants

shura (Arabic)—a council or consultation

SIGINT—signals intelligence

SITREP—situation report

SIM—subscriber identity module, the card in the back of a cell phone that uniquely identifies the phone number and account

snake eater—slang for anyone in special operations

SOCOM—Special Operations Command

Strike Eagle—call sign for F-15E fighter-bombers

T-38—a supersonic aircraft used to train fighter pilots

takfir (Arabic)—the process of excommunication, by declaring another Muslim to be *kafir,* an apostate

TAI—tactical area of interest

talib (Arabic)—a student. The Taliban movement identify themselves first as students of the Koran.

TECHDIV—the Navy's Technical EOD Division at Indian Head, Maryland

TEDAC—the FBI's Terrorist Explosive Device Analytical Center

terp—slang for interpreter

TIC—troops in contact, a popular term for a firefight

TOC—tactical operations center

toshak (Pashto)—sleeping mattress, placed directly on the floor

TOT—time on target

Troy—the counter-IED task force for Iraq

UAV—unmanned aerial vehicle, an older term for an RPA or drone

ummah (Arabic)—the congregation of all Muslims

UPT—undergraduate pilot training

Viper—slang for F-16 fighter jets

VOIP—voice over Internet protocol, a way to make voice phone calls using an Internet connection

NOTES

THIS BOOK IS PRIMARILY BASED on hundreds of hours of interviews with the principle characters. The names (and only the names) of Hayes, Gene Rich, and M——— have been changed, to protect their privacy. Notes listed below reference outside sources or background interviews with others.

PROLOGUE

1   **In the Name of Allah, the Most Gracious**: Nearly all correspondence, field reports, fatwas, and other communication among high-ranking jihadists begin with a prayer and invocation to Allah, to put the content of the message in context.

1   **fight and slay the pagans wherever ye find them, seize them, beleaguer them, and lie in wait for them in every stratagem**: The Sword Verse, Koran 9:5.

1   **fight them until there is no more oppression and all submission is made to Allah alone**: Koran 8:39.

1   **all who are able must kill them in every country upon the earth until all Muslims are free**: Fatwa by Al Qaeda leader Osama Bin Laden, dated February 23, 1998.

1   **thin wire leads**: All descriptions of physical IED evidence in the prologue is based on the Air Force report given to the family of Matt Schwartz.

1   *albuyah nasiffah***:** The most common Arabic term for IED, based upon background interview with Arab linguist.

3   **I want to hear, he said**: In a dozen years of doing demolitions all over the world, every explosives professional I have ever worked with gets quiet right before triggering the shot, in order to listen for fragments that may be hurtling toward your position.

3   **hump and flukes of Yunus's whale**: In Islam, Jonah (of the biblical story Jonah and the Whale) is known as the Prophet Yunus.

CHAPTER 1

12   **Fifteen of my fellow EOD brothers had died in the previous twelve months**: All EOD killed-in-action statistics are available at the EOD Memorial Foundation webpage (www.eodwarriorfoundation.org).

12   **a killed-in-action rate of 5 percent**: Based upon ten operational companies of approximately thirty EOD techs each, the in-country manning at the time, according to background interview with an EOD staff officer.

12   **over ten times the average for American soldiers at the time**: One-half percent killed in action rate based upon 418 killed (per iCasulaties.org) and a 2012 average of 90,000 troops, per the *Washington Post* https://www.washingtonpost.com/world/us-troops-inafghanistan/2014/09/30/45477364–490d-11e4-b72e-d60a9229cc10_graphic.html (retrieved on September 21, 2015).

CHAPTER 2

18   **he was off to Camp Snoopy**: A conversation with Dee Downing, who deployed with Schwartz at the time.

22   **one can read the Wikipedia article**: LAW 80: https://en.wikipedia.org/wiki/LAW_80 (retrieved on September 26, 2015).

24   **"They also serve, who only stand and wait"**: John Milton, "On His Blindness."

25   **bloodiest province in Afghanistan by a two-to-one margin**: See iCasulaties.org: http://icasualties.org/oef/ByProvince.aspx.

28   **The average age of a US soldier killed in Vietnam was twenty-three**: According to the Department of Defense's Combat Area Casualty File, the basis for the Vietnam Memorial wall, average age was 23.11 years.

28   **The average in Iraq and Afghanistan was twenty-six**: For Afghanistan figure, see James Dao and Andrew W. Lehren, "In Toll of 2,000, New Portrait of Afghan War," *New York Times*, August 21, 2012. For the Iraq figure, see Don Babwin and Tom Breen, "NC Soldier, 23, Was Last US Troop Killed in Iraq," *Associated Press*, December 18, 2011.

29   **Department of Defense's only port mortuary**: Air Force Port Mortuary Fact Sheet: http://www.mortuary.af.mil/library/factsheets/factsheet.asp?id=15361 (retrieved on September 21, 2015).

30   **A bum leg kept Zachary Fisher**: Biographic information via the Fisher House website: https://www.fisherhouse.org/about/our-history/zachary-fisher-builder-philanthropist-patriot/ (retrieved on September 21, 2015).

30   **There are now sixty-five such houses**: As per the Fisher House website: https://www.fisherhouse.org/programs/houses/ (retrieved on September 21, 2015).

CHAPTER 3

33   **On April 6, 2007, a 107-millimeter rocket**: Dates and basic information are found on the EOD Warrior Foundation website. Incident information via an interview with Josh Tyler, their tactical commander at the time.

37   **over two hundred thousand total at last count**: As per David Hood, "Patriot Guard Riders' Mission Expands," *Press-Enterprise*, March 31, 2014.

43   **Matt is the fourth of five**: CNN's interactive casualty website provides comprehensive geographical data (http://www.cnn.com/SPECIALS/war.casualties/).

46   **Lieutenant General James Kowalski**: Full biography available at the Air Force website: http://www.af.mil/AboutUs/Biographies/Display/tabid/225/Article/107901/lieutenant-general-james-m-kowalski.aspx (retrieved on September 22, 2015).

49   **The dead included three Arab operatives**: The full story on the drone strikes by Mark Hosenball and Chris Allbritton, "Exclusive: Senior Al Qaeda Figure Killed in Drone Strike," *Reuters*, January 19, 2012.

CHAPTER 4

51   **The Bomber is not the one wearing the suicide vest**: For two even-handed accounts of suicide bombers, see Robert Worth, "Mad

Bombers," *New York Times Magazine*, June 16, 2013, and Adam Lankford, *The Myth of Martyrdom: What Really Drives Suicide Bombers, Rampage Shooters, and Other Self-Destructive Killers* (New York: Palgrave Macmillan, 2013).

51 **Hassan Ghul**: Ghul's presence in Iraq was seen as the indicator of much scheming and planning. For example, Andrea Mitchell, "Al Qaeda Captive in Iraq Talking," *NBC Nightly News*, January 29, 2004.

52 **Invoking a *hadith*, a saying attributed to the Prophet Muhammed, Al Qaeda proscribed**: For essential background on Al Qaeda's application of *hadiths*, see the prologue of Ali H. Soufan, *The Black Banners: The Inside Story of 9/11 and the War Against al-Qaeda* (New York: W. W. Norton, 2011).

52 **al-Walid and al-Khattab:** See Brian Williams, "Unraveling the Links between the Middle East and Islamic Militants in Chechnya," *Central Asia–Caucus Institute Analyst,* February 12, 2003.

53 **We send them straight to Supermax**: See Mark Binelli, "Inside America's Toughest Prison," *New York Times Magazine*, March 26, 2015.

53 **Yahya Ayyash**: Ayyash took the al-Muhandis honorific himself and graduated from Birzeit University with an electrical engineering degree, fitting the profile well (as we'll see later in the book).

53 **for crafting shoe bombs and underwear bombs**: The previously mentioned al-Asiri, the maker of the underwear bomb, was named "The World's Most Dangerous Man" in the August 5, 2013, issue of *Time* magazine. I would beg to differ.

54 **The *Washington Post* says the first IED**: See Rick Atkinson, "The Single Most Effective Weapon Against Our Deployed Forces," *The Washington Post*, September 30, 2007.

54 **the greatest casualty-maker of the last fifteen years:** See the Operation Iraqi Freedom and Operation Enduring Freedom data at the Defense Casualty Analysis System at the Defense Manpower Data Center (www.dmdc.osd.mil).

55 **Yet as late as December of 2004**: Personal experience at Combat Skills Training at Fort Carson, Colorado.

55 **Warlock, Channel**: See Noah Shachtman, "The Secret History of Iraq's Invisible War," *Wired*, June 14, 2011. Also, good background at GlobalSecurity.org: http://www.globalsecurity.org/military/systems/ground/an-vlq-9.htm (retrieved on September 22, 2015).

58 **At that time there were 25,000 US troops in Afghanistan**: As per the *Washington Post* chart: https://www.washingtonpost.com/world/us-troops-in-afghanistan/2014/09/30/45477364–490d-11e4-b72e-d60a9229cc10_graphic.html (retrieved on September 25, 2015).

58 **Meanwhile, in the real state of Texas, there were over 54,000 police officers**: *2009 Crime in Texas Report*, see Chapter 7 (https://www.dps.texas.gov/crimereports/09/citCh7.pdf) (retrieved on September 25, 2015).

58 **The Engineer was back, and the IED-lite days were over**: The Taliban themselves indicate that IED knowledge was transferred between theaters after the Iraq War. "Arab and Iraqi mujahedin began visiting us, transferring the latest IED technology and suicide-bomber tactics they had learned in the Iraqi resistance during combat with US forces." (Sami Yousafzai, "The Taliban's Oral History of the Afghanistan War," *Newsweek*, September 25, 2009.)

58 **The total number of IEDs in Afghanistan doubled**: The best data come from JIEDDO, which can be found here: Anthony H. Cordesman and Jason Lemieux, "IED Metrics for Afghanistan January 2004–May 2010," Center for Strategic and International Studies, Washington, DC, July 21, 2010 (http://csis.org/files/publication/100722_IED_INCIDENTS_IN_AFGHANISTAN.pdf) (retrieved on September 25, 2015).

60 **slowly from the center to the periphery, according to the method of the oil slick**: Joseph-Simon Gallieni, *Neuf ans à Madagascar* (Paris: Librairie Hachette, 1908). See also Thomas Rid, "The Nineteenth Century Origins of Counterinsurgency Doctrine," *Journal of Strategic Studies*, vol. 33, no. 5, 727–58, October 2010.

60 **Victor Krulak called for ink blots**: Frank Everson Vandiver, *Shadows of Vietnam: Lyndon Johnson's Wars* (College Station, TX: Texas A&M University Press, 1997), 187.

62 **any public policy debate about the relative efficacy**: For a well-considered opposing view that highlights the failures of COIN throughout recent history, see Gian Gentile, *Wrong Turn: America's Deadly Embrace of Counterinsurgency* (New York: New Press, 2013).

62 **"The people are the prize."**: See General Stanley McChrystal's November 2009 COIN Training Guidance (http://usacac.army.mil/cac2/AIWFC/COIN/repository/COMISAF_COIN_Training_Guidance.pdf) (retrieved on September 25, 2015).

64 **904 US soldiers, sailors, airmen, and Marines died**: Consistently, the best casualty data is found at iCasulaties.org (http://icasualties. org/IRAQ/index.aspx) (retrieved on September 25, 2015).

64 **By mid-July 2008**: Again, see James Dao and Andrew W. Lehren.

65 **The killed-in-action rate, per capita**: See R. Lechner, G. Achatz, T. Hauer, H. G. Palm, A. Lieber, and C. Willy, "Patterns and Causes of Injuries in a Contemporary Combat Environment," *Unfallchirurg,* February 2010, 113(2):106–13. For an update that includes the Afghanistan Surge, this rate can be calculated by dividing the total number killed by the number deployed in theater. Using the Defense Casualty Analysis System, there were 4,411 American deaths in Iraq among 1.5 million who served in theater, for a rate of 0.3 percent. During the Afghanistan Surge, there were 1,500 deaths among 240,000 who served there, a rate of 0.625 percent.

65 **Left of Boom**: This language was so ubiquitous, Rick Atkinson used it as the title for his special report for the *Washington Post,* published September 30, 2007.

66 **We loved them like a gambler**: Researchers have theorized that we grew much more attached to our robots, to the point of not sending them into harm's way. See Julie Carpenter, "The Quiet Professional: An Investigation of U.S. Military Explosive Ordnance Disposal Personnel Interactions with Everyday Field Robots," PhD diss., University of Washington, Seattle, 2013. I would respectfully disagree.

66 **each of us sent our anointed surrogate into the arena to fight in single combat**: In *The Right Stuff,* Tom Wolfe reminds us that in the 1950s, single combat involved fighter pilots, astronauts, and Sputnik. See Tom Wolfe, *The Right Stuff* (New York: Picador, 1979), 97.

66 **We didn't lose a Marine EOD technician until 2004**: Again, see EOD Warrior Foundation (www.eodwarriorfoundation.com).

69 **mentioned only a handful of times in *The Black Banners***: See Soufan, pages 77, 112, 264, 327, 455, and 481.

69 **Early in *The Outpost***: See Jake Tapper, *The Outpost: An Untold Story of American Valor* (New York: Little, Brown, 2012), 42 and 48.

70 **The 2004 Duelfer Report on Weapons of Mass Destruction**: See volume 1, page 81.

70 **Gopal mentions the Engineer only once**: See Anand Gopal, *No Good Men Among the Living* (New York: Metropolitan Books, 2014), 207.

70 Omar Yousef Hussein: See Mark Kukis, *Voice from Iraq: A People's History, 2003–2009* (New York: Columbia University Press, 2011), 40.

70 accumulation of information on the Internet: While Al Qaeda did compile an *Encyclopedia of Jihad*, they did not believe in creating "virtual training camps" online. As a matter of educational philosophy, they preferred that skills be acquired through experience via hands-on training in each jihadist's home country. See Anne Stenersen, "'Bomb-making for Beginners': Inside an Al-Qaeda E-Learning Course," *Perspectives on Terrorism*, 2013, vol. 7, no. 1.

CHAPTER 5

79 His Arabic was barely passable: Interviews with Hayes and others on background, on the prevalence of Arabic among the Pashto speakers of Afghanistan.

79 shabby box of Chinese batteries: Personal experience collecting evidence and examining reports on completed Afghan IEDs.

79 Sunlight streamed in the open windows: To get a sense of the atmospherics of daily life in Afghanistan, see Ben Anderson's films *The Battle for Marjah* and *This Is What Winning Looks Like*.

80 a small round container, plastic and rubber: A PMN landmine, found throughout the Panjwe and Arghandab Districts. For more information, see page 20 of the Afghanistan Unexploded Ordnance Identification Guide given to US soldiers (http://www.jmu.edu/cisr/research/OIG/Afghanistan/low%20res/08-Landmine.pdf) (retrieved on September 25, 2015).

81 The Great Satan is always searching for a new land of the *ummah* to invade: For an example of this perspective, see Osama Bin Laden's November 2002 open letter to America (http://www.theguardian.com/world/2002/nov/24/theobserver) (retrieved on September 25, 2015).

84 Solesbee and Hamski and six Pathfinders from Fox Company: The six soldiers are First Lieutenant Runkle, Staff Sergeant Mills, Staff Sergeant Osman, Sergeant Ramosvelazquez, Sergeant Bohall, and Specialist Patton (http://www.clarksvilleonline.com/2011/05/29/six-101st-airborne-division-soldiers-killed-in-afghanistan/)(retrieved on September 25, 2015).

91 an expandable metal detector called a MIMID: The MIMID is made by the Schiebel company: https://www.schiebel.net/Products/Mine-Detection-Systems/MIMID/Introduction.aspx (retrieved on September 25, 2015).

CHAPTER 6

102 The NATO Role 3 hospital at the Kandahar Airfield: The hospital was famous throughout Afghanistan for having an extremely high survival rate; between 95 percent and 98 percent of all soldiers who arrived with a pulse lived. For an excellent report on the hospital at the time Fye was treated, see Corinne Reilly, "A Chance in Hell," *The Virginian Pilot*, July 31, 2011 (http://hamptonroads.com/2011/07/chance-hell-part-one-inside-combat-hospital-afghanistan) (retrieved on September 25, 2015).

CHAPTER 7

108 The calibration knobs on the pins could be subtly adjusted: This process is known as the Ilizarov Technique. For a more in-depth discussion of the method and its challenges, see D. Paley, "Problems, Obstacles, and Complications of Limb Lengthening by the Ilizarov Technique," *Clinical Orthopaedics and Related Research*, 1990 Jan (250): 81–104.

108 only 5.6 centimeters: Ibid.

108 a number of medical complications to the frame's use: For infection complications, see Aik Saw, Yp Chua, Golam Hossain, and Subir Sengupta, "Rates of Pin Site Infection During Distraction Osteogenesis Based on Monthly Observations: A Pilot Study," *Journal of Orthopaedic Surgery*, 2012; 20(2):181–4.

109 Surgeons were so inundated with patients that: See Chad Krueger, Joseph Wenke, and James Ficke, "Ten Years at War: Comprehensive Analysis of Amputation Trends," *Journal of Trauma and Acute Care Surgery*, December 2012; 73(6 Suppl 5):S438–44.

109 Compared to Iraq, the average American soldier in Afghanistan had roughly double the chance of losing a limb: All statistics in this paragraph, except where noted below, from Hannah Fisher, "U.S. Military Casualty Statistics: Operation New Dawn, Operation

Iraqi Freedom, and Operation Enduring Freedom," *Congressional Research Service,* February 5, 2013.

109 German researchers found: See Lechner, et al.

109 At the height of the fighting seasons: See Fisher's Congressional Research Report.

110 The wounded to killed ratio in World War II was 2.1: See same Defense Casualty Analysis System and iCasulaties.org for Afghanistan and Iraq. All ratios consider battlefield deaths compared to battlefield wounded. For World War II, an additional 30,000 missing are added to the deaths category, since they constituted such a large percentage of the lost.

110 In World War II, 7 percent of soldiers: Per Department of Veterans Affairs paper titled "Traumatic Amputation and Prosthetics," May 2002: http://www.publichealth.va.gov/docs/vhi/traumatic_amputation.pdf (retrieved on October 1, 2015).

110 multiple amputation rate also jumped to 30 percent: See Krueger, et al.

110 The greatest percentage of amputations, 42 percent of the total: Ibid.

112 HO is frustrating because: For clinical background on HO, see Ted Melcer, Brian Belnap, Jay Walker, Paula Konoske, and Michael Galarneau, "Heterotopic Ossification in Combat Amputees from Afghanistan and Iraq Wars: Five Case Histories and Results from a Small Series of Patients," *Journal of Rehabilitation Research and Development,* 2011; 48(1):1–12.

112 HO was previously classified as "infrequent," but the latest research: See Benjamin Potter, Jonathan Forsberg, Thomas Davis, Korboi Evans, Jason Hawksworth, Doug Tadaki, Trevor Brown, Nicole Crane, Travis Burns, Frederick O'Brien, and Eric Elster, "Heterotopic Ossification Following Traumatic and Combat-Related Amputations. Prevalence, Risk Factors, and Preliminary Results of Excision," *The Journal of Bone and Joint Surgery, American Volume,* March 2007, 89(3):476–86.

CHAPTER 8

130 small entrance known as the Hero's Highway: The hospital in Balad closed down in 2011. For a photo of the flag-draped tent, and a brief retrospective, see http://www.usmedicine.com/agencies/

department-of-defense-dod/end-of-era-us-military-dismantles-its-hospitals-in-iraq/ (retrieved on September 26, 2015).

132 **Whipples were first performed in Europe in the nineteenth century**: For clinical background, see Chandrakanth Are, Mashaal Dhir, and Lavanya Ravipati, "History of Pancreaticoduodenectomy: Early Misconceptions, Initial Milestones and the Pioneers," *HPB (Oxford)*, June 2011, 13(6):377–384.

135 **A 2007 *Washington Post* investigation revealed a system**: Dana Priest and Anne Hull, "Soldiers Face Neglect, Frustration at Army's Top Medical Facility," *The Washington Post*, February 18, 2007.

135 **One of the guys OD'd and died**: Ibid.

137 **The trip was sponsored by World TEAM Sports**: This bike trip was not a one-off; the organization continues to sponsor events around the country (http://worldteamsports.org/).

138 **Jukes would go on to climb 20,075-foot Lobuche**: See Brian Mockenhaupt, "The Other Side of the Mountain," *Outside*, March 2011. For a review of the film, see Jeanette Catsoulis, "Therapy from a Mountaintop," *New York Times*, November 1, 2012.

138 **In October he requested that his left leg be removed**: In some ways, Frost's story is the more typical one. While only 15 percent of Iraq and Afghanistan combat-related amputations occur after twelve weeks (Daniel Stinner, Travis Burns, Kevin Kirk, Charles Scoville, James Ficke, and Joseph Hsu, "Prevalence of Late Amputations During the Current Conflicts in Afghanistan and Iraq," *Military Medicine*, December 2010; 175(12):1027–9), medical studies have also found that patients who choose to have their limbs removed, rather than salvaged, have better long-term outcomes (William Doukas, Roman Hayda, Michael Frisch, Romney Anderson, Michael Mazurek, and James Ficke, "The Military Extremity Trauma Amputation/Limb Salvage (METALS) Study: Outcomes of Amputation Versus Limb Salvage Following Major Lower-Extremity Trauma," *Journal of Bone and Joint Surgery, American Volume*, January 16, 2013; 95(2):138–45).

141 **The holy grail for the industry was an implantable version**: Swedish scientists would later attain this standard: Max Ortiz-Catalan, Bo Hakansson, and Rickard Branemark, "An Osseointegrated Human-Machine Gateway for Long-Term Sensory Feedback and Motor Control of Artificial Limbs," *Science Translational Medicine*, October 8, 2014.

CHAPTER 9

145 On September 11, 2001, hundreds of military EOD technicians: Per background interviews with EOD technicians assigned to work Secret Service duty at the time.

145 nearly 10 percent of the total active duty EOD force: This actually says more about how small the joint EOD force was (only about 2,500 total enlisted operators) prior to 9/11. To fight the wars that followed, the force would more than triple in size.

145 the first medal for heroism earned by an EOD tech: For the entire story of Prewitt on that day, see Stephen Phillips, "A Remembrance of 9/11," *Small Wars Journal*, September 11, 2010.

147 on his left Dr. Doug Owsley: For a profile of Dr. Owsley, see Aaron Elkina, "35 Who Made a Difference: Douglas Owsley," *Smithsonian. com*, November 1, 2005.

147 Maude was a Vietnam veteran, the highest-ranking officer to die at the Pentagon on 9/11: For the official obituary of Lieutenant General Maude, see http://www.nytimes.com/2001/09/22/us/ lt-gen-timothy-l-maude-53-an-army-deputy-chief-of-staff.html (retrieved on September 28, 2015). The last officer of similar rank to die by enemy action was Lieutenant General Simon Bolivar Buckner Jr., the son of Confederate General Buckner, who died after leading the invasion of Okinawa in 1945.

149 Brueghel, Bosch: Of Brueghel, see *The Triumph of Death* and *The Fall of the Rebel Angels*. Of Bosch, see especially *The Last Judgement* and the last panel of the triptych *The Garden of Earthly Delights*.

150 Brassfield-Mora: The *Military Times* series of newspapers keeps small stories of deceased soldiers at http://thefallen.militarytimes. com/.

151 At the height of the Iraq Surge, an average of 175 such incidents: *The Long War Journal* keeps a useful archive of IED statistics in Iraq: http://www.longwarjournal.org/archives/2007/12/iraq_by_the_ numbers.php.

152 The storage area at TEDAC looks like the warehouse: For a peek inside TEDAC, see Del Quinten Wilbur, "Inside the FBI's Giant Bomb Warehouse," *Bloomberg Business*, June 26, 2014.

157 Special Forces only began to send the same units back to the same Afghan villages in 2010: See Linda Robinson, *One Hundred Victories: Special Ops and the Future of American Warfare* (New York: Public Affairs, 2013), 51.

158 ASP 3: Wikileaks is full of reports of ordnance stolen from ASP 3 in Samarra, for example: https://wardiaries.wikileaks.org/id/ DBE88E0D-1072–47D4-B994-AE67FAD2C7AF/ (retrieved on September 28, 2015).

CHAPTER 10

167 When the Taliban ordered a string of assassinations in the summer of 2011: See Julian Borger, "Afghanistan Government Under Threat After Second Assassination in a Week," *The Guardian,* July 18, 2011, and Alyssa J. Rubin, "Assassination Deals Blow to Peace Process in Afghanistan," *New York Times*, September 20, 2011. Also, Linda Robinson's *One Hundred Victories,* page 61.

168 Talon robots cost only $100,000: They cost much more at the start of the war, $250,000 each. But by the end of Iraq and Afghanistan, bulk orders cut the price significantly. According to the latest September 2015 brochure, the cost is even lower, $60,000.

168 Captain Rob Yllescas: See Tapper, page 379. ". . . Yllescas must have been bit by a radio-controlled IED. He'd been singled out and targeted."

168 Casualties during the Iraq Surge leapt 20 percent for Green Berets: See the memorial wall at the Green Beret Foundation: http://www.greenberetfoundation.org/memorial-wall/ (retrieved on September 28, 2015).

168 doubled for EOD techs: See memorial wall at the EOD Warrior Foundation: http://www.eodwarriorfoundation.org/eod-memorial (retrieved on September 28, 2015).

168 SEAL teams didn't lose a single man in Iraq until 2006: See the memorial at the Navy SEAL Foundation: http://www.navysealfoundation.org/about-the-seals/our-fallen-heroes/ (retrieved on September 28, 2015).

172 *Ad Dawla al Islamiyya fin al-Iraq wa al-Sham:* The Islamic State (also known as ISIS) began as the Al Anbar arm of Al Qaeda in Iraq (see Michael Weiss and Hassan Hassan, *ISIS: Inside the Army of Terror* (New York: Regan Arts, 2015)). It evolved through several names as leaders were killed during the Iraqi Surge, and eventually broke from central Al Qaeda over disputes concerning (among other things) the doctrine of killing civilians in "martyrdom" attacks. There is evidence that, in his last years, Osama Bin Laden greatly

regretted the civilian deaths Al Qaeda had inflicted, and had come
to see them as counterproductive (see especially, Mark Bowden, *The
Finish: The Killing of Osama Bin Laden* (New York: Atlantic Monthly
Press, 2012) and Don Rassler, et al, "Letters from Abbottabad: Bin
Laden Sidelined?" *Combating Terrorism Center at West Point*, May 3,
2012).

172 **"You do not care for the widows and orphans of our slain brothers**: Ibid.

172 **"You have lost your focus on the Great Satan brought near**: Ibid.

173 **the warheads all wrapped in aluminum foil**: Background interviews with EOD techs who worked in Tikrit in 2008. They found
many rocket warheads wrapped in aluminum foil.

173 **"We wrap our fingers in tape**: A good demonstration of Iraqi insurgent bomb building procedures can be found in Molly Bingham
(Director) and Steve Connors (Director), *Meeting Resistance* [doc-
umentary], United States: Nine Lives Documentary Productions,
2007.

173 **Battle of Manhattan**: Osama Bin Laden's term for the attacks of
9/11.

173 **"We have not received the remote detonators**: Osama Bin Laden,
when he was a mujahideen leader in Afghanistan in the 1980s, received
remote detonators and surface-to-air missiles from the United States.
See George Crile, *Charlie Wilson's War: The Extraordinary Story of
the Largest Covert Operation in History* (New York: Atlantic Monthly
Press, 2003).

173 **you bring those wishing to be *shaheed* through Syria**: Background
interviews with US military intelligence officers, on the suicide
bomber pipeline and procedures in western Iraq. The two methods
of coercion described here, enticement and shame, were very common. For additional suicide bomber background, see Lankford.

174 **black banners of Khurasan**: Per Soufan, Al Qaeda saw itself as
the champion of Khurasan, a historical designation for an area that
now encompasses large portions of Afghanistan, Pakistan, Iran,
Uzbekistan, Tajikstan, and Turkmenistan.

176 **The final report would determine that Fye was simply unlucky**:
Provided to me courtesy of Fye. The internal report was filed by the
EOD team leader who did the post-blast investigation of Fye's incident, and was communicated via typical SITREP (situation report)
channels.

CHAPTER 11

182 They were contractors: As predicted by P. W. Singer in *Corporate Warriors: The Rise of the Privatized Military Industry* (Ithaca: Cornell University Press, 2003).

182 French police began tabulating the lengths of forearms: The father of French biometrics was Alphonse Bertillon, who, besides measuring noses and arms, invented the mug shot, and in the early twentieth century, wrote influential papers on the science of fingerprinting.

182 Scotland Yard adopted fingerprinting in 1901: This system, known as the Henry Classification System, was widely used by all police departments until the 1990s.

183 Conducting a census of the population is a classic counterinsurgency strategy: General David Petraeus's much-praised counterinsurgency manual *Counterinsurgency, Field Manual 3–24* (Washington, DC: Department of the Army, December 2006), has a section on census operations. See page 3–29: "In some cases, it may be necessary for Soldiers and Marines to go door to door and collect census data themselves." For additional historical background, see Michael S. Shrout, "Biometrically Supported Census Operations as a Population Control Measure in Counterinsurgency," School of Advanced Military Studies (Fort Leavenworth, Kansas: United States Army Command and Staff College).

184 unlike the HIIDE, FBI standard nail-to-nail rolled fingerprints: It took years for the DoD's biometrics system to conform to the standard system used by other government agencies. See, for example: United States Government Accountability Office, *GAO-11–276 Defense Biometrics: DoD Can Better Conform to Standards and Share Biometrics Information with Federal Agencies*, March 2011.

186 Afghanistan's naming convention: For a longer treatment of challenges with Afghanistan's use of names, see Joseph Goldstein, "For Afghans, Name and Birthdate Census Questions Are Not So Simple," *New York Times*, December 10, 2014.

190 Army Colonel A. T. Ball, and he said their mission was "sensor-to-shooter" fusion: In September of 2007, Colonel Ball wrote his own public affairs media release on the mission of Task Force-ODIN: https://www.dvidshub.net/news/12463/task-force-odin-using-innovative-technology-support-ground-forces#.VgVaHqSmDIU (retrieved on September 28, 2015).

191 She read Dick Couch and Linda Robinson: Hard to find a better introduction to the world of Special Forces. See Dick Couch, *Chosen Soldier: The Making of a Special Forces Warrior* (New York: Crown, 2007), and Linda Robinson, *Masters of Chaos: The Secret History of the Special Forces* (New York: Public Affairs, 2005).

191 Soliman also read *War Torn*: Tad Bartimus, Denby Fawcett, Jurate Kazickas, Edith Lederer, Ann Bryan Mariano, Anne Morrissy Merick, Laura Palmer, Kate Webb, and Tracy Wood, *War Torn: Stories of War from the Women Reporters Who Covered Vietnam* (New York: Random House, 2002).

192 The 9/11 Commission Report had recommended: National Commission on Terrorist Attacks Upon the United States, *The 9/11 Commission Report* (New York: W.W. Norton and Company, 2004), pages 385–89.

195 He gestured at the Tea Boy huddled: The exploitation of Tea Boys (also called Dancing Boys) is known as *bacha bazi*, or "boy play" in Pashto, and it has a long and ignoble tradition. To learn more, see Joseph Goldstein, "U.S. Soldiers Told to Ignore Sexual Abuse of Boy by Afghan Allies," *New York Times*, September 20, 2015, and Ben Anderson (Director), *This Is What Winning Looks Like* [documentary], United States: VICE Media, 2013.

196 Say the *Ayatul Kursi* to yourself: The Throne Verse is the 255th verse of the second chapter of the Koran. It is often recited in times of trouble or distress. For a typical example, see Hassan Blasim, *The Corpse Exhibition and Other Stories of Iraq* (New York: Penguin, 2013), 160.

196 She is Nuristani, maybe, or one of Alexander's Greeks: The people of Nuristan, in far northeastern Afghanistan, have red hair and blue eyes, and legends persist that they are descended from Greeks left behind after Alexander the Great's invasion. In *The Outpost* (page 49), Jake Tapper describes this thought as "a long-discredited myth."

198 Dostum put the foot soldiers of his enemies in shipping containers and forgot about them: General Dostum has a long history of such atrocities, including one incident, while he was on the CIA payroll, known as the Dasht-i-Leili Massacre. See James Risen, "U.S. Inaction Seen After Taliban P.O.W.'s Died," *New York Times*, July 10, 2009.

199 an old dry *kariz* maybe: A common tactic. See Robinson, *One Hundred Victories*, page 40.

200 **Afghan Arab movement founded by Abdullah Azzam**: The best background I know on the roots of modern jihad is Steve Coll, *Ghost Wars: The Secret History of the CIA, Afghanistan, and Bin Laden, From the Soviet Invasion to September 10, 2001* (New York: Penguin, 2004).

200 **Khalid Sheikh Mohammed, received a degree in mechanical engineering**: See 9/11 Commission Report, page 146.

201 **his wiring adaptation changed with it**: Personal experience while working in Iraq.

202 **When he uploads a new circuit design to a Chinese specialty manufacturing company**: Background interviews with analysts who worked in CEXC in Iraq and Afghanistan.

203 **sung by Syrian insurgents**: An excellent overview of a few *katibats* in Syria that named themselves for Chechen heroes can be found at this quasi-jihadist news site: http://www.esinislam.com/Articles201306/ WritersArticles_MarkazKavkaz_0603htm#AllahIsGreat (retrieved on September 28, 2015).

203 **In the midst of the worst Russian artillery bombardment**: The best first-person jihadist account of the 1990s wars in Grozny that I have found is Aukai Collins, *My Jihad* (New York: Pocket Star Books, 2002).

204 **Her 2011 article, "Al Qaeda Foot Soldiers**: Anne Stenersen, "Al Qaeda's Foot Soldiers: A Study of the Biographies of Foreign Fighters Killed in Afghanistan and Pakistan Between 2002 and 2006," *Studies in Conflict & Terrorism*, 2011 (34):171–98.

205 **It was just Abu Abdul Raham al-Muhajir**: As previously mentioned, noted a few times in Soufan's *The Black Banners*.

205 **In his Wikipedia profile**: Filed under his given name, rather than his Al Qaeda *hadith* alias. See https://en.wikipedia.org/wiki/Mushin_ Musa_Matwalli_Atwah (retrieved on September 29, 2015).

205 **I eventually found Midhat Mursi**: See Stenersen, "'Bomb-making for Beginners': Inside an Al-Qaeda E-Learning Course."

205 **some misreported**: See, for example, Brian Ross and Habibullah Khan, "U.S. Strike Killed Al Qaeda Bomb Maker," *ABC News*, January 18, 2006, and Dan Darling, "Al Qaeda's Mad Scientist: The Significance of Abu Khabab's Death," *The Weekly Standard*, January 19, 2006.

205 **some correct**: See, among others, Jeffery Simon, "Al-Qaida Confirms Death of Poisons Expert in Pakistan," *The Guardian*, August 3, 2008,

and Aamir Latif, "A Key al Qaeda Bomber Maker Is Killed (Again),"
U.S. News & World Report, July 29, 2008.

205 NBC says the FBI had used the wrong photo: See Lisa Meyers,
"U.S. Post Wrong Photo of 'al-Qaida Operative,'" *NBC News,* January 6,
2006 (http://www.nbcnews.com/id/11042211/#.VgWb0aSmDIU)
(retrieved on September 29, 2015).

206 a gait recognition algorithm: A few months after 9/11, the
Department of Defense started a program called Total Information
Awareness. According to a report in the *New Yorker* (Ryan Lizza,
"State of Deception," *New Yorker,* December 16, 2013), "The T.I.A.
system was intended to collect information about the faces, fingerprints, irises, and even the gait of suspicious people." The program
was shut down in 2003.

209 Their remains were so intermingled: You can see a photo at the
macabre but very useful findagrave.com: http://www.findagrave.
com/cgi-bin/fg.cgi?page=pv&GRid=10540884&PIpi=3168943
(retrieved on September 29, 2015).

**211 Killing him would be the easy part, it was finding him that was
hard**: A sentiment shared by the Special Forces soldiers in Linda
Robinson's *One Hundred Victories* (see page 25).

CHAPTER 12

213 Gary Shroen had been professionally attached: For the full story,
see Gary Shroen, *First In: An Insider's Account of How the CIA
Spearheaded the War on Terror in Afghanistan* (New York: Presidio
Press, 2005).

215 a Predator pilot finished a cup of coffee and did just that: Peter
Singer explores this new idea of "going to war" in the age of drones
in P. W. Singer, *Wired For War: The Robotics Revolutions and Conflict
in the 21st Century* (New York: Penguin Books, 2009), page 327.

216 Drone was a term used by those who don't like them: "A remotely
piloted aircraft—a Predator or a Reaper—is not a drone, Air Force
officers will tell you, and to call it that is practically like spitting on
their shoes." Aram Roston, "The 'D' Word: What to Call a UAV,"
DefenseNews.com, March 26, 2013.

224 Good pilots practice identifying what will kill them first: In *The
Right Stuff,* Wolfe explains this phenomenon with Saint-Exupéry
("The field of consciousness is very small") and notes the comfort

it brings. "I've been here before! And I am immune! I don't get into corners I can't get out of!" See Wolfe, page 270.

226 **This is why it was better to be deployed**: Even Matt Martin, whose book serves as a consistent pitch for Predators, celebrates being closer to the war. "Pilots or mission commanders at Nellis lacked the capability to drive across base and personally interact with army teams, QRFs [quick reaction forces], JTACs, and other commanders." (See page 230 of Matt Martin, *Predator: The Remote-Control Air War over Iraq and Afghanistan: A Pilot's Story* (Minneapolis: Zenith Press, 2010).)

227 **They were blurring, bad now**: In a 2013 study, researchers found that drone pilots experienced anxiety, depression, and post-traumatic stress rates equal to those of pilots of manned aircraft, and that the source of the stress was a combination of battlefield influences and scheduling/workflow dynamics, the constant compartmentalization and dissonance between flying and home life. Jean Otto and Bryant Weber, "Mental Health Diagnosis and Counseling among Pilots of Remotely Piloted Aircraft in the United States Air Force," *Medical Surveillance Monthly Report, Armed Forces Health Surveillance Center* 20, no. 3 (March 2013).

228 **Slim Pickens in a B-52**: Stanley Kubrick (Director), *Dr. Strangelove or: How I Learned to Stop Worrying and Love the Bomb,* United States: Columbia Pictures, 1964.

228 **Saddam actually shot down a Predator the morning of 9/11**: This story ran at 7:50 a.m. on 9/11: http://usatoday30.usatoday.com/news/world/2001/09/11/iraq.htm (retrieved on September 29, 2015).

231 **Prayer is better than sleep**: From the Muslim Call to Prayer, during *fajar*, the first prayer of the day.

231 **He just could not update it regularly enough**: According to Stenersen ("'Bomb-making for Beginners': Inside an Al-Qaeda E-Learning Course"), most jihadist online electronics courses fail because of "their reliance on one or very few online instructors who are not always able to contribute on a regular basis, causing the interest to ebb away."

CHAPTER 13

233 **FREEDOM, ALPHA ROMEO, do you have visual on the Objective**: Nearly all military communications via radio use the same

format: Receiver, Sender, Message. For example, in this case, ALPHA
ROMEO is asking FREEDOM whether they can see the objective.

241 **Task Force 373**: For more on TF 373, see Nick Davies, "Afghanistan
War Logs: Task Force 373—Special Forces Hunting Top Taliban,"
The Guardian, July 25, 2010.

242 *l'as Adolphe Pégoud:* The first-ever fighter ace, Pégoud had at least
six air-to-air kills in World War I. In 1915, at the age of twenty-six,
he was shot down by a German pilot and killed. He had an incredi-
ble moustache.

CHAPTER 14

260 **A 2010 study by George Washington University**: See Steven L.
Schooner and Collin D. Swan, "Dead Contractors: The Un-Examined
Effect of Surrogates on the Public's Casualty Sensitivity," *Journal of
National Security Law & Policy*, April 2012.

261 **A 2013 study by the RAND Corporation**: See Molly Dunigan,
et al, *Out of the Shadows: The Health and Well-Being of Private
Contractors Working in Conflict Environments* (Washington: RAND
Corporation, 2013).

264 **Be polite, be professional, have a plan to kill everybody you meet**:
See page 313 of Tom Ricks, *Fiasco: The American Military Adventure
in Iraq* (New York: Penguin, 2006).

271 **The Armed Forces of the United States are here to seek justice
for our dead**: For the full leaflet verbiage, see http://www.cnn.
com/2001/US/10/18/ret.flyers/ (retrieved on September 29, 2015).

CHAPTER 15

281 **scholarship at her alma mater**: "On Sept. 8 . . . Soliman created
a $25,000 endowment in honor of her former mentor, Dr. Wils
Cooley, professor emeritus in the Lane Department of Computer
Science and Electrical Engineering. The endowment will provide
scholarship assistance to engineering students interested in studying abroad." See http://wvutoday.wvu.edu/n/2011/09/09/finding-a-
way-to-make-the-best-better-endowed-scholarship-honors-former-
mentor (retrieved on September 30, 2015).

283 **The computer doesn't need practice, so the safer system is put
aside for humans to hand fly**: During the Mercury program, the

new astronauts, all former fighter pilots, colluded to refer to the capsule as a "spacecraft" in the hopes that NASA would let them, rather than the computer, fly the machine. See Wolfe, page 152.

293 **Alive Day**: In the modern military, an Alive Day is the day one is blown up but lives.

293 **John rolls himself into a stall**: John's name has been changed to protect his privacy.

297 **there were 184 names on the wall**: All EOD casualty statistics available via the EOD Warrior Foundation (www.eodwarriorfoundation. org).

302 **Major General Timothy Byers**: Full biography available here: http:// www.af.mil/AboutUs/Biographies/Display/tabid/225/Article/108036/ major-general-timothy-a-byers.aspx (retrieved on October 1, 2015).

Selected Bibliography and Reading List

Ackerman, Elliot. *Green on Blue.* New York: Scribner, 2015.

Anderson, Ben. *Battle of Marjah.* Documentary. Directed by Ben Anderson. 2010. United States: HBO Documentary Films.

————. *This Is What Winning Looks Like.* Documentary. Directed by Ben Anderson. 2013. United States: VICE Media.

Badkhen, Anna. *Peace Meals: Candy-Wrapped Kalashnikovs and Other War Stories.* New York: Free Press, 2010.

Blasim, Hassan. *Corpse Exhibition: And Other Stories of Iraq.* New York: Penguin, 2014.

Bonenberger, Adrian. *Afghan Post: One Soldier's Correspondence from America's Forgotten War.* Philadelphia: The Head & The Hand Press, 2014.

Bowden, Mark. *The Finish: The Killing of Osama Bin Laden.* New York: Atlantic Monthly Press, 2012.

Coll, Steve. *Ghost Wars: The Secret History of the CIA, Afghanistan, and Bin Laden, From the Soviet Invasion to September 10, 2001.* New York: Penguin, 2004.

Collins, Aukai. *My Jihad.* New York: Pocket Star Books, 2002.

Crile, George. *Charlie Wilson's War: The Extraordinary Story of the Largest Covert Operation in History.* New York: Atlantic Monthly Press, 2003.

Crumpton, Henry. *The Art of Intelligence: Lessons from a Life in the CIA's Clandestine Service.* New York: Penguin, 2013.

Dao, James, and Andrew W. Lehren. "In Toll of 2,000, New Portrait of Afghan War," *New York Times,* August 21, 2012.

Department of the Army. *Counterinsurgency, Field Manual 3–24.* Washington, DC: December 2006.

Duelfer, Charles. "Comprehensive Report of the Special Adviser to the DCI on Iraq's WMD," vol. I (September 30, 2004).

Fisher, Hannah. "U.S. Military Casualty Statistics: Operation New Dawn, Operation Iraqi Freedom, and Operation Enduring Freedom." *Congressional Research Service* (February 5, 2013).

Gallieni, Joseph-Simon. *Neuf ans a Madagascar*. Paris: Librairie Hachette, 1908.

Gentile, Gian. *Wrong Turn: America's Deadly Embrace of Counterinsurgency*. New York: The New Press, 2013.

Gopal, Anand. *No Good Men Among the Living*. New York: Metropolitan Books, 2014.

Haldeman, Joe. *The Forever War*. New York: St. Martin's Press, 1974.

Halloran, Colin. *Shortly Thereafter*. Charlotte, NC: Main Street Rag Publishing, 2012.

Junger, Sebastian. *War*. New York: Twelve, 2010.

Kapuscinski, Ryszard. *Another Day of Life*. New York: Houghton Mifflin Harcourt, 1987.

Kukis, Mark. *Voice from Iraq: A People's History, 2003–2009*. New York: Columbia University Press, 2011.

Lankford, Adam. *The Myth of Martyrdom: What Really Drives Suicide Bombers, Rampage Shooters, and Other Self-Destructive Killers*. New York: Palgrave Macmillan, 2013.

Lerner, Alexander, et al. *Armed Conflict Injuries to the Extremities: A Treatment Manual*. New York: Springer, 2011.

Lindqvist, Sven. *The Myth of Wu Tao-Tzu*. London: Granta Books, 2014.

Manguso, Sarah. *Ongoingness: The End of a Diary*. Minneapolis, MN: Greywolf Press, 2015.

Martin, Matt. *Predator: The Remote-Control Air War over Iraq and Afghanistan: A Pilot's Story*. Minneapolis, MN: Zenith Press, 2010.

Maurer, Kevin. *Gentlemen Bastards: On the Ground in Afghanistan with America's Elite Special Forces*. New York: Berkley Books, 2012.

Melville, Herman. *Moby-Dick; or, The Whale*. New York: Harper & Brothers, 1851.

National Commission on Terrorist Attacks upon the United States. *The 9/11 Commission Report*. New York: W. W. Norton, 2004.

Omar, Qais Akbar. *A Fort of Nine Towers: An Afghan Family Story*. New York: Farrar, Straus and Giroux, 2013.

Owen, Mark and Kevin Maurer. *No Easy Day: The Firsthand Account of the Mission that Killed Osama Bin Laden*. New York: Dutton, 2012.

Prince, Erik. *Civilian Warriors: The Inside Story of Blackwater and the Unsung Heroes of the War on Terror*. New York: Portfolio, 2013.

Ricks, Thomas E. *Fiasco: The American Military Adventure in Iraq*. New York: Penguin, 2006.

———. *The Gamble: General Petraeus and the American Military Adventure in Iraq.* New York: Penguin, 2009.

Rid, Thomas. "The Nineteenth Century Origins of Counterinsurgency Doctrine." *The Journal of Strategic Studies* 33, no. 5 (2010), 727–58.

Robinson, Linda. *One Hundred Victories: Special Ops and the Future of American Warfare.* New York: Public Affairs, 2013.

Sageman, Marc. *Understanding Terror Networks.* Philadelphia, PA: University of Pennsylvania Press, 2004.

Shachtman, Noah. "The Secret History of Iraq's Invisible War." *Wired,* last modified on June 14, 2011. http://www.wired.com/2011/06/iraqs-invisible-war/.

Shroen, Gary. *First In: An Insider's Account of How the CIA Spearheaded the War on Terror in Afghanistan.* New York: Presidio Press, 2005.

Singer, P. W. *Corporate Warriors: The Rise of the Privatized Military Industry.* Ithaca: Cornell University Press, 2003.

———. *Wired for War: The Robotics Revolutions and Conflict in the 21st Century.* New York: Penguin, 2009.

Soufan, Ali H. *The Black Banners: The Inside Story of 9/11 and the War Against al-Qaeda.* New York: W. W. Norton, 2011.

Stanton, Doug. *Horse Soldiers: The Extraordinary Story of a Band of US Soldiers Who Rode to Victory in Afghanistan.* New York: Scribner, 2009.

Stenersen, Anne. "Al Qaeda's Foot Soldiers: A Study of the Biographies of Foreign Fighters Killed in Afghanistan and Pakistan Between 2002 and 2006." *Studies in Conflict & Terrorism* (2011) 34:171–198.

———. "'Bomb-making for Beginners': Inside an Al-Qaeda E-Learning Course." *Perspectives on Terrorism* 7, no. 1 (2013).

Tapper, Jake. *The Outpost: An Untold Story of American Valor.* New York: Little, Brown, 2012.

Vollmann, William T. *An Afghanistan Picture Show, or, How I Saved the World.* New York: Farrar, Straus and Giroux, 1992.

Vonnegut, Kurt. *Breakfast of Champions.* New York: Delacorte, 1973.

———. *Slaughterhouse-Five, or The Children's Crusade.* New York: Delacorte, 1969.

Wolfe, Tom. *The Right Stuff.* New York: Farrar, Straus and Giroux, 1979.